ALEXANDER POPE

1 Alexander Pope. Oil painting by Charles Gervas. National Portrait Gallery, London.

ALEXANDER POPE
essays for the tercentenary

edited by

Colin Nicholson

ABERDEEN UNIVERSITY PRESS

1791765?
UKM

12-29-88

First published 1988
Aberdeen University Press
A member of the Pergamon Group

© The Contributors 1988

British Library Cataloguing in Publication Data

Alexander Pope: essays for the tercentenary.
1. Poetry in English. Pope, Alexander,
1688–1744—Critical studies
I. Nicholson, Colin
821'.5

ISBN 0 08 036394 6

Printed in Great Britain
The University Press
Aberdeen

Contents

List of Illustrations

Preface

Curious to reflect now upon the vanished heat and dust of literary contention in early-eighteenth-century England, when Swift could write to Gay in attractively gladiatorial tones: 'The Beggar's Opera has knocked down Gulliver. I hope to see Pope's Dulness knock down the Beggar's Opera.' How far away, too, we seem from Savage's account of the excitement which greeted publication by Pope:

> On the day the book was first vended, a crowd of Authors besieg'd the Shop; Entreaties, Advices, threats of Law, and Battery, nay cries of Treason were all employ'd, to hinder the coming out of *The Dunciad*: On the other Side, the Booksellers and Hawkers made as great Efforts to secure it . . .

Rumour soon became rife—that Pope dared not stir abroad without a tall Irishman attending him; that he became virtually a prisoner in his own house. On the evidence of his own sister, though, legends of Pope's incarceration were somewhat premature. 'My brother loved to walk out alone, and particularly went often to Mr Fortesque's at Richmond. Only he would take [his dog] Bounce with him; and for some time carried two pistols in his pocket.'

To recover senses of that emotional pitch requires some exercise of the historical imagination on our part. A culture which marginalises literary processes to the extent that ours does seems unlikely to respond easily to Pope's evident centrality during his life of writing. His axial significance in a varied convergence of discourses—from poetics to politics, from economics to ethics, from form to fashion makes him at once characteristic of his age and almost correspondingly alien to our own. Intriguingly, Pope stands at one of those moments of epochal transition when structures and perceptions we can recognise as germane to our own come into being. Yet, though the Post-Romantic fragmentation of discourse has traceable origins in the world established by the Revolution Settlement, the asymmetrical discontinuities we read as daily actuality in the writing of the first three decades of our own century were as alien to the Augustans as their ordered hierarchies seem to us. Where we experience atomisation and division, a rising bourgeoisie, anxious to perceive itself as participating in a natural hegemony, and educated by such projects as *The Spectator*, sought to translate its own developing ascendancy into kinship and connectedness. For Samuel Johnson, whose early poem *London* received praise and encouragement from Pope, Adam

Smith's *The Wealth of Nations* was as much a work of literature as *Othello*. It is, at least, paradoxical. An era which sought to establish harmony in poetic numbers, to the extent of sometimes seeming to force a metrical equipoise and aesthetic balance upon recalcitrant material, produces nonetheless a literature marked by opposition, conflict and often venomous contestation. The 'peace of the Augustans' was never any such thing, though at a time when politics and poetry were inseparable for those who practised either (and many practised both) such antagonisms could hardly be surprising. After the Revolution Settlement, for example, it had become fashionable in the new political world to distinguish between a traditional, Tory 'landed interest', and a 'moneyed' one which supported Revolution principles, though in reality, as Pope's own network of relationships helps to demonstrate, such clear-cut divisions rarely operated in any simple way. But the widespread acceptance of this central polarisation, and its use in political propagandising does at least point to deep-seated hostilities and fears which attended the new world struggling into existence. Such widespread feelings indicate, too, the extent to which intuitions of a political kind feed into and are articulated by a poetry of statement social in orientation and civic in intent.

Reaching across discursive boundaries then, Pope coordinates, in the *Imitation of Horace, Epistle II, i,* military conquest over France with Anglo-French aesthetic and artistic conjunction. 'Britain to soft refinements less a foe,/Wit grew polite, and Numbers learn'd to flow' (265–6). After this, he goes on in quite explicit ways to elaborate what we might now recognise as a preferred sociology of form:

> Tho' still some traces of our rustic vein
> And splay-foot verse, remain'd, and will remain.
> Late, very late, correctness grew our care,
> When the tir'd nation breath'd from civil war.
> (270–3)

The privileged couplet, technically 'correct" paradigm of balance and harmony, of epigrammatic containment and judicious equilibrium becomes the metrical equivalent of a social perspective seeking concord after strife. And since, in Pope's hands, the couplet shows a remarkable capacity for diversity and variety so, in combination, the imposition of rhyming pentameters upon such heterogeneous material as he displays could emblematise the restoration of order over fractious discontent. Or, where splenetic rivalry survives, the couplet may enclose it, tempering its excess by reducing it to ordered syllables and fixed rhythm. Simultaneously, Pope speaks for, and against, a whole age.

So it is that literary disputes which raged, often vitriolically, between the 'Ancients' and the 'Moderns', signalled oppositions of more immediately social dimensions, and Pope's own identification with Neo-Classical prescriptions carried complex overtones of contemporary significance. His publication of the *Pastorals* in 1709 witnesses his own contribution to a genre which in England had, for more than half a century, been characterised by opposing tendencies known since as the 'neo-classic' and the 'rationalistic'. And if, as has been suggested, the conflict here is fundamentally one between the Ancients on the one hand and self-sufficient Reason on the other, then the disputes which attended Pope's pastorals extend into wider considerations. As his Twickenham editors suggest:

> Here, as in other quarrels in which Pope engaged, there were issues which transcended the purely personal and which reflected not only literary, but also social and political, divisions. On the side of the 'rationalistic' group were such men as Addison, Steele, Tickell, Philips, Dennis and Welsted; the 'neo-classic' sympathisers were men such as Temple, Swift, Walsh, Pope, and Gay.
>
> (p 18)

Accordingly, Pope satirises each of those who opposed him, while praising those with whom he was in agreement. Clearly, political ideology and social attitudes are being articulated in literary form and aesthetic debate. Even the use of the term 'wit' in *An Essay on Criticism* signified participation in this socio-political dialectic since the aesthetic conflict both concealed and expressed considerable social antagonism with middle-class 'men of sense' ranged against aristocratic 'men of wit': or, again in the words of his Twickenham editors, 'the City against the West End' (p 225).

As he wrote *The Rape of the Lock*, such a division was reflected in London's urban geography, with one end of the town being governed by a tangle of Palace, Westminster and City officials, while the other operated virtually as a mercantile republic. By the time of the great Epistles and Imitations of the 1730s Pope is in full cry against the dominance of the City elements over the London from which he was anyway excluded by religious prejudice. Echoes and reconstructions of these and similar oppositions and separations are with us now, perhaps more nationally perceived than they were then. Revolutionary turbulence in economic affairs is as much a part of our sense of the world as it was Pope's, so that in this three-hundredth year since his birth it seems appropriate to look again at the nature of his achievement, at its reception, and at the sources and relationships on which he drew for inspiration and for senses of continuity and stability.

Acknowledgements

My thanks are due to all the contributors to this volume, for their help and support. I must, though, single out one or two who have been encouraging above and beyond the call of duty. From the very beginning, Alastair Fowler's ready advice and willingness to give time generously, made my tasks much easier than they otherwise would have been. To him my particular thanks. I am also grateful to Michael Phillips and to Roger Savage for their suggestions of both detailed and general kinds.

An earlier version of the essay ' "Illusion on the Town": Figuring out Credit in *The Dunciad*', first appeared in *Literature & History*, Vol 12:2 Autumn 1986.

COLIN NICHOLSON

Notes on Contributors

IAN BELL is Lecturer in English Literature, The University College of Wales. His publications include *Defoe's Fiction, Narrators and Narrative in Defoe*

GEOFFREY CARNALL is Reader in English Literature, Edinburgh University. His publications include *Robert Southey and his Art, Robert Southey*, and he is co-author of volume 8 of the *Oxford History of English Literature*

H T DICKINSON is Richard Lodge Professor of History, Edinburgh University. His publications include *Bolingbroke, Walpole and the Whig Supremacy, Liberty and Property: Political Ideology in 18th Century Britain*

ALASTAIR FOWLER is Professor Emeritus, English Literature, Edinburgh University. His publications include *Spenser and the Numbers of Time, Triumphal Forms, Kinds of Literature*

PETER FRANCE is Professor of French, Edinburgh University. His publications include *Racine's Rhetoric, Rhetoric and Truth in France, Diderot*

BREAN HAMMOND is lecturer in Modern English Literature, University of Liverpool. His publications include *Pope and Bolingbroke: A Study of Friendship and Influence, Pope: Harvester New Readings Series*

R D S JACK is Professor of English Literature, Edinburgh University. His publications include *The Italian Influence on Scottish Literature, Scottish Verse 1560–1660, Alexander Montgomerie*

WENDY JONES is Lecturer in Language and Literature, Tokushima Bunri University, Japan. Shortly to be published is her book on *Pope's Correspondence*

MARTIN MALONE is a graduate student at the University of Liverpool

COLIN MANLOVE is Reader in English Literature, Edinburgh University. His publications include *Modern Fantasy, Literature and Reality 1660–1800, The*

Gap in Shakespeare: The Motif of Division from "Richard II" to "The Tempest"

D W NICHOL is Lecturer in English Literature, Memorial University of Newfoundland. Shortly to be published is his book *Pope's Literary Legacy: an editorial correspondence between William Warburton and John Knapton* (1745–1755)

COLIN NICHOLSON is Lecturer in English Literature, Edinburgh University. He co-edited *Tropic Crucible: Self and Theory in Language and Literature*

MICHAEL PHILLIPS is Lecturer in English Literature, Edinburgh University. He co-edited *William Blake: Essays in Honour of Sir Geoffrey Keynes*, and is preparing a biography, *William Blake's Early Life*

JOHN PRICE is Senior Lecturer in English Literature, Edinburgh University. His publications include *The Ironic Hume, David Hume*. He edited Hume's *The Dialogues Concerning Natural Religion*

W W ROBSON is Masson Professor of English Literature, Edinburgh University. His publications include *Modern English Literature, The Definition of Literature, A Preface to English Literture*

ROGER SAVAGE is Senior Lecturer in English Literature, Edinburgh University. He specialises in the drama with a strong interest in operatic production in the seventeenth and eighteenth centuries

1

The Politics of Pope

H T DICKINSON

Pope in his political context

Few periods in British history have seen such a close relationship between politics and literature as the Augustan age. Almost every significant politician was the subject of praise or criticism emanating from the major writers of the day. Some leading politicians wrote propaganda themselves and nearly all of them patronised men of letters and encouraged them to wage a propaganda campaign in support of their principles and their policies. Even Sir Robert Walpole, who was contemptuous of the role of men of letters in society and who attracted the hostility of so many of the leading writers of his day, spent vast sums of money on hiring pro-government propagandists. Although he deliberately refrained from encouraging writers of genius, undoubtedly incurring their resentment as a result, he did not let their satirical criticisms of him and his policies go by default. He sought either to silence his literary critics or to engage them in debate (Goldgar 1976, chapter 1). Though some of his propagandists were very capable journalists, Walpole often put his trust in hack writers. In contrast, many of the most talented writers of the age enlisted in the ranks of the opposition to Walpole. Alexander Pope was one of these, though he could hardly be classed as a very active politician nor as a very profound political thinker. Literature always mattered more than politics to Pope, but there were times in his life when he was so engaged in political debate that his literary output cannot be fully appreciated if divorced from that context.

Historians, as well as literary critics, are now very cautious about regarding imaginative literature simply as the mirror of its time or as an illustration of contemporary attitudes. They recognise that the originality, the imagination and the literary talents of the individual writer, and the art form which he adopts, will inevitably mean that his writings are not meant to, and can never, be accepted as an objective or reliable picture of external reality. Since Alexander Pope was not only a brilliant satirist, but a man who wrote primarily in verse, then this distortion of reality is compounded. Satire and poetry undoubtedly impose more limitations on the straightforward expression of political views than the prose pamphlet or the journalistic essay. Indeed, it was precisely Walpole's recognition of this fact that led him to reject this kind of literature as encouraging distortion and allowing lies to prosper. Walpole regarded politics as a serious business for which literary men did not possess the necessary talent. He preferred 'reason' and 'commonsense' to imagination, and his own propagandists claimed that the satires of more literary men were often little more than libels which encouraged vice and appealed to the worst in human nature (Goldgar, pp 21–4).

There are obviously problems in interpreting any satirist or poet, and Pope presents particular difficulties. It is impossible to be absolutely confident that the 'self' projected in his poems is the same 'self' as the poet in his private life. There is always the danger that Pope is creating a persona in his poems, a mask of rhetoric, which is not to be identified with the real personality of the writer. In his satire Pope may be projecting not himself, but an exaggerated figure for which he does not take full responsibility. Yet, some literary critics would insist, in at least some of his verse his own personality does shine forth and he speaks candidly about his own inner feelings, emotional state and deep-rooted anxieties (Hammond 1984, p 124). Thus, while recognising the danger of accepting too literal an interpretation of Pope's verse satires, this essay will contend that it is a mistake to ignore the context in which Alexander Pope met and responded to political and social issues. The literary critic may quite legitimately be preoccupied with the literary genius of Pope, but he misses a vital element in the poet's satires if he remains ignorant of the particular circumstances and the specific incidents that inspired Pope to express those ideas and emotions which are so apparent in some of his verse. There *is* evidence that Pope's satire was the product of his society and a criticism of it. His poetry does appear to reflect and to give an edge to his understanding of his own world and, in the 1730s in particular, his satires insistently present his subjects in terms of moral conviction and urgency. He regularly referred to specific people, actual places and recognisable incidents and there is an important element of truth behind the satires. Moreover, the poems not only have political content, but were consciously conceived as a form of political action designed to arrest the decline in the nation's moral fibre (Hammond 1984, p 9; Erskine-Hill 1975, part one).

It certainly appears that some of Pope's verse carried conviction with his contemporaries precisely because they themselves appreciated that he was genuinely pained, concerned, and even outraged by the state of the world in which he lived. There can be little doubt that Pope was, at times, very willing to use his literary talents to highlight abuses and to correct the political and moral corruption of Walpolean Britain. In this campaign he clearly believed that his satirical verse was a legitimate, indeed a powerful, weapon. In 1732 he confessed to Swift, 'I know nothing that moves strongly but Satire, and those who are asham'd of nothing else, are so of being ridiculous' (Sherburn 1956, iii, 276). A few years later he told Arbuthnot, 'It was under the greatest Princes and best Ministers, that moral Satyrists were most encouraged; and that then Poets exercised the same jurisdiction over the Follies, as Historians did over the Vices of men' (ibid, iii, 420). This conviction, that satire was a moral teacher, a social therapeutic and a means of preserving law and order, was expressed in several of Pope's poems. In the second dialogue of his *Epilogue to the Satires*, for instance, he boasted:

> Yes, I am proud; I must be proud to see
> Men not afraid of God, afraid of me:
> Safe from the Bar, the Pulpit, and the Throne,
> Yet touch'd and sham'd by *Ridicule* alone.
>
> (208–11)

Before attempting to determine Pope's political views or endeavouring to measure his political influence, however, it is as well to recognise that he was not always an active partisan in the political disputes of his age and to acknowledge that he often expressed a distrust of parties and a dislike of extreme attitudes. There were, no doubt, sound practical reasons for Pope hesitating to become deeply embroiled in the activities of any one particular group in a sharply divided political nation. Pope was a Catholic in a staunchly Protestant country. His father appears to have suffered under the penal laws and, as he claimed in his *Imitation of Horace, Epistle II, ii*, he himself was occasionally inconvenienced by them (58–67). As a Catholic, he could never hope for political office and he knew well that Catholicism was associated in the public mind with the treason of Jacobitism. As a cripple with limited financial resources and a relatively low social station, and as a writer who wished to succeed with his pen without relying on patrons or hiring himself out to the highest bidder, he knew that partisan political comments could alienate those he wished to please. Neither Pope's physique nor his temperament (which was always sensitive to criticism) was well suited for the rough and tumble of public life.

These practical considerations were reinforced by some of Pope's deepest instincts and most cherished beliefs. Although he always took his faith seriously, Pope was no fanatic. While he remained on good terms with Catholic relatives, friends and neighbours, his most intimate friends were not Catholics and two at least, Atterbury and Swift, were Anglican divines who disliked Catholicism. Pope prided himself on his tolerance, he frequently declared his hostility to sectarian attitudes, and he regularly professed his admiration for men of moderate religious opinions. In the *Imitation of Horace, Satire I, ii*, he claimed:

> My Head and Heart thus flowing thro' my Quill,
> Verse-man or Prose-man, term me which you will,
> Papist or Protestant, or both between,
> Like good *Erasmus* in an honest Mean,
> In Moderation placing all my Glory,
> While Tories call me Whig, and Whigs a Tory.
>
> (63–8)

As this last line indicates, Pope also denied that he was a partisan in politics and, in *An Essay on Criticism*, he professed his abhorrence of faction (456–7). When Bolingbroke attacked party divisions as irrelevant and unreal, Pope readily embraced his apparently non-partisan manifesto and, like his lordship, claimed to desire the good of the whole nation. As David Morris has pertinently argued, however, Pope's ideal of moderation does not imply a fixed or restrictive middle state from which he never varied (1984, p 211). As Pope himself put it, in the *Imitation of Horace*, *Epistle I, i*, his moderation moved and flowed between extremes:

> Sworn to no Master, of no sect am I:
> As drives the storm, at any door I knock,
> And house with Montagne now, or now with Lock.
> Sometimes a Patriot, active in debate,
> Mix with the World, and battle for the State,
> Free as young Lyttelton, her cause pursue,
> Still true to Virtue, and as warm as true:
> Sometimes, with Aristippus, or St. Paul,
> Indulge my Candour, and grow all to all;
> Back to my native Moderation slide,
> And win my way by yielding to the tyde.
>
> (24–34)

None the less, while acknowledging that, at times, Pope had good reasons for keeping a low political profile and while accepting the justice of some of his protestations of moderation, it is still possible to detect occasions when he was involved, even sometimes deeply involved, in political issues. As a young man Pope showed some sympathy for the Tory cause even if he enjoyed being courted by the Whigs. He praised Queen Anne, welcomed the Treaty of Utrecht and associated with other Tory writers in the Scriblerus Club. The heavy blows delivered to the Tories by the Hanoverian succession in 1714 and the disaster of the Jacobite rebellion in 1715 appear to have persuaded Pope of the wisdom of retreating to the outer fringes of politics for a number of years. The trial of Bishop Atterbury in 1723 and the suspected involvement of his own kinsmen, Charles and Michael Rackett, in the activities of the Waltham Blacks, aroused his personal sympathies, but probably only served to confirm him in the wisdom of giving political intrigues a wide berth (Thompson 1977, pp 278–94; Rogers 1985, pp 75–92). In the late 1720s, when he was heavily engaged in his literary work, he strove to keep on friendly terms with both Sir Robert Walpole and one of his foremost critics, Lord Bolingbroke. Gradually, however, Bolingbroke's abilities, both political and intellectual, began to exercise such an influence over Pope that he was steadily brought into the Opposition camp. By the early 1730s Pope had become deeply involved in politics for the first time, as an alliance of Tories and anti-government Whigs strove to build up a Country programme which denounced the political corruption and the moral bankruptcy of the Walpolean régime. Country ideology, with its fear of corruption and its praise of civic virtue, appealed to Pope's deepest instincts. It transformed him into one of the leading critics of the government outside parliament. By the end of the 1730s, however, the failure of the Tories and the Opposition Whigs to achieve a genuine and effective coalition based on Country principles, and Pope's distaste for those who were putting their desire for office before the cause they had championed for so long, led to the poet's disillusionment with politics. In his last few years of life he again retreated to a more private world, safe from political strife (Aden 1972, pp 172–99).

Pope's involvement with the Country or Patriot Opposition in the 1730s has attracted most attention from those literary critics who are particularly interested in his political views (e.g. Reichard 1955; Mack 1969; Butt 1969, pp 111–26; Dixon 1968, 1972; Erskine-Hill 1975, 1981–2; and Hammond 1984). Before examining this phase in Pope's political career, however, it is necessary to determine his role in other political contexts. In addition to being the 'Poet Laureate of the Opposition' for a decade, Pope was also deeply enmeshed in the clash of political personalities and was more tenuously linked with the Jacobite cause.

Pope's political friends and enemies

In recent years many historians have become critical of that interpretation of eighteenth-century British politics, assiduously propagated by Sir Lewis Namier and his disciples, which puts much greater stress on personal ambition, petty intrigues and factious disputes than on public opinion, political debate and political ideas. There is now a much better appreciation of the role of political ideas and political principles in late Stuart and early Hanoverian Britain, but this recognition does not mean that historians should ignore the role of personal relations in politics. After all, the political *élite*, even the political nation as a whole, were a small proportion of the population. There were fewer than two hundred peers and only a few thousand men had any realistic chance of winning a seat in the House of Commons. As candidates, these men did not depend on a mass electorate or a highly organised party machine to secure their election to parliament. Success in most, if not all, constituencies depended upon their own social and economic position or on their personal connections with the greater landowners and borough patrons. In such circumstances therefore it is not surprising to find politics degenerating, at times, into a bitter struggle for power waged by a small number of ambitious men. To secure their ends these politicians hired propagandists or enlisted the support of sympathetic writers who could promote their political influence at court, in parliament or with the voters in the larger and more open constituencies where public opinion might determine the result of an election.

Alexander Pope found himself increasingly embroiled in this more personalised form of political conflict until, by the 1730s, he was firmly committed to the leading politicians out of office who were endeavouring to bring down the administration of Sir Robert Walpole. Apart from this period in his life, it has been claimed that Pope was friendly with men of all political shades of opinion. One commentator (Macdonald 1951, pp 56–8) has tried to classify Pope's political friends and he has concluded that Pope had about ten Tory friends and two Tory enemies (Lords Kinnoul and Scarsdale), about fifteen Whig friends and sixteen Whig enemies, and about ten Opposition friends and one Opposition enemy (Lord Carteret). This calculation, however, tends to obscure the extent of Pope's commitment to a particular political group. Some of his friendships with pro-government Whigs were neither warm nor close and he showed no sympathy for their political opinions. His friendship with William Fortescue continued to prosper despite, not because, of the latter's close relationship with Walpole. It has to be admitted that Pope cultivated the friendship of Viscount Cobham in the mid 1720s, when that peer was still an ally of Walpole's. In subsequent years Pope regularly directed his rambles towards Stowe and acted as a sort of landscape consultant for his lordship. On the other hand, it was not until the 1730s that Pope propagated the fame of Stowe in his *Epistle to Burlington* and not until 1734, by which time Cobham had, in fact, joined the Opposition to Walpole, that Pope expressed his admiration for his lordship's public character in his *Epistle to Cobham*. His relations with Burlington developed along similar lines as that Whig peer also deserted Walpole to join the Opposition.

A very high proportion of Pope's closest friends, of those whom he most admired, and of those with whom he usually agreed on public issues, can be categorised as opponents and critics of Sir Robert Walpole. The list would include such Tories as Bolingbroke, Oxford, Atterbury, Wyndham, Bathurst, Peterborough, Polwarth, Marchmont, Sir John Barnard, Sir William Trumbull, Swift, Gay, Arbuthnot, Parnell, John Caryll and Lord Digby, and such Opposition Whigs or Patriots as Pulteney, Carteret, Chesterfield, Argyll, Burlington, Cobham, Lyttleton, and William Murray. Some of Pope's friends, such as Lord Cornbury, shifted from Tory to Opposition Whig, but remained throughout opponents of Walpole's administration. Many of these names appear in Pope's poems, especially in the *Epilogue to the Satires*. Several men who were, or who became, leading opponents of Walpole, including Bathurst, Burlington, Cobham and Bolingbroke, have epistles dedicated to them by Pope.

There can be no doubt at all that the most profound political influence upon Pope was Lord Bolingbroke, who was the most constant and embittered of Walpole's political enemies. There is a wealth of incontrovertible evidence to prove Pope's close attachment to Bolingbroke during the years when the latter was seeking to orchestrate and to coordinate the opposition to Walpole. Joseph Spence recorded several anecdotes in which Pope expressed unqualified admiration for Bolingbroke's talents, openly praised his political works, and acknowledged the influence which Bolingbroke had exerted upon him (Spence 1964, pp 103–4, 115, 176–9, 186–7). Pope's published correspondence includes letters to and from Bolingbroke and joint compositions which they sent to Swift; besides many favourable comments upon Bolingbroke in other letters. It is obvious that Pope and Bolingbroke were not merely near neighbours and close acquaintances, but that they spent many, many hours in deep discussion and in close collaboration about their philosophical ideas, their literary products and their political reactions to public events. Pope was a regular visitor to Bolingbroke's residence at Dawley Farm and he paid extensive visits in 1731 when he was writing *An Essay on Man*. For his part, Bolingbroke stayed with Pope on his visits to England during his second period of exile in France in the late 1730s and he allowed Pope privately to print a few copies of his unpublished political treatise, *The Idea of a Patriot King*. Bolingbroke's influence on Pope's ideas and on his verse was openly acknowledged by the poet himself. Among the concluding lines of *An Essay on Man* is this explicit tribute to Bolingbroke's influence:

> Come then, my Friend, my Genius, come along,
> Oh master of the poet, and the song!
> And while the Muse now stoops, or now ascends,
> To Man's low passions, or their glorious ends,
> Teach me, like thee in various nature wise,
> To fall with dignity, with temper rise;
> Form'd by thy converse, happily to steer
> From grave to gay, from lively to severe;
> Correct with spirit, eloquent with ease,
> Intent to reason, or polite to please . . .
> When statesmen, heroes, kings, in dust repose,
> Whose sons shall blush their fathers were thy foes,
> Shall then this verse to future age pretend
> Thou wert my quide, philosopher and friend?
> (373–82, 387–90)

Some of Pope's leading interpreters, from Warburton to Maynard Mack, have sought to deny that *An Essay on Man* owes a great deal to Bolingbroke's philosophical influence (Evans 1932, pp 71–83; and Mack's introduction to *TE*, III, i). This view has been challenged recently (Hammond 1984; and Wong 1983) and Brean Hammond has proved, quite conclusively in my view, that Bolingbroke had a profond influence on Pope's political views in the early 1730s just when Bolingbroke was making his greatest contributions to *The Craftsman* and Pope's verse was revealing his increased interest in the political issues of the day.

In sharp contrast to the number of favourable references which he made to his political friends in his verse are the numerous attacks which Pope launched upon the allies and dependants of Sir Robert Walpole. After he himself had been attacked by Lord Hervey, an influential pro-government Whig, in *Verses Address'd to the Imitator of . . . Horace* (1733), Pope launched one of the most stinging literary assaults in history. In his *Epistle to Arbuthnot*, he condemned Hervey as a court flatterer and as Walpole's corrupt and spiteful puppet (309–22). Even more significant, though the verse is less vivid, are the satirical blows at Walpole's political allies and dishonest cronies. Among those singled out for criticism, particularly in the *Epistle to Bathurst*, are Gilbert Heathcote, one-time Governor of the Bank of England; Denis Bond, who was expelled from the House of Commons for embezzling the funds of the Charitable Corporation; Sir John Blount, one of the directors involved in the notorious scandal of the South Sea Bubble; John Ward, a Whig MP convicted of fraud and forgery and expelled from the House of

Commons; 'Vulture' Hopkins, who was notorious for his rapacity; Francis Chartres, who was twice pardoned for rape; and Peter Walter, whose business and financial skills made him a fortune. In *The Dunciad*, Pope's attack on hack writers manifests a marked anti-government bias. While he exempts *The Craftsman* from attack and he criticises only three 'dunces' who were associated with the Opposition, he is highly critical of dozens of 'dunces' who were minor government officials or who wrote for the major government journals (Goldgar 1976, pp 75–7). In the 1735 edition of the poem, Pope added a footnote describing Matthew Concanen as 'a hired Scribler in the Daily Courant, where he pour'd forth much Billingsgate against the Lord Bolingbroke and others' (*TE*, v, 152 n).

In view of this, it is perhaps surprising to discover that Pope's attitude to Walpole himself was rather ambivalent. Pope dined with Walpole on a number of occasions in the late 1720s and he tried for a time to live on civil terms with both the chief minister and his leading critics. He even tried to enlist Walpole's support for his efforts to secure court employment for John Gay and it was probably due to Walpole's good offices that he personally received a gift from the court for translating the *Odyssey*. Edward Thompson has argued that Pope's attachment to Walpole, or rather his refusal to attack him in public, was not based on genuine conviction, but was forced out of him by Pope's desire to protect his closest kin, Charles and Michael Rackett, from prosecution. According to this argument the Racketts were not only involved in deer stealing, but had engaged in a Jacobite conspiracy. Walpole might have prosecuted them but held his hand, in part, in order to influence Pope's future conduct. By holding two hostages against Pope, he was able to ensure that for several years, at least until the death of Charles Rackett in 1728, the poet had to tread very warily and had to control his natural desire to attack Walpole and all he stood for (Thompson 1977, pp 278–94). This explanation of Pope's conduct is not very convincing and the flaws in Thompson's thesis have recently been brilliantly exposed by Pat Rogers (1985, pp 75–92). This is not meant to deny, however, that Pope was very likely saying things in Walpole's company that did not entirely square with what he was saying when he dined with Bolingbroke.

Pope's friendly relations with Walpole in the late 1720s were promoted by Mrs Howard, the king's mistress, and by William Fortescue, Walpole's private secretary, who was to remain a lifelong friend of Pope and a vital contact with the administration. At this time Pope was certainly sufficiently friendly with Walpole to be embarrassed by Swift's references to him as a critic of the court in *A Libel on Dr Delany* (Hammond 1984, p 49). By the 1730s Pope had shifted decisively into the Opposition's political camp, but his attacks on Walpole were always more muted or indirect than his criticisms of the régime he headed. Pope may well have been satirising Walpole's extravagance and bad taste in his lines on Timon's villa in his *Epistle to Burlington*, but many of his contemporaries believed that the shaft had been aimed at the princely Duke of Chandos (Mahaffy 1980, pp 315–51). While deploring the consequences of Walpole's political arts, Pope never entirely lost his fascination for the minister's skills. In *The Fourth Satire of Dr John Donne*,

Versifyed, Pope almost certainly had Walpole in mind when he described the arts of a subtle minister, who knows:

> Whose Place is *quarter'd out*, three Parts in four,
> And whether to a Bishop, or a Whore?
> Who, having lost his Credit, pawn'd his Rent,
> Is therefore fit to have a *Government*?
> Who in the *Secret*, deals in Stocks secure,
> And cheats th' unknowing Widow, and the Poor?
> Who makes a *Trust*, or *Charity*, a Job,
> And gets an Act of Parliament to rob.
>
> (136–43)

In the first dialogue of the *Epilogue to the Satires*, Pope overtly satirised Walpole, who was widely known as the 'Screen' because of his role in defending his corrupt political associates after the bursting of the South Sea Bubble:

> His sly, polite, insinuating stile
> Could please at Court, and make AUGUSTUS smile,
> An artful Manager, that crept between
> His Friend and Shame, and was a kind of *Screen*.
>
> (19–22)

But he then went on to write (and at a time, we should remember, when he was bitterly frustrated at the failure of the Opposition to force Walpole out of office):

> Seen him I have, but in his happier hour
> Of Social Pleasure, ill-exchang'd for Pow'r;
> Seen him, uncumber'd with the Venal tribe,
> Smile without Art, and win without a Bribe.
> Would he oblige me? let me only find,
> He does not think me what he thinks mankind.
> Come, come, at all I laugh He laughs, no doubt,
> The only diff'rence is, I dare laugh out.
>
> (29–36)

Pope and Jacobitism

Whereas it can be legitimately argued that it was personal ties above all other influences that eventually brought Pope into the Opposition camp, it is essential to look beyond his friends and enemies in order to identify his political opinions. Few historians would now endorse the Namierite interpretation of the structure of politics in the first half of the eighteenth century; an interpretation which played down the role of organised parties and the significance of political ideas. While historians today are not all in agreement, one with another, recent research has combined to assert the significance of organised political parties in the competition for power, to stress the influence of ideas and opinions in politics, and to demonstrate that political stability was never fully achieved even in the years of Walpole's ascendancy. To understand Pope's politics we need therefore to locate him in the clash between Whigs and Tories and in the public debate between Court and Country ideologies. This section will examine whether Pope can be classed as a Tory, even perhaps as a Jacobite, whereas the next will explore his contribution to that Country or Patriot campaign which tried so hard to defeat political corruption and to promote civic virtue.

In 1717, in perhaps the clearest statement of his religious and political principles that he ever made, Pope stressed his moderation and praised the British constitution. He also implied that he had no reason to give his loyalty to a Catholic Pretender with absolutist principles and he indicated that he hoped to be a loyal subject of George I:

> I am not a Papist, for I renounce the temporal invasion of Papal power, and I detest their arrogated authority over Princes, and states. I am a Catholic, in the strictest sense of the word. If I was born under an absolute Prince, I would be a quiet subject; but I thank God I was not. I have a due sense of the excellence of the British constitution. In a word, the things I have always wished to see are not a Roman Catholick, or a French Catholick, or a Spanish Catholick, but a true Catholick: and not a King of Whigs, or a King of Tories, but a King of England. Which God in his mercy grant his present Majesty may be.
>
> (Sherburn 1956, i, 455)

In a letter to Swift, written on 4 March 1730, Pope even claimed that he was a Whig (Sherburn 1956, iii, 95); but, it must be admitted, there is precious little evidence to suggest that he had much sympathy with any Whig government during his lifetime. His personal friendship with such staunch Whigs as William Fortescue and Ralph Allen do not indicate any firm attachment to the political principles of the government they supported. On the other hand, although Pope's relations with active Tories appear to include more 'political' friendships, his desire to maintain a low political profile and his dislike of extremes prevented him from making many explicit protestations of his commitment to Tory principles. None the less, there are intimations in his writings that his sympathies lay very much more with the Tories than the Whigs.

The distinguishing political principles of the Tories had originally been their attachment to divine right, indefeasible hereditary succession and non-resistance. The Catholicism of James II and the threat which his policies posed to the privileged position of the Church of England led them to abandon their political principles in order to safeguard their religion. Despite this, many Tories were but cool supporters of the Glorious Revolution of 1688 or even of the Hanoverian succession in 1714, and some—the Jacobites— remained loyal to their original principles. Considerable research in recent years has suggested that Pope, despite his caution, maintained at least a sneaking admiration for Tory principles, and may well have entertained

Jacobite sympathies (Erskine-Hill 1975, 1979, 1981–2, 1982; Aden 1972, 1978; and Brooks-Davies 1985) .

Some reasons for reaching such a conclusion have already been mentioned. Pope was a Catholic when most Catholics were suspected of Jacobitism and he, like them, found the penal laws irksome and unjust. In his *Imitation of Horace, Epistle II, ii*, Pope indicated that his own father had suffered because of his refusal to endorse the Glorious Revolution:

> But knottier Points we knew not half so well,
> Depriv'd us soon of our Paternal Cell;
> And certain Laws, by Suff'rers thought unjust,
> Deny'd all Posts of Profit or of Trust:
> Hopes after Hopes of pious Papists fail'd,
> While mighty WILLIAM's thundring Arm prevail'd.
> For Right Hereditary tax'd and fin'd,
> He stuck to Poverty with Peace of Mind;
> And me, the Muses help'd to undergo it;
> Convict a Papist He, and I a Poet.
>
> (58–67)

Pope's nearest kinsmen, Charles Rackett and his son Michael, may have been implicated in Jacobite intrigues, as were a number of Pope's closest friends and political allies, including Bishop Atterbury, Bolingbroke, Oxford, Bathurst, Lord Lansdowne, Lord Cornbury, Lord Orrery, John Caryll, Father Thomas Southcote and Mrs Charles Caesar. At some risk to himself Pope was prepared to affirm his friendship with the arrested Jacobite leader, Bishop Atterbury, and to speak in his favour during his trial in the House of Lords in 1723.

Although it is quite easy to connect Pope with a surprising number of individuals who flirted seriously at some stage in their lives with schemes to promote a Jacobite restoration, it is much more difficult to detect clear evidence of Jacobite sympathies in the poet's published works. Attempts have been made by several literary critics, however, to tease out of his verse some intimations of Pope's attachment to the Jacobite cause, though these efforts have not proved entirely convincing (at least to this more literal-minded historian). Probably Pope's first published verses are a scathing lampoon on the 'Dutch Prince' (William III), who failed to conquer in love or war, and he again reflected severely on Dutch William in his early poem, *The First Book of Statius His Thebais*, which deals with two kinsmen competing for a throne. It is also possible to note both criticism of William III (a usurper in Jacobite eyes) and admiration for Queen Anne (James II's daughter) in a few lines of *Windsor Forest*. Pope pursues the cryptic parallel of William III and William I as conquerors associated with warfare, waste and rapine (79–84), whereas Anne (327–8) is praised for bringing peace through the Treaty of Utrecht (a treaty warmly welcomed by the Tories and condemned by the Whigs). This poem is dedicated to a Tory Jacobite, Lord Lansdowne, and it contains the conspicuous line, 'And Peace and Plenty tell, a STUART reigns' (42). *Windsor Forest* may indicate, as John Aden (1978) has claimed, that

Pope was very concerned at the unhappy state of Britain, torn as it was between two rival claimants to the throne; but it is rather tenuous evidence on which to base the supposition that Pope wished to see a Jacobite restoration and it provides no proof at all that Pope was prepared to work or conspire towards this end. Other evidence from Pope's verse can only hint at an emotional or rhetorical sympathy with the Jacobite cause, but it cannot demonstrate a clear desire for a Jacobite restoration. Howard Erskine-Hill (1979), for example, has tried to argue that *The Rape of the Lock* might allude to the rape of a kingdom, whereas Douglas Brooks-Davies (1985) has endeavoured to interpret Pope's *Dunciad* as a study in emotional Jacobitism; but such evidence can hardly convict Pope of dabbling in treason. His Jacobitism, if such it was, rarely rose above the level of innuendo. There is no evidence at all that he would have welcomed the social unrest which might have followed an invasion and a civil war initiated by the Pretender (Mack 1985, pp 261–6).

Pope and the Country Opposition

The most overt political comments in Pope's verse rarely link him directly with the basic tenets of Toryism and Pope was not, of course, committed to the defence of the privileges of the Church of England as were nearly all the Tories. In order to elucidate Pope's political opinions we need to focus our attention not on his attachment to particular party principles nor on his view of specific political issues, but on his moral and social attitudes to the political world in which he lived. When we do this, we discover that Pope, at least in the 1730s, is best described as one of the most searching critics of the political vices of Walpolean Britain and as one of the most insistent voices raised in support of Country or Patriot principles. It was Country ideology, with its appeal to Tories and Opposition Whigs to unite behind a non-party campaign to restore public virtue, that won Pope's loyalty in the 1730s and influenced most of his satire during that decade (see for example, Butt 1969, pp 111–26; Mack 1969; and Dixon 1968, 1972).

Country ideology was founded on an ethic of civic virtue that maintained that civilised society and civil government could be preserved only by the patriotic actions and the public spirit of men of landed property. Those who possessed a real and substantial stake in the country were the only true citizens and were the natural leaders of those who were merely inhabitants. Their property gave them both independence and a sense of responsibility; hence they alone were in a position to act in the best interests of the nation as a whole. It was essential for such men to play the dominant role in society if harmony and stability were to be achieved and social discord was to be avoided. The landed proprietors must concern themselves with the welfare and morality of those below them in the social hierarchy and they must promote moderation, taste and decorum rather than pursue material advancement or personal ambition. Only by such means could men sustain the traditional moral economy, in which landlords and their rural neighbours were united together in a reciprocal bond of rights and duties.

Pope shared the Country ideal and praised those rural patriarchs who generously contributed to the welfare of their local community and composed unnecessary disputes. This explains his admiration for the Man of Ross in his *Epistle to Bathurst*:

> Behold yon Alms-house, neat, but void of state,
> Where Age and Want sit smiling at the gate:
> Him portion'd maids, apprentic'd orphans blest,
> The young who labour, and the old who rest.
> Is any sick? the MAN of ROSS relieves,
> Prescribes, attends, the med'cine makes, and gives.
> Is there a variance? enter but his door,
> Balk'd are the Courts, and contest is no more.
>
> (265–72)

In Pope's opinion the squirearchy served society well on their rural estates if they lived lives of innocence, simplicity and social responsibility, but the influence of the landed aristocracy quite properly stretched across the nation and deservedly reached even into the towns. Thus, in his *Epistle to Burlington*, Pope wrote:

> His Father's Acres who enjoys in peace,
> Or makes his Neighbours glad, if he encrease;
> Whose chearful Tenants bless this yearly toil,
> Yet to their Lord owe more than to the soil;
> Whose ample Lawns are not asham'd to feed
> The milky heifer and deserving steed;
> Whose rising Forests, not for pride or show,
> But future Buildings, future navies grow:
> Let his plantations stretch from down to down,
> First shade a Country, and then raise a Town.
>
> (181–90)

Unfortunately, as Pope was ready to observe, some landowners no longer maintained the old moral and social order. They neglected their duties, disavowed their responsibilities to their tenants and dependants, and allowed the traditional rural way of life to disintegrate.

Pope believed that the most serious threat to the traditional moral economy stemmed from the recent rise of a new financial interest which endangered the social stability, the political liberties and the moral fibre of the nation. He rightly perceived that, since the early 1690s, a veritable financial revolution had taken place. A small, moneyed *élite*, operating principally in the City of London, had made themselves politically indispensable through their hold on the Bank of England and the great chartered trading companies and through their control of a vast share of the national debt. These men could exert considerable political influence on the government in managing and manipulating the paper securities of the London Stock Exchange. An entire financial sub-culture of directors, monopolists, stock-jobbers, scriveners and usurers, prospered rapidly and enormously, to the alarm of those, like Pope, who did not understand the mysteries of the stock market. By their mastery of high finance these moneyed men secured vast fortunes which seemed out of all proportion to their efforts, their merits or their contribution to society. With their apparently ill-gotten gains they were often able to buy out honest, but poorer, men of landed estates and then to neglect the social role which the traditional proprietors had performed. Money was, and remained, their sole preoccupation. According to Pope, greed, not simplicity, responsibility or virtue, became their guiding light. Thus, in *The Second Satire of Dr John Donne Versifyed*, Pope warned:

> In shillings and in pence at first they deal,
> And steal so little, few perceive they steal;
> Till like the Sea, they compass all the land,
> From Scots to Wight, from Mount to Dover strand . . .
> Piecemeal they win this Acre first, then that,
> Glean on, and gather up the whole Estate:
> Then strongly fencing ill-got wealth by law,
> Indentures, Cov'nants, Articles they draw;
>
> (83–6, 91–4)

The moneyed men drained wealth from both agriculture and commerce and, by their vile trade, they forced others to become their pawns and dependants:

> Alike in nothing but one Lust of Gold,
> Just half the land would buy, and half be sold:
> Their Country's wealth our mightier Misers drain,
> Or cross, to plunder Provinces, the Main:
> The rest, some farm the Poor-box, some the Pews;
> Some keep Assemblies, and wou'd keep the Stews;
> Some with fat Bucks on childless Dotards fawn;
> Some win rich Widows by their Chine and Brawn;
> While with the silent growth of ten per Cent,
> In dirt and darkness hundreds stink content.
>
> (*Epistle I, i*, 124–33)

Pope regarded the whole system of public credit and the new emphasis on pursuing speculative profits at all costs as deeply corrupting. In criticising the corrupting effects on the individual of the new moneyed order, he condemned the mysterious arts of men like Peter Walter (Erskine-Hill 1975, pp 103–31) and he lamented the way in which the pursuit of gain had eroded the character of Sir Balaam and his family (*Epistle to Bathurst*, 369–402). More serious still, however, were the political threats posed by the unbridled pursuit of wealth. In Pope's opinion, public vices could be traced back to a willingness to abandon private virtue in order to gain exorbitant riches. The intensity of his hostility to moneyed men was not due simply to the higher profits made in finance compared to the returns on land. Pope feared that the moneyed men were not independent citizens, but the creatures of the Court. The fortunes of the financial interest depended on their success in lending money to the government. By lending such vast sums, however, the moneyed men greatly extended the range of crown patronage and thus enabled the Court to buy men's political independence in return for places and profits. The Country Opposition feared that the Court was fast approaching the position where it might be able to count upon a subservient majority in parliament to support its every action. If this day ever dawned, then the essential balance of the constitution would be destroyed, the cherished independence of parliament would be sacrificed, and the liberties of the subject would be endangered. These fears underpinned substantial sections of Pope's *Epistle to Bathurst*:

> Blest paper-credit! last and best supply!
> That lends Corruption lighter wings to fly!
> Gold imp'd by thee, can compass hardest things,
> Can pocket States, can fetch or carry Kings;
> A single leaf shall waft an Army o'er,
> Or ship off Senates to a distant Shore;
> A leaf, like Sibyl's, scatter to and fro
> Our fates and fortunes, as the winds shall blow:
> Pregnant with thousands flits the Scrap unseen,
> And silent sells a King, or buys a Queen.
> (69–78)

In Pope's view, if corruption in public life were not arrested, then the whole social order would be inverted and the nation's very security from its external enemies would be undermined:

> At length Corruption, like a gen'ral flood,
> (So long by watchful Ministers withstood)
> Shall deluge all; and Av'rice creeping on,
> Spread like a low-born mist, and blot the Sun;
> Statesman and Patriot ply alike the stocks,
> Peeress and Butler share alike the Box,
> And Judges job, and Bishops bite the town,
> And mighty Dukes pack cards for half a crown.
> See Britain sunk in lucre's sordid charms,
> And France reveng'd of ANNE's and EDWARD's arms!
> (ibid, 137–46)

In order to counter the rise of corruption Pope stressed the need for a revival of public morality and civic virtue. The vigilant defence of virtue was the only effective antidote to the poisonous effects of money, luxury, vice and corruption. To promote this vigilance Pope aimed his satire openly and directly at individual men rather than at government measures. In the *Imitation of Horace, Epistle I, ii* (161–8), Pope praised the virtues of an ordered family life, while in *An Essay on Man* in particular, he advised men to accept the aristocratic, paternalistic and hierarchical social theory known as 'the Great Chain of Being'. This concept of society rested on the belief that God had ordained an hierarchical order not only for human society but throughout the whole of creation. This divinely-ordained order produced both stability and liberty because each man was allotted a role in society that marked out both his duties and his rights. In obedience to God men ought to accept their station in life and, with it, the particular functions and duties incumbent upon them. It was in the public interest to preserve the traditional social hierarchy in which the great majority of men could learn the benefits of living in political, social and economic subordination to the great landowners. The desire for individual advancement and the pursuit of ambition and self-interest were vices which threatened the public interest. To seek to change this natural order was to rebel against God's ordinance and to risk bringing chaos and destruction to civil society:

> On superior pow'rs
> Were we to press, inferior might on ours:
> Or in the full creation leave a void,
> Where, one step broken, the great scale's destroy'd:
> From Nature's chain whatever link you strike,
> Tenth or ten thousandth, breaks the chain alike.
> And if each system in gradation roll,
> Alike essential to th' amazing whole;
> The least confusion but in one, not all
> That system only, but the whole must fall.
> (*An Essay on Man*, i, 241–50)

According to Pope, men should not rely too much on human reason and should be wary of being led astray by pride and ambition. Human arrogance would only produce human misery. Virtue and submission therefore were the best guarantees of stability, cooperation and inter-dependence:

> Cease then, nor ORDER Imperfection name:
> Our proper bliss depends on what we blame.
> Know thy own point: This kind, this due degree
> Of blindness, weakness, Heav'n bestows on thee.
> Submit—In this, or any other sphere,
> Secure to be as blest as thou canst bear:
> Safe in the hand of one disposing Pow'r,
> Or in the natal, or the mortal hour.
> (ibid, 281–8).

Pope recognised corruption as a threat to both personal and public morality. In turn, he was aware that virtue must be cultivated at both the individual and the national level. He was therefore not content to preach a private morality in his satires, but endeavoured to act in a public and political sphere in order to promote civic virtue. As an admirer of Bolingbroke he first enlisted in the Country campaign waged against Walpole and the Court, but he was

soon making an independent contribution to the efforts to encourage civic
virtue. He helped to promote the Patriot plays written by Thomson, Glover,
Mallet and Brooke. After Bolingbroke had retreated once more to France,
in 1735, Pope retained his connections with the leaders of the Opposition and
began to associate more closely with the new generation of young Patriots,
including Lyttelton, Polwarth and Cobham's 'cubs'. Indeed, it is possible to
argue that Pope became one of the leading exponents of anti-government
principles outside parliament itself. In the *Imitation of Horace, Satire I, ii*,
Pope referred to himself as a critic of vice and a friend of virtue:

> Hear this, and tremble! you, who 'scape the Laws.
> Yes, while I live, no rich or noble knave
> Shall walk the World, in credit, to the grave.
> To VIRTUE ONLY and HER FRIENDS A FRIEND
> The World beside may murmur, or commend.
>
> (118–22)

In the *Imitation of Horace, Epistle I, i*, which was dedicated to Bolingbroke
and which provided an ethical and political definition of virtue, Pope again
alluded to his own role in politics:

> Sometimes a Patriot, active in debate,
> Mix with the World, and battle for the State,
> Free as young Lyttleton, her cause pursue,
> Still true to Virtue, and as warm as true.
>
> (27–30)

In 1738 Pope's *Epilogue to the Satires* celebrated most of the leaders of
the Opposition by name and condemned many of the corrupt adherents of
Walpole. Unfortunately, it also acknowledged that the Opposition had failed
in its recent campaign to denounce Walpole's handling of the country's
commercial disputes with Spain. The first dialogue concluded with a vision
of vice's final triumph over virtue:

> Lo! at the Wheels of her Triumphal Car,
> Old *England*'s Genius, rough with many a Scar,
> Dragg'd in the Dust! his Arms hang idly round,
> His Flag inverted trails along the ground! . . .
> Hear her black Trumpet thro' the Land proclaim,
> That 'Not to be corrupted is the Shame'.
> In Soldier, Churchman, Patriot, Man in Pow'r,
> 'Tis Av'rice all, Ambition is no more!
> See, all our Nobles begging to be Slaves!
> See, all our Fools aspiring to be Knaves!
> The Wit of Cheats, the Courage of a Whore,
> Are what ten thousand envy and adore.
> All, all look up, with reverential Awe,
> On Crimes that scape, or triumph o'er the Law:

> While Truth, Worth, Wisdom, daily they decry—
> 'Nothing is Sacred now but Villany'.
>   (151–4, 159–70)

The second dialogue to the *Epilogue of the Satires* appeared two months later, with Pope's resolution appended not to publish any more poems of this kind, but to add, in the most plain and solemn manner, 'a sort of PROTEST against that insuperable corruption and depravity of manners, which he had been so unhappy as to live to see . . . bad men were grown so shameless and so powerful, that Ridicule was become as unsafe as it was ineffectual' (*TE*, iv, 327 n).

The failure of the Opposition's attack on Walpole in 1738 marked a decisive turning point in Pope's political career (Gabriner 1980, pp 585–611). Exhausted and increasingly pessimistic, Pope revealed in his correspondence his growing disillusionment with the leaders of the parliamentary Opposition and with their failure to arrest the tide of corruption (Sherburn 1956, iv, 142–3, 249–50, 260–1, 272–3). Like Bolingbroke, he too came to rest his political hopes upon the accession to the throne of Prince Frederick. Influenced by Bolingbroke's unpublished treatise, *The Idea of a Patriot King*, which he was permitted to circulate among his friends, Pope hoped that the heir to George II might be persuaded to act upon Country principles when he eventually came to the throne:

> For the age is too far corrupted to Reform itself; it must be done by those upon or near the Throne, or not at all: They must restore what we ourselves have Given up. They must save us from our own Vices, and Follies, they must bring back the taste of Honesty, and the Sense of Honour, which the Fashion of Knavery has almost Destroy'd.
>
>   (Sherburn 1956, iv, 139)

In one of his last works—the unfinished poem, *One Thousand Seven and Forty*—Pope clearly revealed his fears that some of the Opposition leaders, Carteret and Pulteney in particular, were ready to sell out to the Court upon receiving the first reasonable offer of place or preferment:

> C(arteret), his own proud dupe, thinks Monarchs things
> Made just for him, as other fools for Kings;
> Controls, decides, insults thee every hour,
> And antedotes the hatred due to Pow'r.
>   Thro' Clouds of Passion P(ulteney)'s views are clear
> He foams a Patriot to subside a Peer;
> Impatient sees his country bought and sold,
> And damns the market where he takes no gold.
>   (5–12)

Even the rank-and-file Tory squires, who had opposed Walpole for many years from the Opposition backbenches, were proving that they were easily duped by their dishonest leaders and were showing that they no longer had the stamina for the regular grind of opposing Walpole and resisting his abuse of power:

> As for the rest, each winter up they run,
> And all are clear, that something must be done.
> Then urg'd by C(artere)t, or by C(artere)t stopt,
> Inflam'd by P(ulteney), or by P(ulteney) dropt;
> They follow rev'rently each wond'rous wight,
> Amaz'd that one can read, that one can write:
> So geese to gander prone obedience keep,
> Hiss if he hiss, and if he slumber, sleep.
> Till having done whate'er was fit or fine,
> Utter'd a speech, and ask'd their friends to dine;
> Each hurries back to his paternal ground,
> Content but for five shillings in the pound,
> Yearly defeated, yearly hopes they give,
> And all agree, Sir Robert cannot live.
>
> (29–42)

The nation and its liberties, Pope feared, could not now be preserved by its political representatives in parliament. The last remaining hope in the struggle against corruption lay in the succession of a virtuous Patriot King. Pope very probably had Prince Frederick in mind here, since he was still associated with his court and he was regularly referring to him in his correspondence, but there is a hint that he might be willing to consider the restoration of the Jacobite Pretender in the lines:

> Whatever his religion or his blood,
> His public virtue makes his title good,
> Europe's just balance and our own may stand,
> And one man's honesty redeem the land.
>
> (95–8)

During the last four years of his life Pope's interest in politics undoubtedly waned as he lost hope of redressing the situation. Even when Sir Robert Walpole finally resigned, in early 1742, he escaped censure and was succeeded by some of his closest disciples, who continued his policies and retained his political methods. Pulteney and Carteret, as Pope had feared four years before, sold out the Country Opposition and took office under their former opponents. Some of Pope's Patriot friends (especially Sir William Wyndham) were now dead, Swift was senile and of unsound mind, whereas Bolingbroke's political career was in ruins. Even Prince Frederick seemed no longer to offer the promise of a new reign of virtue. Pope's political poetry during the 1730s had undoubtedly helped to identify the political and social vices of the day, but he recognised that his satire had failed to combat them or to teach society the merits of civic virtue.

References

Aden, John M 'Pope and Politics: "The Farce of State" ', in Peter Dixon (ed) *Alexander Pope: Writers and their Background* (London: G Bell & Sons, 1972)
—— *Pope's Once and Future Kings* (Knoxville: Univ of Tennessee Press, 1978)
Brooks-Davies, Douglas *Pope's* Dunciad *and the Queen of Night: a study in emotional Jacobitism* (Manchester: Manchester UP, 1985)
Butt, John 'Pope and the Opposition to Walpole's Government', in Geoffrey Carnall (ed) *Pope, Dickens and Others: Essays and Addresses by John Butt* (Edinburgh: Edinburgh UP, 1969)
Dixon, Peter *The World of Pope's Satires* (London: Methuen, 1968)
—— (ed) *Alexander Pope: Writers and their Background* (London: G Bell & Sons, 1972)
Erskine-Hill, Howard *The Social Milieu of Alexander Pope* (New Haven: Yale UP, 1975)
—— 'Literature and the Jacobite Cause', *MLS* 9 (1979) 15–20
—— 'Alexander Pope: The Political Poet in His Time', *ECS* 15 (1981–2) 123–48
—— 'Literature and the Jacobite Cause: was there a Rhetoric of Jacobitism?', in Eveline Cruickshanks (ed) *Ideology and Conspiracy: Aspects of Jacobitism, 1689–1759* (Edinburgh: John Donald, 1982)
Evans, A W *Warburton and the Warburtonians* (London: Oxford UP, 1932)
Gabriner, Paul 'Pope's "Virtue" and the Events of 1738', in Maynard Mack and James A Winn (eds) *Pope: Recent Essays by Several Hands* (Brighton: Harvester Press, 1980)
Goldgar, Bertrand A *Walpole and the Wits: The Relation of Politics to Literature, 1722–1742* (Lincoln: Univ of Nebraska Press, 1976)
Hammond, Brean *Pope and Bolingbroke: A Study of Friendship and Influence* (Columbia: Univ of Missouri Press, 1984)
Macdonald, W L *Pope and His Critics* (London: J M Dent, 1951)
Mack, Maynard *The Garden and the City: Retirement and Politics in the Later Poetry of Pope 1731–1743* (London: Oxford UP, 1969)
—— *Alexander Pope: A Life* (New Haven: Yale UP, 1985)
Mahaffy, Kathleen 'Timon's Villa: Walpole's Houghton', in Maynard Mack and James A Winn (eds) *Pope: Recent Essays by Several Hands* (Brighton: Harvester Press, 1980)
Morris, David B *Alexander Pope: The Genius of Sense* (Cambridge, Mass.: Harvard UP, 1984)
Reichard, Hugo M 'The Independence of Pope as a Political Satirist', *JEGP* 54 (1955) 309–17
Rogers, Pat 'Blacks and Poetry and Pope', in Pat Rogers, *Eighteenth Century Encoun-*

ters: Studies in Literature and Society in the Age of Walpole (Brighton: Harvester Press, 1985)

Sherburn, George *The Correspondence of Alexander Pope*, 5 vols (Oxford: Clarendon Press, 1956)

Spence, Joseph *Anecdotes, Observations and Characters of Books and Men*, new edn (London: Centaur Press, 1964)

Thompson, E P *Whigs and Hunters: The Origin of the Black Act* (Harmondsworth: Penguin Books, 1977)

Wong, Constant T S 'The Poet and the Philosopher: Pope, Bolingbroke and "An Essay on Man" ', unpublished PhD thesis, Monash University, 1983.

2

Pope and Churchill

BREAN S HAMMOND and *MARTIN MALONE*

An appropriate way of celebrating the tercentenary of a great poet might be to consider what happened to his work after he died. How did he influence the generations of poets immediately succeeding him? The answer, in Pope's case, is bleaker than in Jonson's or Dryden's, since there is a general consensus that verse satire went into decline after Pope died. In the case of satire, at any rate, Pope's *Dunciad* prophecy was realised—the Muse obey'd the Pow'r of Dulness. Only one not very bright star gleams in that extinguishing firmament—Charles Churchill.

A reader who can be persuaded to attend to Churchill's uptake on Pope is in for a surprise. The natural assumption might be that Churchill would eagerly shelter under Pope's aegis, or, more ambitiously, assume his mantle. Superficially at least, Churchill lived in analogous times to those of Pope. After the relatively soporific era of Pelham and Newcastle, genuine political differences seemed to re-emerge. In contrast to the inclusive tactics of the Broad-bottoms, there were once again 'outs' and 'ins', once again heroes like Pitt and Wilkes and villains like Bute. Conditions were again propitious for militant satire and it would have seemed sensible for a writer whose talents lay in that direction to arrogate to himself the Popean role of opposition laureate. Pope, producing his imitations of Donne's second and fourth *Satires*, had conceived his enterprise as analogous to Horace's sophistication of Lucilius (Erskine-Hill 1983, p 90). Might not Churchill have aspired to occupy a branch on that illustrious family tree?

In fact, Churchill was at pains to put as much distance between himself and Pope as he possibly could. Recording in verse his failure to obtain any significant patronage from Warburton, Churchill writes:

> Much did I wish, tho' little could I hope,
> A Friend in him, who was the Friend of POPE.
> (*Dedication to the Sermons*, 85–6)[1]

a comment typical of the sideswiping that goes on whenever Churchill has occasion to mention his eminent predecessor. In *An Epistle to William Hogarth* for instance, he attributes to malicious envy Pope's attack on Addison (though the accusation against Pope here is very versatile and could equally refer to the Timon's Villa passage in the *Epistle to Burlington* or even, conceivably, to Pope's publication of Bolingbroke's *Patriot King*):

> Had I (which Satirists of mighty name,
> Renown'd in rhyme, revered for *moral* fame,
> Have done before, whom Justice shall pursue
> In future verse) brought forth to public view
> A Noble Friend, and made his foibles known,
> Because his worth was greater than my own;

Here, Churchill hints at a more comprehensive attack on Pope that he never lived to make, but that he threatened in an anecdote preserved by Thomas Davies in his *Life of Garrick*:

> He was a great admirer of Dryden, in preference to Pope. . . . He held Pope so cheap, that one of his most intimate friends assured me, that he had some thoughts of attacking his poetry; and another gentleman informed me, that in a convivial hour he wished the bard of Twickenham was alive, that he might have an opportunity to make him bring forth all his art of Poetry, for he would not only have a struggle with him for pre-eminence, but endeavour to break his heart.
>
> (Grant 1956, p 538)

The note of fierce competitiveness struck here sounds again in a comment Churchill made in a letter to Wilkes of August 1763:

> Several poems I shall have out soon . . . Mr. Pope ought surely to feel some instinctive terrors, for against him I have double pointed all my little Thunderbolts, in which, as to the design, I hope I shall have your approbation, When you consider his heart
>
> (Grant, p 539)

His hostility towards Pope was obvious enough to men of his own time to be mentioned in satirical attacks on him such as *Churchill Dissected*, which contains the following lines:

> Or would not Envy suffer him to raise
> Round POPE's fair Tomb, the Tribute of his Praise?
> POPE, thy great Master in Satyric Art,
> Without thy hellish Rancour at his Heart.

Yet it is abundantly clear, despite his own disclaimers, that Churchill's poetry is massively dependent on Pope's, to an extent that makes for unconscious irony. The *Epistle to Dr Arbuthnot* and *Epilogue to the Satires* are intertexts evoked by several of Churchill's poems. His classic *pronunciatum* on prosody, delivered in *The Apology*, is a repudiation of Pope in favour of Dryden; but the passage is a virtual template over a celebrated section of the *Essay on Criticism* (337ff):

In polish'd numbers, and majestic sound,
Where shall thy rival, Pope, be ever found?
But whilst each line with equal beauty flows,
E'en excellence, unvary'd, tedious grows.
Nature, thro' all her works, in great degree,
Borrows a blessing from VARIETY.
Music itself her needful aid requires
To rouze the soul, and wake our dying fires.
Still in one key, the Nightingale would teize:
Still in one key, not BRENT would always please.

(*The Apology*, 366–87)

How hard Churchill tries to make the sound echo the sense in the boring dactyls 'excellent, unvaried, tedious', and to conform to Pope's onomatopoeic manifesto in the anaphoric 'Still in one key', the dependence culminating a few lines later in the frank verbal borrowing of 'What if some dull lines in cold order creep?'

By now, Churchill's borrowing of lines, structural devices like the dialogue form in poems like *The Candidate* and *The Farewell* and his deployment, albeit half-hearted, of *The Dunciad*'s satiric mythos in *The Rosciad* and elsewhere, is quite well-documented (Brown 1943, Weatherly 1946, Winters 1961). It is nevertheless worth pausing a little to show just how deeply Pope's work is sedimented in Churchill's, so that the conundrum of his repudiation will strike the reader with full force.

We might, for instance, follow a strand of thinking in Churchill's verse. In *Gotham* 3.63ff, he imagines the satisfactions to be gained from being a 'PATRIOT KING', a paternal, benevolent monarch who would subdue factions, abolish 'Corruption', patronise the arts and create a brotherhood of man. The vision is Bolingbroke's as expressed in *The Idea of a Patriot King* and is underpropped by the social theory memorably expressed in Epistle 3 of the *Essay on Man*, that love of self can be adjusted perfectly to patriotism, or love of one's nation. In *The Farewell*, the poet's persona gives a virtual summary of Pope's Epistle, enlivened by the same tropes of ladder and river:

Those ties of private nature, small extent,
In which the mind of narrow cast is pent,
Are only steps on which the gen'rous soul
Mounts by degrees till She includes the whole.
That spring of Love, which in the human mind,
Founded on self, flows narrow and confin'd,
Enlarges as it rolls, and comprehends
The social Charities of blood, and friends,
Till smaller streams included, not o'er past,
It rises to our Country's love at last,
And He, with lib'ral and enlarged mind,
Who loves his Country, cannot hate mankind.

(*The Farewell*, 289–300)

More suggestively, we might examine one of Churchill's most interesting, if least assured, performances—*The Prophecy of Famine*. This poem is billed as a 'Scots Pastoral', a label that will be received by the reader as a comic paradox since Scotland is not the most likely country in which to situate the classical *locus amoenus*.

Perhaps, the reader conjectures, it will be an attempt to renegotiate the decorum of pastoral along the serio-comic lines of John Gay's *The Shepherd's Week*? At all events, the reader will be alerted to a debate over the status of contemporary pastoral in which Alexander Pope was a key spokesman. Pope's own pastorals, and the *Discourse* in which he justified them, had argued for the acclimatisation of Arcadia to England. The pastoralist must give the classical eclogues of Theocritus and Virgil a local habitation: and it was Philips' attempt to domesticate them more radically (which upstaged Pope's *Pastorals* in critical notice when both sets were printed in Tonson's *Miscellany*) that drew Pope's famous ironic *Guardian* attack on native pastoral. Churchill's poem opens by situating itself within this debate over pastoral ideology, declaring himself in favour of native pastoral:

> Clad, as your nymphs were always clad of yore,
> In rustic weeds—a cook-maid now no more—
> Beneath an aged oak LARDELLA lies—
> Green moss, her couch; her canopy, the skies.
> From aromatic shrubs the *roguish* gale
> Steals *young* perfumes, and wafts them thro' the vale.
> The youth, turn'd swain, and skill'd in rustic lays,
> Fast by her side his am'rous descant plays.
> Herds lowe, Flocks bleat, Pies chatter, Ravens scream,
> And the full chorus dies a-down the stream.
> The streams, with music freighted, as they pass,
> Present the fair LARDELLA with a glass,
> And ZEPHYR, to compleat the love-sick plan,
> Waves his light wings, and serves her for a fan.
> (*Prophecy*, 15–28)

Clearly, the poet is handling the pastoral idiom and conventions with tongs here and doubtless his actual belief is Johnson's, that the pastoral as a vehicle for serious expression of feeling is dead. For polemic purposes, however, he expresses faith in an unsophisticated form of it and goes onto argue that in this era of a tyrannical '*great man*' (Bute, of course), such honest rustication has been replaced by 'Ostentation' and 'Pride'. Reason makes a sacrifice of instinctive pastoral (Jack's desire to woo Jill in song) and replaces it by 'NONSENSE with *Classic* ornaments'. Lest we forget who is responsible for such nonsense, the next paragraph alludes to the opening of Pope's *Spring* and goes on to guy the idealised landscape depicted in *Summer*:

> Then the rude THEOCRITE is ransack'd o'er,
> And *courtly* MARO call'd from MINCIO's shore;

Sicilian Muses on our mountains roam,
Easy and free as if they were at home;
NYMPHS, NAIADS, NEREIDS, DRYADS, SATYRS, FAUNS,
Sport in our floods, and trip it o'er our lawns;
Flow'rs which once flourish'd fair in GREECE and ROME,
More fair revive in ENGLAND'S meads to bloom;
Skies without cloud exotic suns adorn;
And roses blush, but blush without a thorn;
Landscapes, unknown to *Dowdy* Nature, rise,
And new creations strike our wond'ring eyes.

(*Prophecy*, 47–58)

The lines in *Spring* read:

First in these Fields I try the Sylvan Strains,
Nor blush to sport on *Windsor's* blissful Plains:
Fair *Thames* flow gently from thy sacred Spring,
While on thy Banks *Sicilian* Muses sing;
Let Vernal Airs thro' trembling Osiers play,
And *Albion's* Cliffs resound the Rural Lay.

(*Spring*, 1–6)

Churchill's actual target, as it appears in the next paragraph, is not directly Pope, but rather the poets of the 'ode and elegy and sonnet' school, specifically William Mason and George, Lord Lyttelton. These poets exemplify for Churchill the new decadence, defined not quite as Pope had defined it in terms of state-sponsored propaganda, but rather as a poetic form in which individual feeling has been subdued by collective 'Taste':

For bards, like these, who neither sing nor say,
Grave without thought, and without feeling gay,
Whose numbers in one even tenor flow,
Attun'd to pleasure, and *attun'd* to woe,
Who, if *plain* COMMON-SENSE her visit pays,
And mars one couplet in their happy lays,
As at some Ghost affrighted, start and stare,
And ask the meaning of her coming there;
For bards like these a wreath shall MASON bring.
Lin'd with the softest down of FOLLY's wing;
IN LOVE'S PAGODA shall they ever doze,
And GISBAL kindly rock them to repose;
My lord—to letters as to *faith* most true—
At once their patron and example too—
Shall *quaintly* fashion his love-labour'd dreams,
Sigh with sad winds, and weep with weeping streams,
Curious in grief, (for real grief, we know,
Is curious to dress up the tale of woe)
From the green umbrage of some DRUID's seat,
Shall his own works in his own way repeat.

(*Prophecy*, 59–78)

But in an almost subliminal way, Churchill's anger is focused on Pope, whom he cannot forgive for the stifling of 'natural' poetry. The attack on monotony recapitulates his strictures on Pope's couplet art in *The Apology*: and Mason's 'wreath' is the poem that made his reputation in 1747, *Musaeus: a Monody to the Memory of Mr Pope, in Imitation of Milton's 'Lycidas'*. This poem has a catalogue of poetic mourners paying tribute to the deceased Pope in pastiche verse—Chaucer, Spenser and Milton. Milton gets carried away with rapture over Pope's grotto and fulsomely celebrates his mastery of rhyme (in blank verse!), confessing his own error in trying to subdue 'uncouth dirge' with blank verse. At this point, Pope interrupts to stress that sweet verse is juvenile trifling if it is not pressed into the service of patriotic and virtuous themes, after which he is embraced by the goddess Virtue herself and ravished to the sky. Lyttelton, both 'patron and example' of fustian like this, had also written a *Monody* in 1747, 'To the Memory of Lady Lyttelton', which certainly outvies *Lycidas* in its articulation of what Churchill calls 'curious' grief:

> Where were ye, Muses, when relentless Fate
> From these fond arms your fair disciple tore;
> From these fond arms, that vainly strove
> With hapless ineffectual love
> To guard her bosom from the mortal blow? . . .
> Nor then did Pindus, or Castalia's plain,
> Or Aganippe's fount, your steps detain,
> Nor in the Thespian valleys did you play;
> Nor then in Mincio's bank
> Beset with osiers dank,
> Nor where Clitumnus rolls his gentle stream,
> Nor where, through hanging woods,
> Steep Anio pours his floods:

Churchill's interest in pastoral might also have stretched to Lyttelton's early eclogues *The Progress of Love*, inscribed to Pope, that continued the tradition of artificial pastoral:

> POPE! to whose reed, beneath the beechen shade,
> The nymphs of Thames a pleased attention paid,
> While yet thy Muse, content with humbler praise,
> Warbled in Windsor's grove her silvan lays,
> Though now, sublimely borne on Homer's wing,
> Of glorious wars and godlike chiefs she sing;
> Wilt thou with me revisit once again
> The crystal fountain and the flowery plain?
> Wilt thou, indulgent, hear my verse relate
> The various changes of a lover's state;
> And while each turn of passion I pursue,
> Ask thy own heart if what I tell be true?

Equally significant is the verse epistle 'To Mr Pope' that Lyttelton addressed to him from Rome lamenting the debased poetic tradition of that once glorious city and suggesting, through the ghost of Virgil, that Pope should 'shun that thorny, that unpleasing way' of satire and compose a British epic 'to sing the land, which yet alone can boast/That liberty corrupted Rome has lost'. Since Lyttelton was instrumental in spurring Pope on to even greater efforts in the cause of Patriot opposition to Walpole, Churchill would have regarded him as midwife at the birth of the poetry of public virtue that was his aversion.[2]

We have done enough to show how deeply involved Churchill's poetry is with Pope's, despite the fact that he denied that involvement. There is a very straightforward account of this paradox, which is given by the anonymous eighteenth-century editor of Letters to and from Mr Wilkes, who has the virtue of being in close contact with Churchill's feelings:

> Mr Churchill thought meanly of *Pope*'s private character, and was always disgusted with the extravagant compliments paid by the minor critics to him, as the *first* of our poets . . . The writings of *Pope*, almost the only truly correct, elegant, and high-finished poems in our language, breathe the purest morality, the most perfect humanity and benevolence. In the commerce of life however he shewed himself not scrupulously moral, and was a very selfish, splenetic, malevolent being. The friends, whom he most loved, were the sworn enemies of the liberties of his country, Atterbury, Oxford and Bolingbroke, on which he lavished the sweet incense of a delicate, exquisite praise, which ought only to have been purchased by virtue.
>
> (1769, I, pp 310–11)

In short, Churchill considered that Pope was an inauthentic poet, whose poetry created a censored version of his life. Although nowadays more allowances are made for the part played by the generic demands of formal verse satire in the construction of Pope's poetic self-image, this inauthenticity is still a fundamental problem for all biographers, including Maynard Mack. Certainly, Churchill's explanation is too simplistic. It cannot explain the absorption of so much of Pope's form and substance into Churchill's verse. Only a biographical method that is adequately theorised to handle the notion of the 'poetic unconscious', and does not confine us to what was in Churchill's conscious knowledge, can hope to deal with the paradox of his rejection of Pope. Since 1973, such a theory has been available: this looks like a paradigm case of Harold Bloom's 'anxiety of influence'.

Bloom's *The Anxiety of Influence* (1973) 'offers a theory of poetry by way of a description of poetic influence, or the study of intra-poetic relationships' (p 5). Bloom defines poetic influence thus:

> Poetic Influence is the sense—amazing, agonizing, delighting—of other poets, as felt in the depths of the all-but-perfect solipsist, the potentially strong poet.

For the poet is condemned to learn his profoundest yearnings through an awareness of other selves. The poem is within him, yet he experiences poems—outside him. To lose freedom in this center is never to forgive, and to learn the dread of threatened autonomy forever.

(pp 25–6)

Did Churchill, then, feel as a result of an acute awareness of Pope a 'loss of freedom'? In Bloom's terminology, his persistent rejections of Pope would be represented as the efforts of a strong new poet to throw off his 'Covering Cherub'. With Bloom's theory in mind, it is worth glancing again at the lines from *The Apology* in which Churchill dismisses the tedious excellence of Pope in favour of Dryden's 'noblest vigour':

> Here let me bend, great DRYDEN, at thy shrine,
> Thou dearest name to all the tuneful nine.
> What if some dull lines in cold order creep,
> And with his theme the poet seems to sleep?
> Still when his subject rises proud to view,
> With equal strength the poet rises too.
> With strong invention, noblest vigour fraught,
> Thought still springs up and rises out of thought;
> Numbers, ennobling numbers in their course,
> In varied sweetness flow, in varied force;
> The pow'rs of Genius and of Judgment join,
> And the Whole Art of Poetry is Thine.
> (*The Apology*, 376–87)

This passage seems to encapsulate a form of anxiety which Bloom calls *tessera*. *Tessera* expresses the relationship between poet, precursor and Muse by reference to Freud's articulation of the same kind of triangular structure in the more common circumstances of the family.

The poet, then, allows his work to take on an unnecessary bias as a defence against annihilation. His agony is nicely demonstrated in a passage from *Gotham*, 3. 419–22, where Churchill pays a compliment to Dryden:

> Have I, at your command, (i.e. STUDY's) in verse grown grey,
> But not impair'd, heard DRYDEN tune that lay,
> Which might have drawn an Angel from his sphere,
> And kept him from his office list'ning here.

After this passage, according to the annotations on Wilkes's copy of Churchill's poems, he had intended to insert the lines:

> Whilst Pope, with envy stung, enflam'd with pride,
> Pip'd to the vacant air on t'other side
> (Grant 1956, pp. 538–9)

Thus anxiety results in acts of misprision, as Churchill credits Dryden with a debt of influence that he actually owes to Pope.

Suggestible though Bloom's account is as a solution of the Pope/Churchill enigma, it is not possible to allow the matter to remain there. The hermetic quality of Bloom's model has come under telling attack from other literary theorists. Frank Lentricchia puts the general point very well:

> In (Bloom's) refusal to recognize any longer the constitutive role of extraliterary forces ("differences in religion and politics") upon identity, Bloom turns himself into a remarkably odd scholarly creature: the historian as aesthete . . . The unspoken assumption is that poetic identity is somehow a wholly intraliterary process in no contact with the larger extraliterary processes that shape human destiny.
>
> (Lentricchia 1980, p 326)

It is not merely to the inherent implausibility of Bloom's attempt to determine the relation of influence entirely in psychoanalytic terms that we should object. Virtually all recent commentators on Churchill's poetry have stressed his importance in *forming* a concept of originality as radical as the one Bloom conceives poets trying to protect. They stress the Mannerist quality of his writing, which is the result of various kinds of 'stretching'; whether in the direction of a sentimentalised Juvenalian declamation, as W B Carnochan has argued, or of an aesthetic criterion that licenses ruggedly individualistic behaviour ('Fancy' rather than 'Truth'), as Alan Fisher has suggested (Carnochan 1970; Fisher, 1973). The most thorough study of Churchill's poetry to date, by Thomas Lockwood (1979), shows satire gradually abandoning its commitment to the idea of permanently existent, shared values in favour of a coherence bestowed by the satirist's wayward genius alone. Vincent Carretta (1983), accepting this description of generic mutation, argues that it derives from a loss of faith in historical explanation, specifically in the tradition of exemplary historiography that provided the satirist with a secure position from which to speak. From all sides, there is evidence that Churchill would not possess, at any level of consciousness, the attitude towards originality that is typical of at least one isolationist strand of Romantic thought— though it is a measure of Churchill's importance that he is in some degree responsible for this *Gestalt*-switch.

Do we therefore have to abandon Bloom's theory altogether as a result of its perverse anti-historicism, or are there ways in which we can open it up to other kinds of more positivist influence while retaining its insight into what does indeed seem to be a case of 'misprision'? In our view, Churchill's compulsion to define himself in antithesis to Pope does not altogether need to be explained by reaching into the dark recesses of the psyche. It is clear that the psychological pressures Churchill was experiencing shaking off Pope's ghost were also being felt by others under the pressure of a mid-century crisis in defining the poet's role. We therefore think that there are means of recuperating the valuable parts of Bloom's approach while avoiding being imprisoned by its anti-historicism. To our minds, Pope's poetic embodiment of Addison holds a vital clue. It has been noticed that the Atticus portrait in the *Epistle to Dr Arbuthnot* carries a peculiar biographical supercharge, which the critic Dustin H Griffin accounts for by arguing that Addison is an 'antiself' to Pope. 'Pope's sense of himself seems to have been strengthened and clarified by the presence of a real or imagined other against which he himself might thrust' (1978, p 173). This sense of difference within a general field of similarity is confirmed by Maynard Mack in the recent biography of Pope:

> They were too much alike in some ways: both vain, both exquisitely sensitive to criticism, both too fond of the aristocratic pose of the literary amateur for whom writing is simply an amusement, both secretive and on some occasions devious. At the same time, they were such clear opposites in temperament . . . , in way of life, and in their responses to experience that misunderstandings could almost be counted on.
>
> (1985, p 272)

As Addison was to Pope, so, we believe, Pope was to Churchill. Pope is one of Churchill's 'antiselves'. In *An Epistle to William Hogarth*, as well as in many other places in his verse, Churchill mythologises the abstractions of 'Prudence' and 'Candour', the latter quality being the distinguishing feature of his own satire. 'Candour' was a term that had already begun its career as a watchword of the Radical Dissenters, in the sense of 'freedom from mental bias, openness of mind; fairness, impartiality, justice' (*OED* 3), and Churchill also arrogates it to himself in its more domestic significations of 'freedom from malice' and 'outspokenness'. As an example of 'Prudence' in action, Churchill alludes to Pope's Atticus portrait:

> Had I (which Satirists of mighty name,
> Renown'd in rime, rever'd for *moral* fame,
> Have done before, whom Justice shall pursue
> In future verse) brought forth to public view
> A Noble Friend, and made his foibles known,
> Because his worth was greater than my own;
> (*An Epistle to William Hogarth*, 141–6)

'Prudence', in Churchill's usage, is an ironised label for inauthenticity, a form of hypocrisy particularly odious when encountered in a satirist of Pope's standing. As is said in *The Farewell*:

> Poets, accustom'd by their trade to feign,
> Oft substitute creations of the brain
> For real substance, and, themselves deceiv'd.
> Would have the fiction by mankind believ'd.

To Churchill, Pope's claims to moral probity were bogus. In the terms created by the poem *Night*, Pope was a poet of the 'Day', whereas Churchill was a poet of the 'Night'; that is to say, where Pope is associated with politics, 'patriotism' and prudence, Churchill's ambience is freedom and ease and 'candour'. Despite Pope's professed love for confession ('I love to pour out all myself, as plain,/As downright *Shippen*, or as old *Montagne*'), Churchill would have found in Pope no admission as frank as his own in *The Conference*, 101ff, where the poet confesses his needy past and his bankruptcy. True, Churchill lived the life of a rake while Pope was constitutionally unable to do other than piddle on broccoli and mutton; and this made it difficult for him to accept domestic morality as the basis for normative satire. But the differences are deeper than matters of personal lifestyle. Whereas Pope collapsed the distinction between the public and the private domain in presenting his own exemplary life as the guarantee for his politics, Churchill in *The Conference* wishes to re-instate the distinction between his guilty private life and his unblemished record of public service. Whereas in the *Epistle to Dr Arbuthnot*, Pope had claimed independence not only of patronage but also of the market-place (as *The Dunciad* implicitly does in condemning 'hacks' who write for bread), Churchill is proud of the fact that his own independence has been gained from public patronage, from marketing his assets:

> That I no longer skulk from street to street,
> Afraid lest Duns assail, and Bailiffs meet;
> That I from place to place this carcase bear,
> Walk forth at large, and wander free as air;
> That I no longer dread the aukward friend,
> Whose very obligations must offend,
> Nor, all too froward, with impatience burn
> At suff'ring favours which I can't return;
> That, from dependance and from pride secure,
> I am not plac'd so high to scorn the poor,
> Nor yet so low, that I my Lord should fear,
> Or hesitate to give him sneer for sneer;
> That, whilst sage Prudence my pursuits confirms,
> I can enjoy the world on equal terms;
> That, kind to others, to myself most true,
> Feeling no want, I comfort those who do,
> And with the will have pow'r to aid distress;
> These, and what other blessings I possess,
> From the indulgence of the PUBLIC rise;
> All private Patronage my Soul defies.
> By Candour more inclin'd to save, than damn,
> A gen'rous PUBLIC made me what I Am.
> All that I have, They gave; just Mem'ry bears
> The grateful stamp, and what I am is Theirs.
>
> (*The Conference*, 129–52)

This could scarcely be further away from the aristocratic base of the predicated relationship between poet and reader that is found in Pope.

It is this awareness of the value of the market-place that provides the ideological justification for the new breed of self-dependent satire that Lockwood perceives as being the identifying feature of late-century satire (1979, pp 45–60). Churchill's satire is downwardly mobile socially compared to Pope's, as befits the supporter of 'Wilkes and Liberty'; and this is a timely reminder that the main differences between Pope and Churchill are to be found in a domain no more recherché than politics.

Robert Southey, in a review of Churchill's poems published in the *Annual Review* for 1804, helps us to locate the sphere of greatest distinction between the two poets.

> It was [Churchill's] intention to write an epic poem upon the battle of Culloden. Modern warfare is even less poetical than picturesque; it would have been curious to see how an event so recent could have been modified to his purpose, and a General of the year 1745 elevated into an epic hero . . . Churchill would have done justice to the Jacobites; he would have delineated strongly the absurdity of their principles, but he would not have forgotten the virtues by which that absurdity was fostered.[2]

We find no reason to share Southey's confidence over Churchill's depiction of Jacobite virtues, but he does remind us of the inordinate esteem in which Churchill held the Duke of Cumberland, and of the prominent part played by the Jacobites in the mythology of his satires. He was, after all, a war-child of the Jacobite Rebellion. When he was a boy of twelve, London was in a state of increasing panic over the Pretender's march south. A vivid sense of this is conveyed in Fielding's nightmarish vision of London sacked by a Highland host of outer Barbarians published in the *True Patriot* for 19 November 1745:

> The first sight which occurred to me as I passed through the streets . . . was a young lady of quality, and the greatest beauty of this age, in the hands of two Highlanders, who were struggling with each other for their booty. The lovely prize, though her hair was dishevelled and torn, her eyes swollen with tears, her face all pale, and some marks of blood both on that and her breast, which was all naked and exposed, retained still sufficient charms to discover herself to me, who have always beheld her with wonder and admiration. Indeed, it may be questioned whether perfect beauty loses or acquires charms by distress. This sight was matter of entertainment to my conductors, who, however, hurried me presently from it, as I wish they had also from her screams, which reached my ears to a great distance.
>
> After such a spectacle as this, the dead bodies which lay everywhere in the streets (for there had been, I was told, a massacre the night before), scarce made any impression: nay, the very fires in which Protestants were roasting, were, in my sense, objects of much less horror; nay, such an effect had this sight wrought on my mind, which hath been always full of the utmost tenderness for that charming sex, that for a moment it obliterated all concern for my children, from whom I was to be hurried for ever without a farewel, or without knowing in what condition I left them; or indeed, whether they had hitherto survived the cruelty which now methought raged every where, with all the fury which rage, zeal, lust, and wanton fierceness could inspire into the bloody hearts of Popish priests, bigots, and barbarians.[3]

Doubtless, such apocalyptic imaginings had a lasting effect on the poet's sensibility, since Jacobite-inspired invasions of marauding Scotsmen figure prominently in his poems. It is too often overlooked that the last Jacobite attempt at an invasion of mainland Britain was as recent as 1759, so that Churchill's Jacobites are not entirely the children's bogeymen that they might seem if we take 1745 to be the final destruction of the cause. The main role for Bute and the Jacobites in Churchill's verse, however, is as a substitute for the powerful figure of Walpole, who provides such a magnetic centre for the satire of the earlier era. Bute, a Stuart related to the Pretender's family, can be represented as the figurehead of a Caledonian plot to dispossess the English of their lands and wealth, as he is in *The Prophecy of Famine*.

We have already considered the allusions to Pope in the earlier part of the poem, but these become even richer when it discovers its true theme. In a mock-pastoral dialogue (comically imitating Allan Ramsay's *The Gentle Shepherd*), Jockey and Sawney are lamenting the defeat of the Jacobites in the Fifteen and the Forty-Five.[4] They are located in a cave that bears more than a passing resemblance to the *Dunciad*'s 'Cave of Poverty and Poetry', but fitted with the tartan decor of thistles, briars and (indispensable to any Scottish cave) spiders. To the two rebels appears the Goddess of Famine, who makes them a prophecy of future glory as the occupiers of a subdued England. The prophecy is in imitation of Virgil's fourth *Eclogue*, but to this as embodied in *Windsor Forest*. Pope's splendid vision of peace and commercial prosperity is appropriated by the Goddess of Famine and turned upside down. *Windsor Forest* meets *The Dunciad* in a climax of sectarian exploitation:

> For us, the earth shall bring forth her increase;
> For us, the flocks shall wear a golden fleece;
> Fat Beeves shall yield us dainties not our own,
> And the grape bleed a nectar yet unknown;
> For our advantage shall their harvests grow,
> And *Scotsmen* reap, what they disdained to sow;
> For us, the sun shall climb the eastern hill;
> For us, the rain shall fall, the dew distil;
> When to our wishes NATURE cannot rise,
> ART shall be task'd to grant us fresh supplies.
> His brawny arm shall drudging LABOUR strain,
> And for our pleasure suffer daily pain;
> TRADE shall for us exert her utmost pow'rs,
> Her's, all the toil; and all the profit, our's;
> For us, the Oak shall from his native steep
> Descend, and fearless travel thro' the deep,
> The sail of COMMERCE for our use unfurl'd,
> Shall waft the treasures of each distant world;
> For us, sublimer heights shall science reach,
> For us, their Statesmen plot, their Churchmen preach;
> Their noblest limbs of counsel we'll disjoint,
> And, mocking, new ones of our own appoint;
> Devouring WAR, imprison'd in the north,
> Shall, at our call, in horrid pomp, break forth,
> And when, his chariot wheels with thunder hung,

Fell Discord braying with her brazen tongue,
Death in the van, with Anger, Hate, and Fear,
And Desolation stalking in the rear,
Revenge, by Justice guided, in his train,
He drives impetuous o'er the trembling plain,
Shall, at our bidding, quit his lawful prey,
And to meek, gentle, gen'rous Peace give way.
(*The Prophecy of Famine*, 455–86)

For Churchill, this travesty of Pope's Stuart panegyric must have been especially satisfying, since his predecessor's presumed commitment to the Jacobite cause was an especially prickly thorn in his flesh. The account given of English history in *Windsor Forest* could not be further away from that in his own *Gotham* 2.250ff, where Churchill ranges himself against the Restoration and hails William III as the Protestant saviour.

This is why a short and relatively minor poem of Churchill's is especially significant to a consideration of his relationship with Pope. 'Verses written in Windsor Park', printed in the *London Chronicle* in August 1763 celebrates the Duke of Cumberland as Keeper of the Forest just as Pope had earlier paid tribute to Sir William Trumbull in the same capacity:

WHEN POPE to Satire gave its lawful way,
And made the Nimrods of mankind his prey;
When haughty WINDSOR heard thro' ev'ry wood
Their shame, who durst be great, yet not be good;
Who drunk with Pow'r, and with Ambition blind,
Slaves to themselves, and monsters to mankind,
Sinking the Man to magnify the Prince
Were heretofore, what STUARTS have been since;
Could he have look'd into the womb of time,
How might his spirit in prophetic rhyme,
Inspir'd by Virtue, and for Freedom bold,
Matters of different import have foretold!
How might his Muse, if any Muse's tongue
Could equal such an argument, have sung
One WILLIAM who makes all Mankind his care,
And shines the Saviour of his country there;
One WILLIAM who to every heart gives law;
The Son of GEORGE, the image of Nassau.

Vincent Carretta comments that this poem 'acknowledged the importance of political satire in Pope's *Windsor Forest* and sought to enlist his great predecessor in the current political struggle (1983, p 244). This is surely to miss the irony of the verses. It is scarcely conceivable that Churchill could have thought Pope recruitable to an anti-Stuart position, given that Pope's presumed Jacobitism was an open secret in his lifetime. So many of Churchill's satiric targets are Jacobites and some of these are former friends of Pope's, most notably William Murray, 1st Earl Mansfield, who was the dedicatee of Pope's *Imitation of Horace, Epistle I, vi*, a poem that, it has been argued, was written to gain Murray's support for the anti-Walpole opposition (Aden 1969, pp 69, 74). It is of course still a live issue in Pope biography how far he was a Jacobite and it is very unlikely that anything will be proven about this because being a Jacobite supporter in the period is rather like being a socialist now. The church is a broad one. There is much distance between an 'emotional' supporter of the cause and an armed insurrectionist; and as Bruce Lenman points out in his study of the Jacobite movement (1980, pp 205ff), the Jacobite cause in England after 1725 became 'essentially a verbal exercise', a means of expressing contempt for King George. Lenman's example of an 'insubstantial' Jacobite, William King, Principal of St Mary's Hall, Oxford, is an excellent one, a man who actually met the Pretender, but whose Jacobite innuendos were really a knee-jerk reaction to aspects of English life that he disliked. He is an excellent example, too, because he was a friend of Pope's, and because the insubstantiality of his Jacobite opinions did not prevent him from being attacked in verse by Churchill (*The Candidate*, 703–16). The fact remains that whatever the truth about Pope and Jacobitism, and there is much circumstantial evidence to suggest that he was at least emotionally committed to the cause, that he was widely accused of Jacobitism in his own time and that this is the reputation Churchill would have absorbed.

Perhaps we are now in a position to offer a solution to the biographical detective story we have been unfolding. A great bear of a man with coarse features (even in physical appearance, the anti-type of the finely-chiselled Pope), former Anglican clergyman and anti-Jacobite, Churchill's opinions and attitudes were in most respects opposed to those of Pope. Nevertheless, he was engaged on a self-conscious mission to restore the satirist to the position of public prominence that Pope's poetry had gained for him. Changes in the nature of politics and in the *Zeitgeist* of poetry had, however, already rendered his aspirations redundant. Pope's independence, the basis of his *ego contra mundum* mythology, derived from his sense of speaking for an aristocratic alternative government, an aristocracy, not only of rank but of talent, whose values were based on collective morality. This mythology was largely closed to Churchill, to whom it was unsuitable temperamentally and in most other ways. Since absolute originality is quite inconceivable, Churchill needed to borrow many of the forms of Pope's poems, but also needed to 'inhabit' these forms in a way that created a presence appreciably different to Pope's. Sadly, most readers agree that this new presence lacks the Popean conviction; the diminution of moral energy ensures that Churchill would, in Byron's terms, 'flame the meteor of a day'. It is altogether unlikely that, in the year 2032, admirers of his work will gather together to celebrate his tercentenary with a collection of essays like this.

NOTES

1 All citations of the poetry are to Grant 1956.
2 Although it was not until late in Pope's career that it became known that he was contemplating writing an epic poem, *Brutus*, it is interesting to note that as early

as 1730 Lyttelton was urging him to it. He returned to this suggestion a decade later when co-ordinating the Patriot opposition.

3   *The True Patriot* No. 3 (19 Nov 1745) in *The Works of Henry Fielding*, 10 vols (London, 1806), 8, 81.

4   It is perhaps more than mere coincidence that Churchill uses the unusual nickname 'Sawney' in this dialogue. Pope was given the name 'Sawney' in pamphlet attacks. The pamphlet published in the *Daily Post* for 31 August 1742, *Sawney and Colley, A Poetical Dialogue*, was a well-known reflection on Pope's quarrel with Cibber, and this may be alluded to in Churchill's dialogue between Sawney and Jockey.

References

Aden, John M *Something Like Horace: Studies in the Art and Allusions of Pope's Satire* (Nashville: Vanderbilt UP, 1969)

Bloom, H *The Anxiety of Influence* (Oxford: Oxford UP, 1973)

Brown, W C 'Charles Churchill: a Revaluation', *Studies in Philology* 40 (1943), 402–24.

Caretta, V *The Snarling Muse: Verbal and Visual Political Satire from Pope to Churchill* (Philadelphia: Philadelphia UP, 1983)

Carnochan, W B 'Satire, Sublimity and Sentiment: Theory and Practice in Post-Augustan Satire', *PMLA* 85 (1970), 250–67

Erskine-Hill, Howard *The Augustan Idea in English Literature* (London: Edward Arnold, 1983)

Fisher, A 'The Stretching of Augustan Satire: Charles Churchill's "Dedication" to Warburton', *JEGP* 72 (1973), 360–77.

Grant, D (ed) *The Poetical Works of Charles Churchill* (Oxford: Oxford UP, 1956)

Griffin, D H *Alexander Pope, The Poet in the Poems* (New Jersey: Princeton UP, 1978)

Lenman, Bruce *The Jacobite Risings in Britain 1689–1746* (New York: Holmes and Meier, 1980)

Lentricchia, F *After the New Criticism* (Chicago: Chicago UP, 1980)

Lockwood, T *Post-Augustan Satire: Charles Churchill and Satirical Poetry 1750–1800* (Seattle: Univ of Washington Press, 1979)

Mack, M *Alexander Pope: A Life* (New Haven: Princeton UP, 1985)

Southey, R *Annual Reviews 1804*

Weatherly, E H 'Churchill's Literary Indebtedness to Pope', *Studies in Philology* 43 (1946), 56–69

Winters I 'The poetry of Charles Churchill', *Poetry* 98 (1961), 44–53.

3

Pope And The Scottish Enlightenment Universities

JOHN VALDIMIR PRICE

Pope is the most correct and elegant, perhaps, of all the English poets. He has most happily elucidated and adorned every subject he has undertaken; and his poetry, instead of being embarrassed or debased by rhyme, seems rather to have acquired by that means energy and sprightliness. We regret, however, that a writer of his genius should not have been more an original. Even the translation of Homer, and the imitations of Horace, seem scarcely adequate to the talents of such a genius.

That, at least, was what William Barron was telling his students at the University of St Andrews during his tenure (1778–1803) as Professor of Logic, Rhetoric and Metaphysics (Barron, I, 439). Barron draws attention to and quotes from Pope often throughout his lectures, and his high estimation of him is not unique. A short distance away in Edinburgh, Hugh Blair frequently illustrated his better-known lectures with examples from Pope.

When Blair was appointed to the newly-created Chair of Rhetoric and Belles Lettres at the University of Edinburgh on 7 April 1762, he became the first 'official' professor of English literature in the world. It is clear from his lectures that he expected his students to have a fairly detailed knowledge of the ancient as well as modern writers. Though Blair can seem, and sometimes is, superficial, he was attempting a more comprehensive survey of literature, literary theory, types, and genres than any similar lecturer before, and to a certain extent after, him. Barron's lectures, in contrast, were part of a much larger framework, as is evident from the title (*Lectures on Belles Lettres and Logic*) of his work and Blair's title (*Lectures on Rhetoric and Belles Lettres*). His discussions of genre, for example, are not so detailed as those of Blair.

One of the genres (more accurately, sub-genres) that Blair distinguishes is 'Didactic Poetry', in which, he asserts, 'Mr Pope's Ethical Epistles deserve to be mentioned with signal honour, as a model next to perfect of this kind of Poetry. Here, perhaps, the strength of his genius appeared.' Pope's most conspicuous qualities are 'judgment and wit, with a concise and happy expression, and a melodious versification'. Blair praises both the quantity and quality of Pope's wit, calling *The Rape of the Lock* 'the greatest masterpiece that perhaps was ever composed, in the gay and sprightly Style', while in Pope's more serious works, such as *An Essay on Man* and the *Moral Essays*, 'his wit just discovers itself as much, as to give a proper seasoning to grave reflexions' (Blair, II, 368–9).

Blair's numerous mentions of Pope are made with the confidence of a teacher who knows that his students are familiar with the works in question. His analyses are not often detailed, but that is probably a result of the organisation of his material rather than anything else. He does analyse in detail several *Spectator* papers, as well as a passage from Swift, while Pope is used as a reference point for certain fundamental literary qualities. The generalised comments by Blair on *An Essay on Man* can be contrasted with those of Barron:

> The Essay on Man admitted fewer embellishments and episodes than the poems I have mentioned [Armstrong: *The Art of Preserving Health*; Virgil: *Georgics*; Lucretius: *De Natura Deorum*]. The author's design was more serious than that of any other writer of his class. Instruction was his main object, and no ornaments are introduced but what are manifestly subservient to this end. He employs metaphors frequently, and sometimes comparisons, but they are never mere addresses to the fancy of the reader, they always contribute to illustrate and impress the matter.
>
> This famous essay is literally a system of morals . . . The discussion is ingenious and instructive. We, however, desiderate that distinct and lucid arrangement which we discern in the productions of the other two eminent moderns [Leibniz and Shaftesbury]. Neither has the versification all the merits which shine in his other works; it is frequently abrupt, if not obscure, and possesses not the melody and flow of his other poetry. The abstract nature of the subject, perhaps, and his sincere desire to instruct, rather than to please, may furnish an apology.
>
> (Barron, II, 162–3)

Barron attributes the origin of Pope's argument to Plato, whose 'celebrated doctrine' was developed in the eighteenth century by Leibniz and Shaftesbury. Barron's comments on the style, the manner, and the conduct of Pope's argument perhaps indicate a reluctance to examine the poem for its ideas or its doctrine, or they may simply reflect indifference to the ideas; but he does acknowledge that ideas are at work in the poem.

Some other indication, however, that *An Essay on Man* was intellectually respectable can be gained from a student at Edinburgh University during Hugh Blair's time as Professor. George Gregory (1754–1808) gave up a business career to study at the University and attained the degree of DD in 1792. In some Chesterfieldian letters to his son, he agreed with Samuel Johnson's opinion about *An Essay on Man*, asserting that 'the metaphysics are execrable', while affirming that its 'morality is pure, and sometimes sublime', its knowledge of human nature 'profound' and the poetry itself 'incomparable'; the best passages in the poem are its delineations of character. He seems also to have the distinction of being one of the first, if not the first, to assert that Bolingbroke borrowed from Pope rather than the other way around:

> There is extant a posthumous work of Lord Bolingbroke, purporting to be the substance of several conversations between him and Mr Pope, the object of which is to prove that the whole matter of the Essay on Man was dictated by his lordship, while Mr Pope was little more than a versifier. To me it appears that the work in question was rather taken from the Essay on Man than the Essay from it; and neither Lord Bolingbroke nor Mr Pope was the author of the system on which it is founded; for it is undoubtedly borrowed altogether from King's Origin of Evil: a work abundantly ingenious, but fallacious in its principles, and inaccurate in its conclusions.
>
> (Gregory, II, 168, 169)

Gregory's acceptance of Johnson's remark about the 'execrable' metaphysics in the work was not universally shared in the Scottish universities. Dugald Stewart, Professor of Moral Philosophy at the University of Edinburgh, 1785–1820, was rather more appreciative not only of what Pope was trying to do but what he achieved. *An Essay on Man*, he said, 'contains a valuable summary of all that human reason has been able hitherto to advance in justification of the moral government of God' (Stewart, *Works*, VII, 133).

These various comments illustrate certain aspects of *An Essay on Man* that none of its commentators specifically mention: the ubiquity as well as the multiplicity of its appeal, its variousness as well as its diversity. Yet no one credits Pope with any originality, and appreciation of the work seems to be made more difficult by Pope's determination to incorporate 'metaphysical' as well as moral ideas in the work. Most of the comments carry a tacit assumption that Pope was definitely trying to do something 'new and different' in this poem, and none of these comments focuses on exactly the same features. The diversity of opinions and responses that *An Essay on Man* inspired may be in part attributable to its generic waywardness: putting the ideas of someone else into verse is not something that immediately demands to be classified as 'Didactic Poetry'.

An Essay on Man clearly caused some genuine bewilderment on the part of its Scottish university readers, but the most serious attention that it attracted as a philosophical document came from James Beattie, who at the age of twenty-five had been appointed to the Chair of Moral Philosophy and Logic at Marischal College, Aberdeen. Pope appears to have been a regular constituent of his lectures, despite the fact that his ostensible subjects were logic and moral philosophy. We are able to judge, or at least to make inferences about, his inclusion of Pope's writings in his lectures from the published version of these which first appeared in 1790–3. In the case of *An Essay on Man*, he seems to have been eager to prevent his students from reading it with anything but censorious eyes: 'Pope's Essay on Man has many beautiful and sublime passages; but is founded on an erroneous system, whereof Bolingbroke was the author, and which it appears that Pope did not distinctly understand. The first draught of it in prose, in Bolingbroke's handwriting, has been seen by persons now alive' (Beattie 1817, II, 376–7). It is not clear whether Beattie is being generous or insulting to Pope here: to suggest that Pope would not have adopted Bolingbroke's philosophy had he understood the unChristian perniciousness of it begs the obvious question. The relevance of the remark about the notorious prose draft in Bolingbroke's handwriting is a red herring that a professor of logic ought to be ashamed of. Oddly enough, he is only repeating Hugh Blair's contention about Bolingbroke's role: writing to James Boswell on 21 September 1779, Blair affirms that Lord Bathurst had told him that the work had been originally composed in prose by Bolingbroke (Boswell, II, 402–3).

Beattie's objection to *An Essay on Man* is not so much an objection to Pope *per se*, but more of a reflection of his fear that so forceful and aphoristic a writer might subvert young minds without intending to do so. His own mind was sufficiently secure, apparently, to resist its apostate blandishments. The enthusiasm he had for it as a young man was restrained by his concern for its doctrine, but his admiration was full of superlatives. Writing in November, 1766, to his acquaintance, Charles Boyd, brother of Lord Errol, Beattie's patron, he confesses, 'Pope's "Essay on Man" is the finest philosophical poem in the world; but it seems to me to do more honour to the imagination than to the understanding of its author: I mean, its sentiments are noble and affecting, its images and allusions apposite, beautiful, and new: its wit transcendently excellent; but the scientific part of it is very exceptionable. Whatever Pope borrows from Leibniz, like most other metaphysical theories, is frivolous and unsatisfying: what Pope give us of his own is energetic, irresistible, and divine' (Forbes, I, 94). Like too many educators, Beattie distinguishes between his own enthusiasm for and appreciation of a particular work and his judgement about its suitability for young minds.

Beattie's preoccupation with the subject matter of *An Essay on Man* and its possible heterodoxy was not of concern to another distinguished professor. When Adam Smith began lecturing on rhetoric and belles lettres on his appointment to the Chair of Logic and Rhetoric at the University of Glasgow in 1751 (he was translated to the Chair of Moral Philosophy in April, 1752), he called his students' attention to the beauty of *An Essay on Man*: 'Two of the most beautifull passages in all Popes works are those in which he describes the state of mind of an untaught Indian; and the other in which he considers the various ranks and orders of beings in the universe' (Smith, p 33; *An Essay on Man*, I, 99–112 and 233–44). Since this particular lecture is on various figures of speech (Pope's passages illustrating figurae verborum and figurae sententiarum), he perhaps does not wish to raise the question of Pope's authority for describing the state of mind of an untaught Indian, but the emphasis on the beauty of the work is not something we might have expected from the famous economist. Smith is rather more sceptical of Pope's professed reasons for writing *An Essay on Man*, as we find in a later lecture: 'Mr Pope tells us that the reason which induced him to write his *Essay on Man* in verse rather than in prose was that he saw he could do it in a much shorter and concise manner. I much doubt indeed whether this was his real motive; but it shews he was very sensible of the great superiority of poetry over prose in this respect' (Smith, pp 117–18). It is unlikely that Smith's students, or anyone else for that matter, would have any doubts about the superiority of poetry for short and concise expression, and it is unfortunately not clear what Smith thinks Pope's motives for preferring poetry to prose for *An Essay on Man* might have been. Obvious achievement as poet seems almost *too* obvious.

Pope had been in his grave only a few years when Beattie and Smith began lecturing on him to their undergraduates, but he was already being perceived by university critics as having a variety of features to be emphasised for different audiences. That Beattie was genuinely worried about the efficacy of the ideas in *An Essay on Man* is without doubt; equally without doubt is Smith's clear-headed intention to get his students to approach the work first as a poem and secondly (if at all) as a philosophical text. What seems to me most revealing about all these comments on the origin of the poem, on its form, on the attribution to various authors of the 'matter' or 'design' of the poem to philosophers or quasi-philosophers rather than Pope is not so much an assumption about Pope but one about the nature of poetry and the skills of a poet. The possibility that a poet could actually think, that a poem might contain an argument, and might actually initiate new ideas is not raised by any of the authors or readers I have mentioned. If, as readers ourselves, we cast our minds back to one of the poems which inspired Pope, we might remember that in writing *Paradise Lost*, Milton was putting into epic form what readers of the Bible already knew, and the development of that poem is a narrative one. Pope, vindicating the ways of God to man, is not developing his 'epic' in a narrative manner. The organisation of Milton's material had not only historical precedent behind it but the authority of the Church as well. Pope had to face rather different problems, and while his poem has never lacked admirers (or detractors), it has certainly provoked a wider range of intellectual response than *Paradise Lost*.

Pope's role in the curriculum of the Scottish Enlightenment universities thus makes Barron's criticism of *An Essay on Man* of especial importance, as he perceives the difficulty in the organisation and development of the work: it lacks the 'distinct and lucid arrangement' that is to be found in the works of Leibniz and Shaftesbury. Blair says nothing about the organisation of the poem, nor about the development of an argument in the work, though unlike Barron but like Smith he finds the versification attractive. Equally, the student Gregory is attracted by its incomparability, as Beattie is by Pope's own irresistibility, while both find the 'metaphysical' part unacceptable. Gregory praises in particular the delineations of character in the poem, and his 'finest' passages come, unlike Smith's, from the fourth book, lines 193–308. Beattie has little to say about the arrangement or organisation of the work, but, curiously, his own choice of words for the cosmological and teleological parts of the poem is 'scientific'. The difficulties caused by Pope's attempt to develop philosophical ideas poetically are reflected in the problems his advocates in the Scottish universities have in describing what they regard as defective in the poem. It is curious that Barron wants to apologise for the work, thinking it to fail because Pope was revolutionary enough to wish to bring philosophy into poetry. We all remember what Addison proposed in

Spectator 10 to do with philosophy, to bring it out of closets and libraries and into coffee-shops and onto tea-tables. To Addison's new environment for philosophy Pope added a means of accommodating philosophy with coffee-shops and tea-tables. Few seemed to think Addison's act was inadvisable; many thought Pope's was.

To a certain extent, then, these observations set a tone and a trend for approaches and reactions to *An Essay on Man*. Johnson's notorious dismissal—'Never were penury of knowledge and vulgarity of sentiment so happily disguised' (Johnson, III, 243)—begs at least two questions but was echoed by Pope's nineteenth-century readers and editors, with the honourable exception of Byron. Pope was not, of course, the only poet in the Augustan period to try his hand at philosophical poetry, nor was he the first: Dryden's *Religio Laici* and *The Hind and the Panther* certainly take precedence, though they are more obviously theologically slanted (albeit in different directions) than *An Essay on Man*. *An Essay on Man* was a difficult poem for its readers: it denied easy generic classification, though it had distinguished classical antecedents as well as modern ones. That Pope was the author did not help much either: published anonymously, the poem was widely admired and applauded until the identity of the author was revealed.

Johnson was not the only reader who was more happy exercising traditional critical judgements about Pope's poetry than in thinking about what Pope was saying. Though James Beattie is more interested than Johnson in what Pope is actually saying, he also has the Johnsonian inclination (several years before Johnson) to compare Pope and Dryden:

> Critics have often stated a comparison between Dryden and Pope, as poets of the same order, and who differed only in *degree* of merit. But, in my opinion, the merit of the one differs considerably in *kind* from that of the other. Both were happy in a sound judgement and most comprehensive mind. Wit, and humour, and learning too, they seem to have possessed in equal measure; or, if Dryden may be thought to have gone deeper in the sciences, Pope must be allowed to have been the greater adept in the arts . . . If Dryden founds any claim of preference on the originality of his manner, we shall venture to affirm, that Pope may found a similar claim, and with equal justice, on the perfection of his taste; and that, if the critical writings of the first are more voluminous, those of the second are more judicious; if Dryden's inventions are more diversified, those of Pope are more regular, and more important. Pope's style may be thought to have less simplicity, less vivacity, and less of the purity of the mother-tongue; but it is at the same time more uniformly elevated, and less debased by vulgarism, than that of his great master:—and the superior variety that animates the numbers of the latter, will perhaps be found to be compensated by the steadier and more majestic modulation of the former.
>
> (Beattie 1776, pp 360n–361n)

Johnson's comment may be more eloquent, but it is not more persuasive:

> The notions of Dryden were formed by comprehensive speculation, and those of Pope by minute attention. There is more dignity in the knowledge of Dryden, and more certainty in that of Pope . . . The style of Dryden is capricious and

varied, that of Pope is cautious and uniform; Dryden obeys the motions of his own mind, Pope constrains his mind to his own rules of composition. Dryden is sometimes vehement and rapid; Pope is always smooth, uniform and gentle.

(Johnson, III, 222)

Eighteenth-century readers would probably have derived more from such generalised comments on the respective merits of the two poets than modern readers do, as the application of the generalised remark to a particular poem would have remained the prerogative of the reader. But such generalisations have something of a self-perpetuating quality about them: these features become ones to look for and respond to, and critical readers would search for passages or poems to fit such generalisations. It is not surprising, therefore, to discover that Beattie found Johnson's life of Pope 'excellent', though he signally failed to remark on the similarity of Johnson's comment to his earlier one (Forbes, II, 91).

A specific poem can thus elicit responses which suggest that critical consensus was quickly being structured. (Just what the causal elements in this structure were remains to be seen.) Another example can be found in assessments of *Eloisa to Abelard*. Johnson had said of this poem that Pope had 'excelled every composition of the same kind' (Johnson, III, 105), and Beattie had been saying much the same thing to his students for years: classifying it generically as an 'Epistolary Elegy', he declared it to be the 'finest in our language, or perhaps in any language' (Beattie 1817, II, 374). Hugh Blair described it as a 'very beautiful poem', 'almost his only sentimental production', but of its kind, 'excellent' (Blair, I, 334–5). Perhaps a remarkable thing that all these observations have in common is their tacit acceptance or carefully-mustered silence about the poem's eroticism. One must also wonder about Beattie's failure to voice some uneasiness about the theological implications of the poem, not to mention the absence of a certain kind of moral didacticism. More remarkable still is Beattie's ranking it not only above the elegies of Donne and Milton, but those of Anacreon, Ovid, Propertius, etc whose classical status might otherwise have ensured their precedence. It is, however, a 'modern' poem, having been published in 1717, but its subject was sufficiently distant in time and capable of being tinged with a certain amount of sentimentality by the reader: the emotional phenomena that it delineates have a beauty and an appeal that are more readily comprehended and psychologically assimilated than the aphoristic epistemology of *An Essay on Man*.

That the poem had moments of psychological verisimilitude for its readers was not in doubt, and Adam Smith was able to articulate more specifically what was contained within the generalisations just cited. Arguing that when we feel strongly about something, a particular idea will make its way forward in our consciousness, completely out of the sequence in which we might otherwise expect it, Smith cites as his example Pope's poem:

Eloisa regrets her vain endeavours to check her Passion and the treachery of her heart.

> In vain lost Eloisa weeps and prays
> Her heart still dictates and her hand obeys.

Make it

> Lost Eloisa weeps in vain and prays
> Still her heart dictates and her hand obeys,

the line tho still a pretty one has lost much of its force. (Smith, p 18; ll 15–16 of the poem)

'Prettiness' is not enough for the poem to have the effects Smith admires: it must have some additional cogency and that is achieved by word arrangement. Smith is linking the psychological reactions or perceptions of the reader to the aesthetic sequence the poet chooses for revealing the information the lines contain.

Smith comes closer than either Beattie or Blair to making a comment on the nature of Eloisa's passion, but even the assertion that Eloisa regrets her attempts to restrain her passionate feelings for Abelard (presumably Smith thinks the poem presents her as wishing she had indulged them more), contrasts with the comment about the 'treachery of her heart', a phrase which implies that she had little control over those passions. So, Smith no doubt sympathises with Eloisa's feelings, but the morality of sex in the cloister is discreetly avoided.

Though Smith is able to admire the representation of the passions in Eloisa, he is not an uncritical admirer. In a later lecture, he takes Pope to task for his diction, asserting that he 'frequently applies adjectives to substantives with which they can not at all agree' (Smith, p 77). His example is taken from *Eloisa to Abelard*, though he slightly misquotes these lines:

> Deepens the murmur of the falling floods,
> And breathes a browner horror on the woods
> (169–70)

The second line is misquoted—Smith was doubtless doing so from memory— as 'and shades a browner horror ore the woods', but his objection is not therefore nullified, since, as Smith puts it, 'Brown joined to horror conveys no idea at all' (Smith, p 77). What Smith would have said about a breathing, brown horror is, alas, not known, but he might have been constrained to admire the audacity of the poet.

Hugh Blair had admired the skilful rhymes in *Eloisa to Abelard*, their 'elegance, and sweetness of sound' (Blair, II, 333), and had commented on the poem's tenderness and excellence. However, in his lecture on metaphor, the lines immediately preceding the ones Smith had quoted in approving Eloisa's passionate feelings are cited by Blair as inapposite personification:

> Dear fatal name! rest ever unreveal'd
> Nor pass these lips in holy silence seal'd.
> Hide it my heart, within that close disguise,

Where, mix'd with God's, his lov'd Idea lies.
O write it not, my hand—The name appears
Already written—wash it out, my tears!
(9–14)

(Blair has also slightly misquoted the last two lines, writing 'his name' and 'Blot it out' rather than the lines quoted above.) Having described the poem itself as 'very beautiful', Blair proceeds to examine the 'propriety' of the personification. He finds no problems with Abelard's name, nor with Eloisa's injunction to her heart, 'a dignified part of the human frame', to hide his name. Then the trouble starts:

> But, when from her heart she passes to her hand, and tells her hand not to write his name, this is forced and unnatural; a personified hand is low, and not in the style of true passion: and the figure becomes still worse, when, in the last place, she exhorts her tears to blot out what her hand had written: 'Oh! write it not,' &c. There is, in these two lines, an air of epigrammatic conceit, which native passion never suggests; and which is altogether unsuitable to the tenderness which breathes through the rest of that excellent Poem.
>
> (Blair, I, 335)

Blair's unfortunate substitution of the word 'wash' for Pope's 'blot' changes the nature of the conceit: 'wash' implies, obviously, that the falling tears literally wash away the lines, while 'blot' can suggest that it is Eloisa's vision itself that blurs and obscures the name; or at least 'blot' has a decent ambiguity for a literary critic to relish.

The difference between Blair's objection and Smith's is straightforward. We might disagree with Smith and argue that the idea of 'brown' joined to the idea of 'horror' may not convey an idea, but it is no worse a poetic licence than 'blind mouths'. Smith's criticism is a linguistic or an epistemological one, while Blair's seems to be more a matter of taste. The kind of passion that Smith finds in the two lines he quotes about Eloisa's regrets and her treacherous heart are certainly full of emotion and psychological force, more so than the 'epigrammatic conceit' that Blair finds. More interestingly, they both *want* Eloisa's passion to be strongly conveyed, they *want* the poem to have the appropriate psychological and emotional effect on the reader. It is this emphasis on Pope's poetry as a window to the heart that makes their appreciation of him different in kind and tone from that of Pope's contemporaries and indeed of their English counterparts.

Another striking example of the difference between Blair's approach to and treatment of Pope's poetry can be seen in a comment he makes on a passage from *The Rape of the Lock*, which is also analysed by George Campbell, Professor of Divinity and Principal of Marischal College. Campbell first came to Scottish literary attention in 1762 with his shrewd analysis of Hume's essay 'Of Miracles' in *A Dissertation on Miracles*. His most lasting achievement, however, was his *Philosophy of Rhetoric* (1776), a work not reprinted until 1801, but then reprinted over forty times in the nineteenth century and used as a textbook in British and American universities.

Both Blair and Campbell comment on these lines (II, 105–10) from *The Rape of the Lock*:

> Whether the Nymph shall break *Diana*'s Law,
> Or some frail *China* Jar receive a Flaw,
> Or stain her Honour, or her new Brocade,
> Forget her Pray'rs, or miss a Masquerade,
> Or lose her Heart, or Necklace, at a Ball;
> Or whether Heav'n has doom'd that *Shock* must fall.

Blair's observations about this passage occur in a lecture on figures of speech, specifically antithesis, 'the beauty of which consists, in surprising us by the unexpected contrasts of things which it brings together'. Such antitheses can give evidence of wit but belong only in 'pieces of professed wit and humour', not in 'grave compositions'. Describing Pope as 'happy' in the use of antithesis, he quotes the above lines, and adds, 'What is called the point of an epigram, consists, for the most part, in some Antithesis of this kind; surprising us with the smart and unexpected turn, which it gives to the thought; and in the fewer words it is brought out, it is always the happier' (I, 355). Blair's mention of 'thought' indicates that he is at least aware that the wit depends on the poet's having something to say, but 'happy' is rather a back-handed compliment.

Perhaps Blair expected that a mere hint to his students was sufficient for them to make their own inferences regarding the subject matter of the antithesis and the thought behind it. In contrast, Campbell's account is more specific:

> This is humorous, in that it is a lively sketch of the female estimate of mischances, as our poet's commentator [Warburton] rightly terms it, marked out by a few striking lineaments. It is likewise witty, for, not to mention the play on words . . . a trope familiar to this author, you have here a comparison of—a woman's chastity to a piece of porcelain,—her honour to a gaudy robe,—her prayers to a fantastical disguise,—her heart to a trinket; and all these together to her lap-dog, and that founded on one lucky circumstance (a malicious critic would perhaps discern or imagine more) by which these things, how unlike soever in other respects, may be compared, the impression they make on the mind of a fine lady.

(Campbell, p 19)

Campbell's syntax and punctuation leave much to be desired, and his interpretation of these lines would doubtless provoke dissent, but he has tried to indicate what specifically makes the lines 'work', and he has additionally disclosed an awareness of the sexual imagery. Campbell's criticism occurs in his section on humour, while that of Blair was made in his on figurative language. Blair's is thus a more technical consideration, while Campbell is pleased by the psychological shrewdness the poet displays (a psychological shrewdness likely to be disputed by most female readers). Elsewhere in his book on rhetoric, Campbell cites Pope not only for technical examples of various rhetorical devices, but also for the beauty of his poetry. Often, he links the two; for example, when he is discussing tropes, Pope provides an example of the individual used for the species. Quoting these lines (249–50) from *An Epistle to Dr Arbuthnot,*

> May some choice Patron bless each gray goose quill;
> May ev'ry *Bavius* have his *Bufo* still!

Campbell asserts,

> Here, by a beautiful antonomasia, Bavius, a proper name, is made to represent one whole class of men, Bufo, also a proper name (it matters not whether real or fictitious), is made to represent another class. By the former is meant every bad poet, by the latter every rich fool who gives his patronage to such. As what precedes in the Essay secures the perspicuity (and in introducing tropes of this kind, especially new ones, it is necessary that the perspicuity be thus secured), it was impossible in another manner to express the sentiment with equal vivacity.
> (Campbell, p 300)

Campbell's explication of this couplet is perhaps one of the most successful ones, though it is not one that would immediately occur to many of us when seeking examples of 'beautiful antonomasia'; indeed, without some specific historical figure to stand for Bufo or Bavius, it is not easy to see why this is an example of antonomasia. It may be that Campbell is finding beauties where none exist, or that professors of divinity writing books on rhetoric have access to insights or inspiration denied to lesser, mundane mortals. Yet it is not so much the possible mis-readings of Pope that catches the readers of Campbell's book, as it is the number of times he resorts accurately and persuasively to Pope for examples. The discussion of the function of sound in poetry regularly draws on Pope; the notorious portrait of Addison in the *Epistle to Dr Arbuthnot* is cited as an example of antithesis brilliantly used, drawing forth this praise: 'With what a masterly hand are the colours in this picture blended; and how admirably do the different traits, thus opposed, serve, as it were, to touch up and shade one another' (Campbell, p 378). He also makes the point that admiration for Pope's craftsmanship in such lines is not to be taken for assent to the justness of the portrait.

That feature of Campbell's criticism—the distinction between Pope the poet and Pope the man—is something he shares with the rest of his colleagues in the Scottish Enlightenment universities. The vitriolic personal attacks on Pope that elsewhere passed for literary criticism, particularly during his lifetime, are pleasantly absent from the Scottish criticisms and evaluations of his poetry. Even when a commentator feels that something must be said about Pope's personality, the phrasing is almost deferential. Barron is virtually the only one who mentions Pope's letters at length, and he notes that Pope has difficulty separating ideas of his own dignity from his writings, and that is perhaps one cause for the personal attacks on Pope. Even when corresponding with the 'fair sex', Pope is, however, 'studied and correct'. He 'seems afraid that some circumstances should discover Mr Pope was not a great man' (Barron, II, 35). That said, Barron regrets that Pope's letters do not have the charm that one would expect from personal letters and that no sense of intimacy with the author emerges from reading the letters. But the strictures are made more with regret than with any sense of malice or hostility. His observations have the additional effect of suggesting that whether Pope was a great *man* or not doesn't really matter: what is incontestably great is his poetry.

None of Pope's academic admirers in the Scottish Enlightenment universities have any doubts about his greatness, though they are divided about which poems and which particular portions of those poems are great. The critical vocabulary is often the same: Pope is applauded for his wit, praised for the sprightliness of his verse, extolled for his exquisite taste, and loved for the beauty of his poetry. Perhaps it is the frequent description of Pope's poetry as beautiful that will appear curious to post-Romantic readers, who have been taught to regard beauty as a grand ennobling quality, rather than a by-product of the heroic couplet. Against this, one might cite the appreciation of Pope's elegance, energy, and imagery, an appreciation we share, though, again, we might not regard elegance as a particularly valuable commodity, nor is energy a phenomenon likely to be discovered in heroic couplets. The urgency of Pope's wit seems, to some ears, deflected by the elegance of the heroic couplet.

The poem that seems to cause the most difficulty is *An Essay on Man*, which even today is hard-pressed to find defenders or admirers. Beattie was eager to prevent his students from reading it for fear they might acquire 'wrong' ideas, and he is genuinely puzzled about what Pope was attempting in the poem. Blair as well can only describe or criticise the poem in generalities, and almost everyone seems to think that Pope must have got his ideas from another person. Pope is given very little credit either for having ideas, or for being able to think, and this is perhaps the only area where certain preconceptions about what it meant to be a poet over-ride critical disinterestedness. Writers and readers in the eighteenth century were not so obsessed about generic demarcation disputes in literature as we are in this century, but surprise and bemusement were general reactions to *An Essay on Man*. It was unlike anything that Pope had undertaken before, indeed in scope and epistemological orientation, unlike anything that any 'modern' poet had attempted. Readers were more opposed to the indecorousness of what Pope was doing than they were inclined to assess the feat on its own terms.

There is one final quality which Pope's Scottish university commentators particularly relish: his clarity. Smith adverts to his clarity implicitly in his lectures, as does Barron, and Beattie is very specific: 'There are but few words in Milton, as *nathless, tine, frore, bosky*, &c; there are but one or two in Dryden as *falsify*; and in Pope, there are none at all, which every reader of our poetry may not be supposed to understand' (Beattie 1776, p 527). Like

David Hume before him, James Beattie had compiled a list of Scotticisms and was keen to extirpate them from his writings as well as from those of his countrymen. Pope could therefore be looked up to as a model of propriety and correctness, a poet whose writings were beautiful, irresistible, and accessible to a wide range of readers because they democratised the poetic vocabulary without at the same time vandalising the language.

References

Barron, William *Lectures on Belles Lettres and Logic*. 2 vols (London: Longman, Hurst, Rees, & Orme, 1806)

Beattie, James *Elements of Moral Sciences* (1790–93), 3rd edn, 2 vols (Edinburgh: Archibald Constable, 1817)

Beattie, James *Essays* (Edinburgh: William Creech, 1776)

Blair, Hugh *Lectures on Rhetoric and Belles Lettres*, 2 vols (London: W Strahan, 1783)

Boswell, James *The Life of Samuel Johnson* (1791), George Birkbeck Hill and L F Powell (eds), 6 vols (Oxford: The Clarendon Press, 1934–64)

Campbell, George *The Philosophy of Rhetoric* (1776), Lloyd F Bitzer (ed) (Carbondale: Southern Illinois UP, 1963)

Forbes, William *An Account of the Life and Writings of James Beattie*, 2 vols (Edinburgh: Archibald Constable, 1806)

Gregory, George *Letters on Literature, Taste, and Composition*, 2 vols (London: Richard Phillips, 1808)

Johnson, Samuel *The Lives of The English Poets* (1779–81), George Birkbeck Hill (ed), 3 vols (Oxford: The Clarendon Press, 1905)

Smith, Adam *Lectures on Rhetoric and Belles Lettres* (1762–63), J C Bryce (ed) (Oxford: The Clarendon Press, 1983)

Stewart, Dugald *The Philosophy of the Active and Moral Powers of Man* (1828), in *The Collected Works*, William Hamilton (ed), 11 vols (Edinburgh: Thomas Constable, 1854–69).

4

'Not Lucre's Madman': Pope, Money, and Independence

IAN A BELL

Pope is the most insistent of poets. In his prefatory remarks to the *Essay on Man* (1734), he claimed that the 'science of Human Nature is, like all other sciences, reduced to a *few clear points*' (Twickenham, III, i, 7). In all his later poetry, Pope sought to identify and articulate the few clear points of the sciences of politics and public affairs. As he began to speak out more strongly on public issues throughout the 1730s, Pope reiterated and fantastically elaborated upon the few most important points about the decline in standards in public life. The impression of range and diversity which the poems convey comes not from the fundamental variety of subject, but from the extraordinary imaginativeness and invention with which the recurrent concerns are sketched and figured. His later poetry creates and exploits a graphic contrast between the world as it predominantly seemed to be, and the world as it might, at its best, manage to be. The figurative process which conducts this analysis is one of extreme and exhaustive polarisation. The heroic and the bathetic are offered as mutually exclusive and exhaustive categories in which Pope's world might be construed. Walpole, his 'Robinocracy', and its delibitating effect on national culture offer the bathetic images; Pope, his intimates, and a remote classical past offer the heroic possibilities. Each category is defined by its exclusion of the qualities of the other, and that technique of schematic polarisation lies beneath all of Pope's most imaginative flights of rhetoric.

Pope was, amongst other things, striving to focus dissent and hostility to Walpole's regime, to legitimise and naturalise the ideology of what is called 'the country party'. From a public world full of chicanery, hidden purposes, and a new financial rhetoric which many found wholly baffling, Pope tried to identify the 'few clear points' which would make bizarre events morally comprehensible. He believed, as many others did, that Walpole's success lay partly in his talents as mystifier and disguiser of motives. Once the villainy of the government was made clear, it would no longer be able to claim moral authority. Pope was eager to unveil the duplicity of government, and so to unite the opposition by making obvious the regime's moral poverty. Even the most baffled or out-of-touch country member would have his intuitive reaction against Walpole focused and clarified by Pope's efforts as a satirist.

As a maker of images, Pope used prominent figures and events as symbols of the widespread decline in standards. His chief dunces, Tibbald and Cibber, embody the disastrous decline in standards in the world of polite letters. Walpole and the first two Georges represent the destruction of the civilized arts of government. Through a similar process of identification and reduction, Pope analysed the morality of government by concentrating on its fiscal policies and practice. In his *Drapier's Letters* (1724), Swift had seen the government's cynical manipulation of coinage and currency as symbols of its insensitivity and obtuseness. In *The Beggar's Opera* (1728), Gay had collapsed the moral distinction between Walpole's circle and a gang of thieves. Pope, however, went further than the other Scriblerians in his analysis of finance, and more insistently dissected the insanity of the new world of moneyed men.

For Pope, the maintenance of an honest system of revenue was indicative of the moral health of a nation. In public and in private life, the ability to distribute and retain wealth fairly was a central ethical issue, and that ability or the lack of it forms the substance of much of his moral critique. In an earlier poem, *Windsor Forest* (1713), Pope celebrated the moral integrity of the Stuarts by showing the richness and orderly variety of the world under Anne,

> Rich Industry sits smiling on the Plains,
> And Peace and Plenty tell, a STUART reigns.
>
> (41–2)

That conjunction of peace and plenty both provides and legitimises the monarch's authority. Under the house of Hanover, as conducted by Walpole, Pope saw an illegitimate attempt to construct 'plenty', not from honest industry, but from the chaotic introduction of a new system of revenue. In the *Moral Essays*, Pope most strongly anatomised the new corruptions in government. The system was typified by the extraordinary affair of the South Sea Bubble and by the (for Pope) iniquitous system of public credit which enabled it to occur. In the famous attack upon paper-credit in the *Epistle to Bathurst*, he gave concentrated expression to his sense of the moral depravity of such a method of circulating revenue. In this case, the iniquities arose from power devoid of authority. The paper-credit system was seen by Pope as a licence to print money, leading to an appalling destabilisation of the national economy and its moral basis.

Throughout the *Moral Essays* and the *Imitations of Horace*, Pope explored the notion that avarice was a kind of frenzy, capable of producing nothing but madness and perpetual frustration. The public credit system fed avarice and so was a principal mover in the universal madness of the day. He saw what he described as 'lucre's sordid charms' lying at the base of most of the insane or extravagant behaviour in his contemporary society, which he pictured intensely and insistently throughout these later poems. In his *Imitation of Horace, Epistle I, vi*, he made clear the futility of the frenzied pursuit of money,

> Is Wealth thy passion? Hence! from Pole to Pole,
> Where winds can carry, or where waves can roll,
> For Indian spices, for Peruvian gold,
> Prevent the greedy, and out-bid the bold:
> Advance thy golden Mountain to the skies;
> On the broad base of fifty thousand rise,
> Add one round hundred, and (if that's not fair)
> Add fifty more, and bring it to a square.
> For, mark th' advantage; just so many score
> Will gain a Wife with half as many more,
> Procure her beauty, make that beauty chaste,
> And then such Friends—as cannot fail to last.
> (69–80)

Pope's sarcastic presentation here reinforces the madness of the acquisitive and the impossibility of their success. The outlook for the avaricious is bleak, in that their wealth increases their instability rather than providing a consolation or compensation. The avaricious person seeks control over destiny, but is pictured by Pope as a helpless creature blown by the winds or pulled by the tides.

Behind Pope's critique, of course, lay the traditional Christian disdain for laying up treasures upon earth. Drawing on this pattern of argument on a number of occasions, Pope used it to dismiss the values of property. In his *Imitation of Horace, Satire II, ii*, he addressed Swift in terms which show the reversal of the owner/servant relationship. When wrongly perceived, property takes over its owner,

> What's *Property*? dear Swift! you see it alter
> From you to me, from me to Peter Walter,
> Or, in a mortgage, prove a Lawyer's share,
> Or, in a jointure, vanish from the Heir,
> Or in pure Equity (the Case not clear)
> The Chanc'ry takes your rents for twenty year:
> At best, it falls to some ingracious Son
> Who cries, my father's damn'd, and all's my own.
> Shades, that to Bacon could retreat afford,
> Become the portion of a booby Lord;
> And Hemsley once proud Buckingham's delight,
> Slides to a Scriv'ner or a City Knight.
> Let Lands and Houses have what Lords they will,
> Let Us be fix'd, and our own Masters still.
> (167–80)

The helpless owners of property are the bathetic images of the futile attempt to hold on to wealth. In Pope's perception, the world he lived in offered the temptations of sudden fortune, but also the endless frustrations of managing it and trying to hold on to it. The images in the passage above, like one of Hogarth's sequences, show the progressive degradation of once-noble estates, falling into the hands of a *nouveau riche*, a 'City Knight'.

Pope expanded this disdain in one of his later imitations, that of *Imitation of Horace, Epistle II, ii*, with more pointed and specific examples,

> Heathcote himself, and such large-acred Men,
> Lords of fat *E'sham*, or of Lincoln Fen,
> But every stick of Wood that lends them heat,
> Buy every Pullet they afford to eat.
> Yet these are Wights, who fondly call their own
> Half that the Dev'l o'erlooks from Lincoln Town.
> The Laws of God, as well as of the Land,
> Abhor, a *Perpetuity* should stand:
> Estates have wings, and hang in Fortune's pow'r
> Loose on the point of ev'ry wav'ring Hour;
> Ready, by force, or of your own accord,
> By sale, at least by death, to change their Lord.
> *Man*? and *for ever*? Wretch! what woud'st thou have?
> Heir urges Heir, like Wave impelling Wave:
> All vast Possessions (just the same the case
> Whither you call them Villa, Park, or Chace)
> Alas, my BATHURST! what will they avail?
> Join *Cotswold* Hills to Saperton's fair Dale,
> Let rising Granaries and Temples here,
> These mingled Farms and Pyramids appear,
> Link Town to Towns with Avenues of Oak,
> Enclose whole Downs in Walls, 'tis all a joke!
> Inexorable Death shall level all,
> And Trees, and Stones, and Farms, and Farmer fall.
> (240–63)

Pope's satire in this passage seems to be taking all human activity as eventually absurd. Even landscape gardening, one of his great loves, is here figured as futile and fleeting. The satirist is here reminding his readers of the inevitability of death, and its omnipotence deflates human pretensions to grandeur or permanence. Such a perspective makes the pursuit of money even more absurd, and makes the triumphs of the moneyed men of little fundamental importance. This passage is reminiscent of the climax of the magnificent description of Timon's absurd villa in the *Epistle to Burlington*, where, after a full and elaborate enumeration of Timon's efforts to impose himself on the landscape, the description concludes,

> Another age shall see the golden ear
> Imbrown the Slope, and nod on the Parterre,
> Deep Harvests bury all his pride has plann'd,
> And laughing Ceres re-assume the Land.
> (173–6)

Even Timon's fantastic efforts at permanence will soon matter little. The satirist's moral perspective renders Timon's deeds finally bathetic, and dismisses him as a figure of significance. In Pope's political analysis, these images enact the eventual triumph of land over money, of the country over the city.

The most prominent of Pope's few clear points about economics is thus that avarice and profusion are essentially self-defeating. From such a view, it follows that the political party most associated with the pursuit of money will eventually be humiliated by the grotesquely unsatisfactory achievement of their aims. As Pope put it in the aftermath of the South Sea episode, 'God has punish'd the avaritious as he often punishes sinners, in their own way, in the very sin itself: the thirst of gain was their crime, that thirst continued became their punishment and ruin' (Sherburn II, 53). Pope's long perspective, however, did not dismiss entirely the role of money in society. His contemporary world was drowning under a surfeit of money. To clarify the image, Pope offered a caricature of its polar opposite, a world without the necessary intermediary of coinage. In the *Epistle to Bathurst*, a system of barter is envisaged, as tangibly absurd as the extreme nominalism satirised in Book Three of *Gulliver's Travels*. Such a method of trading, Pope shows, would make card-playing very inconvenient, and would by extension be surrounded by more practical difficulties,

> Poor Avarice one torment more would find:
> Nor could Profusion squander all in kind.
> Astride his cheese Sir Morgan might we meet,
> And Worldly crying coals from street to street,
> (Whom with a wig so wild, and mien so maz'd,
> Pity mistakes for some poor tradesman craz'd).
> Had Colepepper's whole wealth been hops and hogs,
> Could he himself have sent it to the dogs?
> His Grace will game: to White's a Bull be led,
> With spurning heels and with a butting head.
> To White's be carried, as to ancient games,
> Fair Coursers, Vases and alluring Dames.
> Shall then Uxorio, if the stakes he sweep,
> Bear home six Whores, and make his Lady weep?
> (47–60)

So money itself is not the root of the problem. Again, with full Christian precedent, Pope is attacking avarice, and the love of money, as well as the specific and local political organisation which encourages it.

Pope's *Epistles* and *Imitations*, then, contain a gallery of portraits of the avaricious and the profligate. As well as Timon, there are the elder and younger Cotta, Sir Balaam, Blunt, Walter, and many others, all of whom are used to figure the insensitivity of the new men, and the folly of worldly wealth being either stored or squandered. The miserly and the spendthrift offer a repository of images, so savagely reinforced that they seem to be an exhaustive catalogue of the possible uses of wealth. However, it would be a great mistake to see Pope as a radical thinker advocating the tearing down of property and the re-distribution of resources. Though the needy were by far the largest social group of the time, they were not the prime object of Pope's concern. He was more animated by his attempt to define the conditions under which a rich man could enter the kingdom of heaven. Despite all the difficulties, Pope offered his well-off readers a course in suitable moral instruction, leading to the golden mean of enlightened philanthropy.

Avarice clearly benefited neither the avaricious nor anyone else. Profligacy did not benefit the profligate but might, by accident, improve the lot of others. As an aside to the portrait of Timon's villa, Pope mentions the possibility that such grandiose enterprises might have temporary beneficial side-effects,

> Yet hence the Poor are cloath'd, the Hungry fed;
> Health to himself, and to his Infants bread
> The Lab'rer bears: What his hard Heart denies,
> His charitable Vanity supplies.
>
> (173–6)

For once, a utilitarian judgement gains pre-eminence over the morality of the satirist. It constitutes a further stab at Timon, showing again the inevitable frustration of his purposes, and reinforces Pope's view in the overall justice of Providence. The optimism of the *Essay on Man* is glimpsed here, as a positive balance to the moral emptiness of Timon's creation. Although it is tempting to see Mandeville's private vice/public virtue idea here, Pope does not exploit the paradox. It remains in the poem as a casual aside against Timon, rather than a fully created avenue for exploration.

However, elsewhere in these poems, Pope does define the proper forms of conduct for the well-off man. In his portrait of the Man of Ross, Pope offers the clearest figure of his golden mean. Central to his notion is the idea that money has to be used to be beneficial, and that an active life is necessary if the moral mean is to be achieved. As he puts it in the *Epistle to Bathurst*,

> Wealth in the gross is death, but life diffus'd,
> As Poison heals, in just proportion us'd
>
> (233–4)

The Man of Ross deliberately used his portion to improve the lot of others, and his kindly and enlightened charity is offered as the polar opposite of both the grasping and the wasteful,

> Behold the Market-place with poor o'erspread!
> The MAN of ROSS divides the weekly bread:
> Behold yon Alms-house, neat, but void of state,
> Where Age and Want sit smiling at the gate:
> Him portion'd maids, apprentic'd orphans blest,
> The young who labour, and the old who rest.
> Is any sick? the MAN of ROSS relieves,
> Prescribes, attends, the med'cine makes, and gives.
> Is there a variance? enter but his door,
> Balk'd are the Courts, and contest is no more.
>
> (263–72)

The Man of Ross then, functions to smooth out the difficulties in the life of the poor, in a dignified and high-minded way. Pope does not admit into the poem any radical critique of Ross, that by making the system of Alms-houses and poverty run more smoothly he helps to perpetuate it—not until Blake and Wordsworth were such radical arguments taken seriously in British poetry. Rather Pope emphasises the quiet efficiency of Ross, a man of independent means, but not enormous wealth,

> 'Thrice happy man! enabled to pursue
> What all so wish, but want the pow'r to do!
> Oh say, what sums that gen'rous hand supply?
> What mines, to swell that boundless charity?'
> Of Debts, and Taxes, Wife and Children clear,
> This man possesst—five hundred pounds a year.
> (275–80)

It is clear that Pope wishes readers to be astonished that such huge benefits could be created by a sum which he contrives to make small. Five hundred pounds may well be a lot less than that thrown away by Timon or possessed by Bathurst, but it still seems a mighty amount in contemporary terms. Some indication of the relative enormity of this amount can be given by remembering that at the end of the century Thomas Paine outraged many by his suggestion that those over sixty be given a pension of ten pounds per annum. It is only by a trick of Pope's perspective that the Man of Ross can be seen as humble and relatively poor. Pope's perspective, needless to say, starts from the wealthy and looks down.

Still, the Man of Ross puts his store to good use, and is less arbitrary than Timon in his generosity of spirit. He stands for the appropriate moral conduct in private life of the man of limited substance. By this image, Pope creates the notion that money imposes duties on its holders, and these duties increase as the portion increases. The Man of Ross represents generosity in private life, and the image of responsible generosity in public life comes at the conclusion to the *Epistle to Burlington*. In a ringing tribute to Burlington himself, Pope develops the notion of civic responsibility,

> You too proceed! make falling Arts your care,
> Erect new wonders, and the old repair,
> Jones and Palladio to themselves restore,
> And be what'er Vitruvius was before:
> Till Kings call forth th' Idea's of your mind,
> Proud to accomplish what such hands design'd
> Bid Harbors open, public Ways extend,
> Bid Temples, worthier of the God, ascend,
> Bid the broad Arch the dang'rous Flood contain,
> The Mole projected break the roaring Main;
> Back to his bounds their subject Sea command,
> And roll obedient Rivers thro' the Land;

> These Honours, Peace to happy Britain brings,
> These are Imperial Works, and worthy Kings.
> (191–204)

The proper activity of the wealthy man is thus to devote himself to the public good in a series of far-sighted and high-minded civic projects. Not for his own glory should he build, but for the improvement of the nation.

The twin images of Ross and Burlington share a vision of altruism and enlightened charity. In each case, the wealth of the benevolent man enables his philanthropy, and secures him from political sway. In the case of Burlington, his patrimony enables him to avoid having to resort to place-seeking or bribery, and opens up the possibilities of a benign use of financial power. The possession of money allows for independence of ties, and that alone leads to effective public works.

In these poems, the rich are seen as either avaricious or profligate, with only a few exceptions. The poor are but scantly sketched, and seem to exist as mirrors in which the virtues of Ross and Burlington may be more gloriously displayed. The golden mean of independent, enlightened activity is created, but made only tentatively present—Burlington's great deeds are all in the future, and Ross is dead and virtually forgotten. In the present, for Pope, there could be little from which to draw comfort. No-one, it appears, fulfils the requirements of the enlightened, independent philanthropist. No-one, that is, except perhaps Pope himself.

In the *Imitations of Horace*, Pope creates a version of himself which gives great space to his independence and his sensitive handling of money. In a powerful self-description in his *Epistle to Dr Arbuthnot*, Pope immersed his rejection of avarice in a catalogue of denials. The context shows a very interesting conjunction of values, and shows Pope at his most deliberate in creating an image of himself.

> Not Fortune's Worshipper, nor Fashion's Fool,
> Not Lucre's Madman, nor Ambitions Tool,
> Not proud, not servile, be one Poet's praise,
> That, if he pleas'd, he pleas'd by manly ways;
> That Flatt'ry, ev'n to Kings, he held a shame,
> And thought a Lye in Verse or Prose the same:
> That not in Fancy's Maze he wander'd long,
> But stoop'd to Truth, and moraliz'd his song:
> That not for Fame, but Virtue's better end,
> He stood the furious Foe, the timid Friend,
> The damning Critic, half-approving Wit,
> The Coxcomb hit, or fearing to be hit;
> Laugh'd at the loss of Friends he never had,
> The dull, the proud, the wicked, and the mad;
> The distant Threats of Vengeance on his head,
> The Blow unfelt, the Tear he never shed;
> The Tale reviv'd, the Lye so oft o'erthrown,
> Th' imputed Trash, and Dulness not his own;
> The Morals blacken'd when the Writings scape;
> The libel'd Person, and the picture'd Shape;

Abuse on all he lov'd, or lov'd him, spread,
A Friend in Exile, or a Father, dead;
The Whisper that to Greatness still too near,
Perhaps, yet vibrates on his SOVEREIGN's Ear—
Welcome for thee, fair Virtue! all the past:
For thee, fair Virtue! welcome e'en the *last*!

(334–59)

Coming as it does immediately after the picture of the vile, fawning Sporus, this self-advertisement creates a dignified and noble Pope. Without being frenzied, Pope has built up sufficient social standing, created a dignified life, and been an independent, high-minded commentator on the times. In return, he has been slandered and abused. Pope seems to have been trying to give a version of himself in this passage which privileged his independence, both moral and financial. That notion of independence was repeated throughout his verse, when he explicitly denied strict party loyalty, or disdained the trifling strife of party against party. His fundamental loyalty, according to that passage from *Arbuthnot* and many others, was to virtue alone.

This extremely high-minded version of the poet would be persuasive if it was the only information we had about Pope. However, when put in context with other existing versions of his personality, it begins to look less unquestionable. We should remember when reading Pope's self-descriptions that they are very deliberate constructions. Pope stage-managed his own image to such a degree that we become increasingly aware of the disparities between the 'Pope' of the poems and the Pope who wrote them. In creating a very schematic typology for the contemporary world, organised round the treatment of financial matters, Pope left a space for his own image, which was to be the most effective example of the golden mean in his writing. The 'Pope' in the poems conducts himself always with propriety, has nothing to reproach himself with, and has been scandalously misunderstood. He has been properly generous when appropriate, properly censorious when the occasion demanded it, and above all constantly loyal to high principles. Unfortunately, this version looks more and more doubtful the more it is examined.

Pope was always very conscious of what we might now call marketing an image of himself. In terms of portraiture, the case is clear. We are familiar with the whole range of anti-Pope iconography, in which he is pictured as an ape, a spider, or as hideously deformed. In contrast to these, there are a vast number of authorised portraits in which Pope always appears alone (so that his dimunitive stature is less obvious), aloof, and crowned with the garlands of poetic fame. Psychologically, Pope's authorisation of these flattering images might have been compensation for his disabilities. More importantly, however, they collaborate with the enterprise of the poems in creating a sanitised and heroic version of the author, seen as high-minded and independent. As David Piper (1982) puts it, Pope's campaign 'reads like a willed highly controlled projection by Pope of his person into posterity'. The 'person' thus projected was only one of various versions in circulation, and Pope used his extraordinary skills to try to make it the pre-eminent one.

With this in mind, it is worth comparing Pope's claims to financial and moral independence with his actual practice, as far as it can be reconstructed. The closer the attention paid to Pope's practice, the more self-conscious he seems to be, and the more consciously he seems to be 'laundering' his image. One example of this process would be seen in the way he re-edited his letters for publication, to emphasise his prescience and dignity. In the references to money in his correspondence, he shows a combination of embarrassment and eagerness which illustrates how hard he had to strive to gain financial security and the sense of independence it could offer. In a letter to Caryll in 1712, he said,

> I plead this excuse for suffering any consideration so dirty as that of money to have place in a letter of friendship, or in any thing betwixt you and me.
>
> (Sherburn, I, 155)

That note of embarrassment occurs again and again, as though Pope is being reluctantly drawn to mention something distasteful.

Such a mood is in keeping with the poems, where money is an unfortunate necessity for the morally clean life. However, Pope was more active in his pursuit of money than either his embarrassment or his rhetorical disdain would suggest. As a Roman Catholic, Pope was not only politically marginalised for most of his adult life, he was also circumscribed financially. Under William III, Roman Catholics were subject to greater taxation than Protestants, given less security over their property, forbidden to own arms, and not allowed to possess a horse of any value. According to Sherburn (1934), it was Pope's Catholicism which instigated the family's move out of London. It also made Pope acutely sensitive to his financial deprivations and conscious of the need to rectify them,

> But knottier Points we knew not half so well,
> Depriv'd us soon of our Paternal Cell;
> And certain Laws, by Suff'rers thought unjust,
> Deny's all Posts of Profit and of Trust:
> Hopes after Hopes of pious Papists fail'd,
> While mighty WILLIAM's thundring Arm prevail'd.
> For Right Hereditary tax'd and fin'd,
> He stuck to Poverty with Peace of Mind;
> And me, the Muses help'd to undergo it;
> Convict a Papist He, and I a Poet.
>
> (*Epistle II, ii*, 58–67)

Of course, this notion of 'poverty' is purely relative—Pope's family were scarcely poor in any strict sense of the term. However, for Pope to achieve the kind of freedom from constraint that he sought, he had to have money, and to acquire money, he had to be vigilant for opportunities.

In his correspondence, there are hints that he ran the family finances, with his repeated anxiety over his father's French investments, and his requests that friends help him buy a suitable annuity. He also seems to have done another image of frustration and inconstancy, as so much of his poetry tries to trace the consistencies in inconstant behaviour.

Faithful to his sense of man as a mixed, confused creature, Pope's thinking on money and independence is complex and even contradictory. Writing against the moneyed interest, he required his audience to be philanthropic and scrupulous in their financial affairs. Despite his efforts to present himself as heroic and proper in his own dealings, he emerges as at times a bathetic figure, driven by a restless desire for repose and striving to be effortless. The paradox of the frugal generous man, or the hospitable miser, two images which describe the Pope who emerges from this perspective, is well handled by Dr Johnson, in his *Life of Pope*. Though the overall presentation of Pope by Johnson is unreliable, it does contain this passage which catches the complexities dealt with above.

> Of his domestic character frugality was a part eminently remarkable. Having determined not to be independent, he determined not to be in want, and therefore wisely and magnanimously rejected all temptations to expense unsuitable to his fortune. This general care must be universally approved; but it sometimes appeared in petty artifices of parsimony, such as the practice of writing his compositions on the back of letters, as may be seen in the remaining copy of the *Iliad*, by which perhaps in five years five shillings were saved; or in a niggardly reception of his friends and scantiness of entertainment . . .
>
> He sometimes, however, made a splendid dinner, and is said to have wanted no part of the skill or elegance which such performances require. That this magnificence should be often displayed, that obstinate prudence with which he conducted his affairs would not permit; for his revenue, certain and casual, amounted only to about eight hundred pounds a year, of which, however, he declares himself able to assign one hundred to charity.
>
> Of this fortune, which as it arose from public approbation was very honourably obtained, his imagination seems to have been too full: it would be hard to find a man so well entitled to notice by his wit that ever delighted so much in talking of his money . . . The great topic of his ridicule is poverty: the crimes with which he reproaches his antagonists are their debts, their habitation in the Mint, and their want of a dinner. He seems to be of an opinion, not very uncommon in the world, that to want money is to want everything.

Johnson's sketch is eloquently consistent with the version of Pope that this paper has sought to discuss. The paradox of his disdain for earthly wealth existing side by side with his very careful enumeration of its properties can be found in all his poetry, from *The Rape of the Lock* onwards. In that poem, Belinda's trivia were taken seriously and lovingly, however damning her love of trinkets might be made to seem. In his later poetry, Pope adopted a consistently hostile attitude to the newly wealthy, to the frenzy of acquisitiveness, and to the debasement of financial dealings. However, at the same time, he was acutely aware of the benefits that money could bring, and the tension between these two sets of ideas is never dispersed.

That there was a tension is indisputable, and is consistent with Pope's view of the essentially confused state of mankind. More locally, the tension shows some of the contradictions involved in his notion of 'independence'. It is fair of Pope to have claimed independence in the sense of not being beholden to anyone—a significant claim in an age of extensive patronage. It is also fair of him to have rejected the accusations of the frantic pursuit of money for its own sake. All his lucrative projects were, at least in part, high-minded literary projects, and he could fairly set himself in the opposed category to his dunces. However, Pope was not, and could not be, 'independent' in the sense of being able to ignore financial demand or the need to earn money. Throughout his career, he was impelled both by the desire to make money and the desire to dismiss it. His images of the balanced use of money, in the Man of Ross and Burlington, do not seem fully to correspond with Pope's own activities, and part of his own enterprise was to make these images seem as compatible as possible.

In the *Essay on Man*, one of the 'few clear points' is expressed in a pertinent way,

> Two Principles in human nature reign;
> Self-love, to urge, and Reason, to restrain.
> (*Epistle II*, 53–54)

Pope's energies as a satirist all served to restrain his audience. He persistently revealed their errors, their follies, and their iniquities, and demanded that they try to repair them as far as possible. At the same time, his self-love was operative, in its creation of an image of the dignified satirist, and in his steady accumulation of cash. The sense of anti-climax felt in realising that Pope was as money-conscious as his targets makes his stage-management of his own image a bathetic project. His simultaneous insistence on the dreadfulness and the necessity of money is one of the paradoxes or contradictions that lie at the heart of his thinking. The rigorist and the utilitarian in him were perpetually at odds, and his inability to reconcile that conflict is symptomatic of some of the central contradicitons of his age.

monstrous height we now behold them. And that which was first a corruption is at last grown necessary. By this means, the wealth of the nation, that used to be reckoned by the value of land, is now computed by the rise and fall of stocks.

(p 6)

Swift is writing a decade before the South Sea debacle. Looking back on it ten years after the event, Pope articulates a recognisably similar structure of feeling, wherein a whole social order is felt to be shifting, and traditional frameworks for social action and social discourse dissolving. Thus the general drift of property in the sixty years after 1690 which according to Habbakuk 'marks one of the great changes in the disposition of English landed property' (1939–40, p 3), is associated in the poetry with an irresistible and sedulous fraud and deception.

> What's *Property*? Dear Swift! you see it alter
> From you to me, from me to Peter Walter.
> (*Satire* II, ii, 187–8)

Walter being one of the few crooks in the service of the new finance who was actually exposed.

> Piecemeal they win this Acre first, then that,
> Glean on and gather up the whole estate:
> Then strongly fencing ill-got wealth by law
> Indentures, Cov'nants, Articles they draw.
> (*Donne II*, 91–4)

Inevitably, the process outlined here must wreak equally transforming effects at the level of individual subornation, the temptation of Balaam being the finest example:

> The Tempter saw his time; the work he ply'd;
> Stocks and subscriptions pour on every side,
> 'Till all the Daemon makes his full descent,
> In one abundant show'r of Cent. per Cent.,
> Sinks deep within him and possesses whole,
> Then dubs Director, and secures his soul.
> (*Bathurst*, 369–74)

The rape of Danae by Zeus transformed to a shower of gold vies in the narrative with a parody of the Biblical Fall. In fusion they emphasise a wider cultural deformation implicit in the single archetype of corruption. As episode, these lines resonate with the moment in *The Dunciad* where the goddess of Dulness relates how her Angel is 'sent to scatter round/Her magic charms o'er all unclassic ground' (III. 257–8), the corruption there, as everywhere in *The Dunciad*, being presented as a decay in the artistic life of the nation. Such intertextual echoes further suggest the Goddess's miasmal omnipresence, and we find ourselves almost taking refuge in the world of recognisable historical event, hunting a correlative patterning which might anchor in some way Pope's devastating transvaluation of his time and experience.

That, too, is a nebulous business, yet the interactive echoings between text and text and between text and context gradually develop a persuasive kind of power. We can anyway, I think, confidently allow that taken all together, the incorporation of the Bank of England in 1694, the rash of joint-stock companies which then flourished and died recurrently, and particularly around the South Sea year of 1720, the rapid growth of insurance brokerage and the inauguration of the National Debt, fundamentally altered the frames of reference in the social scheme of things. We are then saying that in a chronological sense at least, Pope's life and writing corresponds almost exactly with the institutionalising phase of an economic differentiation which progressively dismantled and then restructured the ways in which individuals saw themselves and their society. It was both an end and a beginning: the great satires of the age interlock with and give expression to the bizarre confusions engendered by the whole process and as Isaac Kramnick comments (1968), 'It was really the new composition of English finance, not Walpole, which was the nemesis that brought to an end the traditional constitution in which, since the days of the Tudors, the aristocracy and gentry had stood paramount' (p 61). A convenient way of registering the emergence of the new apparatus of power is by recalling that in conjunction with the exchequer bill system built up by Walpole after the South Sea collapse, on eight occasions between 1721 and 1742 the government floated a variety of loan schemes, some of them part-lotteries, in which the Bank played a leading part. The public loans of the 1740s were entirely administered by the Bank of England, whose ascendancy by this time was unchallenged; its control over government borrowing complete. Wars had been waged and won without any attempt to balance the books: the attempt to construct a Tory rival to the power of the Bank, in the shape of the South Sea Company, had disintegrated ignominiously, with the bank swallowing up its wreckage. Credit finance and deficit finance had become signs of economic strength rather than frailty.[2] And everywhere, like the Goddess of *The Dunciad*, public credit 'rul'd, in native Anarchy, the Mind' (I, 16).

Years earlier, in an effort to communicate his own notion of the transcendent glory of public credit, Daniel Defoe made God chairman of the board of the greatest trading company of them all, with Credit as a kind of handmaiden:

> Credit is not the effect of this or that wheel in the Government . . . but of the whole movement, acting . . . according to the exquisite design of the Director of the whole frame.

> (1710, p 13)

Given the jaundiced bathos with which Pope viewed this nationwide elevation, it seems in keeping with the satiric elasticity of the poem to reflect that the adaptable ironies of the 'Prolegomena of Martinus Scriblerus', attached to the 1729 *Dunciad Variorum*, might extend their flexibility in this direction too:

> A *Person* must be fix'd upon to support this action . . . This *Phantom* in the poet's mind must have a *name* . . . He finds his name to be *Tibbald*, and he becomes of course the hero of the poem.
>
> (*TE*, V, 51)

Tibbald, like everyone else, obeys the whim of the dusky queen. So, although we are told that 'the personification of Credit as an inconstant female figure . . . is a device of Whig rather than Tory writers' (Pocock 1975, p 452), the enthronement of the goddess Dulness increasingly appears to be the *terminus ad quem* of all such figures as far as the Opposition writers are concerned. But what is beyond dispute is that all of these writers greeted the advent of the money market with a mixture of fear and suspicion. The great business flotations of the 1690s had brought in their wake a massive influx of tellers, scriveners, and stockjobbers, and with them an invading strangeness of terms and jargon. Such was the extent of this alteration, that Defoe, wielding his pen in the service of changing political expediency, was sure of a widely sympathetic response when he criticised how 'these people can ruin silently, undermine and impoverish by a sort of impenetrable artifice, like poison that works at a distance, can wheedle men to ruin themselves, and fiddle them out of their money, by the strange and unheard of engines of interest, discounts, transfers, tallies, debentures, shares, projects, and the devil and all of figures and hard names' (1710, p 22).

Evidently, the hardest of them all was public credit: 'What all people are busy about, but not one of forty understands: every man has a concern in it, few know what it is, nor is it easy to define or to describe it' (Defoe 1710, p 6). Even Swift found it all 'such a complication of knavery and cozenage, such a mystery of iniquity, and such an unintelligible jargon of terms to involve it in, as were never known in any other age or country in the world' (Davis III, p 6). And Swift shared with Pope the perception that rapidly expanding and shrinking values of currency were undermining once stable values associated with the blood-ties of family and with the land. In Pope's case, the perception had been tested on his own pulse. He had gambled as feverishly as the next during the 'bubble' year of 1720, and after the collapse he writes tellingly to Caryll: 'I think that all the morals that were among us are gone: that is to say, all the pretence to morals' (Sherburn II, p 57). But that was afterwards. Pope had learned by then, and at first hand, how easily *credo* had slipped into credit; how belief, worth and value were dissolved into speculative opinion, transformed into desired and desirable fictions and fantasies which increased or diminished according to the operations of the money-market. He both observed and participated as the rise and fall of the stocks became an increasingly accepted yard-stick for measuring the size and scope of a person's moral, or at least public, reputation. During the frenzied period of stock-trading when Pope bid directly for a sudden influx of wealth, a letter to Digby which as his editor remarks, 'tends to arouse suspicion as to Pope's gains from his South Sea stock', catches in its inflated hyperbole the hectic tones of disappointed expectation:

> What Words, what Numbers, What Oratory or what Poetry, can suffice, to express how infinitely I esteem, value, love and desire you all, above all the Great ones, the rich ones and the vain ones of this part of the World! above all the Jews, Jobblers, Bubblers, Subscribers, Projectors, Directors, Governors, Treasurers, &c, &c, &c, &c, in *saecula saeculorum*!
>
> (*Correspondence* II, p 50)

All of this is a far cry from the chastened and sombre tones adopted after the mighty fall. Pope, it appears, sold his shares and after the devastation laments 'for may part all I *see* is ruin and mischief: all I *wish* is quiet and resignation' (p 57).

We can see then, that his own participation in the share-dealings of the South Sea Company could not help but instruct Pope in the monetarisation of morality, the fictionalisation of confidence, and the engulfing fantasy of expectation. 'I have borrowed mony upon ours and Mr Eckersals orders', he writes to Martha Blount in March 1720, 'and bought 50011 stock S. Sea, at 180. It is since risen to 184. I wish us all good luck in it' (*Corr.* II, p 38). In May he is telling Caryll that 'there is no gain till the stock is sold . . . So that, instead of wallowing in money, we never wanted more for the uses of life, which is a pretty general case with most of the adventurers, each having put all the ready money they had into the stock. And our estate is an imaginary one only: one day we were worth two or three thousand, and the next not above three parts of the same' (p 42). Pope continued to invest, but it is his recognition of the imaginary nature of these speculative riches that is significant for our purposes here. The same kind of perception, though given slightly different emphasis, can be seen in Richard Steele's pamphlet of 1720, *A Nation a Family: Being the Sequel of The Crisis of Property*. Steele describes how, 'to the disadvantage of the whole community, private persons are made immoderately rich, and every day growing richer by artificial rumours, whereby self-interested men affect the public funds, for their own gain, tho' to the apparent hazard of their country' (Blanchard 1944, p 581). These early attempts to manipulate public confidence created and demolished dreams of acquisition and consequently fuelled public and private suspicions and discontents. After the crash, Pope included himself somewhat remorsefully among those who were lucky enough 'to have the good fortune to remain with half of what they imagined they had' (*Corr.* II, p 53). And as late as 1727, nine months or so before the first appearance of *The Dunciad*, Pope confided to the Earl of Oxford, 'I have withdrawn my little stake from the Turmoil of the Stocks, and out of suspitions which gave me disquiet. What to do with it any other way? I am like a man that saves, and lays together, the planks of a broken Ship, or a falling House; but knows not how to rebuild out of them, either one, or the other' (*Corr.* II, p 444).

Rumour and suspicion, it had long been evident, were able to jeopardise the realisation of wealth in these new proceedings. Worries are being expressed here about its insubstantiality as well as its inconstancy, worries which already went back for more than a quarter of a century, when Daniel Defoe had expressed bemusement at the way so many people could be persuaded to part with their money for shares in what he called 'new-nothings'. Defoe goes on to talk about 'shares in joint-stocks, patents, engines and under-takings, blown up by the air of great words, and the name of some Man of Credit concerned' (1710, pp 12–13), and we catch a fleeting prefiguring of Pope's Sir Balaam whose 'word would pass for more than he was worth' (*Bathurst* 344). While naming the age in his *Essay upon Projects*, Defoe also described the 'Multitude of projectors . . . who besides the Innumerable conceptions which die in the bringing forth, and (like Abortions of the Brain) only come into the Air, and dissolve, do really every day produce new Contrivances, Engines, and Projects to get money, never before thought of' (1697, p 4). Typically, Defoe had been one of the first to suggest in more detail the insubstantiality of paper credit which, 'like the soul in the body . . . acts all substance yet is itself immaterial; it gives motion, yet it self cannot be said to exist, it is neither quantity nor quality . . . it is the essential shadow of something that is not' (1710, p 6). Such a context of shared apprehensions helps us to identify and locate the significance of the ballooning in size and subsequent miniaturisation to which Lemuel Gulliver is subjected after his ship first sets sail on 'a voyage to the South Sea' (Davis II, p 20). Gulliver's mutations are contextualised as only one of the many literary metaphors devised to give shape and utterance to the fundamental transfiguring of human possibility in the developing social and economic world of the time.

It is perhaps to this context, its literature as well as its history, that the 'Argument' of *The Dunciad*'s third book makes ironic reference:

> The Goddess transports the King to her Temple, and there lays him to slumber with his head on her lap; a position of marvellous virtue, which causes all the visions of wild enthusiasts, projectors, inamoratos, castle-builders, chemists and poets.

In the newly mobile and dissimulating world of credit, as Pope cuttingly remarks, 'things change their titles as our manners turn' (*Bathurst* 379), and when in 1720 the gigantic bubble inevitably burst and for so many the assumption of wealth instantly dematerialised, he turned biblical cadence to the service of an image which was to recur in his verse. 'They have dreamed out their dream, and awaking have found nothing in their hands' (*Corr.* II, p 54). What is being registered is the first collective experience of a stock-market crash, and apocalyptic imagery seemed appropriate for a letter to Atterbury. 'Methinks God has punish'd the avaritious . . . The universal deluge of the S. Sea, contrary to the old deluge, has drown'd all except a few *Unrighteous* men' (Corr. II, p 57). That too was a tone and a mode which proved fertile in the poetry of Pope's mature period.

The fledgeling system of economic management soon showed that it had survived, and would survive intact. As far as its installation as the 'economic

Areopagus of the nation'[3] was concerned, the reign of Credit was secure, and the fantasies of wealth continued:

> But nobler scenes Maria's dreams unfold,
> Hereditary realms, and worlds of gold.
> *(Bathurst*, 131–2)

> Hence the Fool's paradise, the Statesman's scheme,
> The air-built Castle, and the golden Dream.
> *(Dunciad* III, 10–11)

> Sore sighs Sir Gilbert, starting at the bray,
> From dreams of millions, and three groats to pay.
> *(Dunciad* IV, 281–3)

A chimerical aspect infiltrates the texture of the verse, as unreal fantasy merges with a fantastic reality. And when Pope gives this movement figurative density, we receive an open invitation to connect explicitly those genealogies of image which the poetry insinuates. One such moment occurs with culmination of Pope's attack on paper-credit in the *Epistle to Bathurst*:

> Blest paper-credit! last and best supply!
> that lends Corruption lighter wings to fly,
> Gold imp'd by thee, can compass hardest things,
> Can pocket States, can fetch or carry Kings;
> A single leaf shall waft an army o'er,
> Or ship off Senates to a distant Shore;
> A leaf, like Sybil's scatter to and fro
> Our fates and fortunes as the wind shall blow:
> Pregnant with thousands flits the scrap unseen,
> And silent sells a King or buys a Queen.
> (69–78)

To James Sutherland's notes we can add that 'A single leaf shall waft an army o'er' gains further point from the fact that in the eighteenth century the fighting services had their own systems of credit. But what is intriguing is the way in which we are able to track the development of an image connecting paper-credit here, 'pregnant with thousands', with the hatching of a myriad insect life from the dirt and darkness where 'hundreds stink content' quoted earlier. The same fascinated attention to an increasingly unnatural autonomy with which wealth, or the appearance of wealth, seems first to generate, and then to fashion human dreams and desires in its own image, is caught in a letter to Broome dated 14 July 1723:

> Every valuable, every pleasant thing is sunk in an ocean of avarice and corruption. The son of a first minister is a proper match for a daughter of a late South Sea director,—so money upon money increases, copulates, and multiplies, and guineas beget guineas in saecular saeculorum.
> *(Corr.* II, p 182)

This movement is subsequently registered in *The Dunciad* when, immediately following the lines which refer to Swift's successful campaign against an attempt to debauch Ireland's currency by the introduction of 'Wood's Half-pence,' Pope puns upon the use of 'Saturnian' to signify a poetical Golden Age, as he testifies to the Goddess Dulness's unchallenged sway in the poem's contemporary England:

> Here pleas'd behold her mighty wings outspread,
> To hatch a new Saturnian age of Lead.
>
> (*Dunciad* I, 25–26)

We see also in the *Bathurst* lines a further continuity of image and of emphasis which through the mention of 'a leaf, like Sybil's', priestess to Apollo, connects us with the God to whom the Emperor Augustus was devoted. Apollo, we recall, concerned himself not only with the arts but with the establishment of cities, with constitutions, with codes of law and their interpretation. For Pope's original audience, this vital tissue of cultural memory and mythic relationship was a far more spontaneous affair than it is for us. He could confidently expect the linkage with a debased literature and *polis* of his own time, and its ritualised perversion in the realm of Dulness to register upon his contemporaries with a power as silent, and as transforming, as that of the stock-market.

As 'gingling' gold (*Bathurst*, 67) learned to move in secrecy, and thus invisibly to possess its owners entirely, so Pope develops corresponding patterns of imagery. In the first book of *The Dunciad*, a note by Pope refers to the abolition of the post of laureate to the City of London, 'so that upon [Elkanah] Settle's demise, there was no successor to that place' (88n). To fill this vacuum, the Queen of Dulness surveys past City laureates:

> She saw with joy the line immortal run,
> Each sire imprest and glaring in his son.
>
> (I, 97–8)

and while there is almost certainly an historical reference in these lines to the new gold, silver and copper coinage struck for the accession of George II, the literary interest of the image lies more in its application of terms from monetary production to the creation of poets and the invention of poetry. The Goddess's 'joy' springs from her recognition of the dominance of 'City' values. By 1735, with the addition of an 'author's DECLARATION' (*TE*, V, 237), the running metaphor of the corruption of the literary imagination is extended to include 'Critics and Restorers who have taken upon them to adulterate the common and current sense of our Glorious Ancestors, Poets of this Realm, by clipping, coining, defacing the images, mixing their own base allay, or otherwise falsifying the same; which they publish, utter, and vend as genuine'. The careful imbrication of literary and monetary terminology renders them indistinguishable; the process of counterfeit expression is at once 'invented', recorded and condemned. Then, in Book 2, after the race to gain 'a poet's form' evaporates into nothing, the goddess invites the bookseller Curl to 'turn this whole illusion on the town' (132), and the business of counterfeit production in contemporary literature is presented as a grotesque promissory note on the future:

> Be thine my stationer! this magic gift;
> Cook shall be Prior, and Concanen, Swift:
> So shall each hostile name become our own,
> And we too boast our Garth, and Addison.
>
> (137–40)

Where, in his correspondence, Pope could appear to urge a friend to 'Turn your Eyes and Attention from this miserable mercenary Period: and turn yourself, in a just Contempt of these Sons of Mammon, to the Contemplation of Books' (*Corr*. II, p 50), in the world of the poetry no such separation seems possible nor any such escape.

Appropriately enough, the fourth book of *The Dunciad* dramatises most fully both the reification of human aspirations and the perverted deification of money-objects. The numismatist Mummius describes how the forger and counterfeiter Annius concealed stolen Greek coins from pirates:

> 'Down his own throat he risq'd the Grecian gold;
> Receiv'd each Demi-God with pious care,
> Deep in his Entrails—I revered them there,
> I bought them, shrouded in that living shrine,
> And at their second birth, they issue mine.'
>   'Witness great Ammon! by whose horns I swore,
> (Reply'd soft Annius) this our paunch before
> Still bears them, faithful; and that thus I eat,
> Is to refund the Metals with the meat.'
>
> (382–90)

For this marvellously compact moment, a sentence from the young Marx, struggling in his own time to express an understanding of the same complex design, seems as marvellously apposite. 'Money has not been transcended in man within the credit system, but man is himself transformed into money, or, in other words, money is *incarnate* in him.'[4] Pope presents this incarnation of money as a perversion of eucharistic communion; a festival of consumption in which idolatry, blasphemy and cuckoldry contextualise the excremental rebirth of a filched Classical symbolism. As the human form becomes a literal embodiment of this figurative process of possession and displacement, so the poetic imagery contains within itself echoes of a once divinely-inspired order of epic *virtu* in the world. Alexander the Great visited the oracle of the Egyptian god Ammon, whom the Greeks identified with Zeus, and the Romans with Jupiter, special protector of Rome. After his visit, Alexander had coins struck showing his own head adorned with the curling ram's horns of the god. An invocation of antique grandeur thereby suffers comic deflation as the Lilliputian denizens of *The Dunciad* whore after their own false gods, each of them, as it were, 'wrapt up in Self, a God without a thought' (485). At this individual level, after prolonged exposure to such deforming experience, 'ev'ry finished son returns' (500) to the service of the Goddess. And with that return, the supremacy of a usurping system of values is acknowledged, while the justly balanced 'oeconomy' celebrated in *To Bathurst* (223–4) is over-turned by the pervading currency of Dulness's domestic empire. In the words of Silenus:

> Now to thy gentle shadow all are shrunk,
> All melted down, in Pension, or in Punk.
> (509–10)

Images of the gradual but inexorable emergence of an alien and dominating sector in the prevailing order of things echo and re-echo throughout *The Dunciad*. In its all-embracing Goddess we witness a darkly comic exfoliation of forces which seem to be simultaneously figures in the human brain and actual motors of human behaviour in daily life. What is at first inexplicable comes to assume a natural dominance in the structure of the poetry. The fantastic figures of Pope's invention acquire social attributes and become parodied representations of an equally burlesqued history. But the Goddess survives her alienating mission: in the society of the poem a whole educational system is enslaved in her service. In an exhilarating self-awareness, *The Dunciad* informs us that the process is sufficiently sophisticated 'to confine Youth to the study of *Words* only in schools, subject them to the authority of *Systems* in the universities, and delude them with the name of party-distinctions in the World' (IV, 501n). It all sounds strangely familiar, but it does at least suggest that any attempt to confine the significance of Pope's goddess to the level of personality, even one as historically evidential as Walpole's, will never quite do justice to the reach of her metaphorical embrace. The profusion of personal references which have been read as disfigurements in the later poetry are indeed, many of them, motivated by personal malice on the poet's part. But practically all of those so scathingly included had associated with the ministry which ushered in and protected the institutions that enriched them all. In so far as they actively supported Walpole's administration with their pens, and a vast majority of them did, they function in the satirical reaction of Pope's vision as a clerisy of the damned, their Lilliputian scribblings forming part of the infrastructure of a power system which both dwarfed and transcended them. Sorry successors to the aediles of ancient Rome, they were the functionaries who first either manned or piloted the huge impersonal machinery of a bureaucratic state partly devised and significantly developed by Walpole.

'These are,' the poem falters over such ephemeral officers of the fledgeling state in a highly comic deconstruction of its own epitaph for them, '—ah no! these were, the Gazetteers' (II, 314). It is a good joke, and like so many in

The Dunciad one which is detonated by the machinery of annotation into which the rhyming couplets spill. Quoting from a report of the Parliamentary Committee of Secrecy (1742) to the effect that upwards of fifty thousand pounds had been paid out to authors and contributors to government newspapers in the decade from 1731 to 1741, the note to the transient gazetteers concludes: 'Which shows the Benevolence of One Minister to have expended, for the current dulness of ten years in Britain, double the sum which gained Louis XIV so much honour in annual Pensions to learned men all over Europe' (314n). We should not, then, be surprised when Walpole too falls victim to the powers for which he had acted as such an astute midwife and manager. When the goddess asserts that 'Princes are but things/Born for First ministers' (IV, 601–2), it must inevitably follow that at her yawn, as part of 'the Nation's sense' (IV, 611) being lost, 'Ev'n Palinurus [Walpole] nodded at the helm' (IV, 614). Since the movement of Dulness embraces everyone, the minister should hardly feel disconcerted by his own submission to a force in the poem greater than himself. For ultimately, *The Dunciad* both states and embodies the premise that even 'The Muse obeys the Pow'r' (IV, 268). And as part of this disconcerting ambience we encounter lines which might strike us as disturbingly self-referential to the poem's own performance:

> There motley Images her fancy strike,
> Figures ill pair'd, and Similes unlike.
> She sees a Mob of Metaphors advance,
> Pleas'd with the madness of the mazy dance:
> How Tragedy and comedy embrace;
> How farce and epic get a jumbled race.
> (I, 65–70).

In one reading, *The Dunciad* is gorged on a surfeit of its own inventiveness.

The poem's central deconstructive attribute might then be read as a result of this surfeit of trickery; that is to say, its progressive weakening, amounting at times to a virtual dismantling of the couplet's ability to contain the world it anathematises. In Pope's hands the balance, the judicious regulation and the controlled variability of the couplet form offered the possibility of a technical correlative for an ideal society, an appropriate mode of discourse for the desired Polybian balance of a stable, mixed constitution. But to borrow a phrase from Dickson (1967, p 90), in 'the new English state initiated so precariously in 1688' the days of this balance were to be numbered in a very different sense. While the occasions and stratagems of an emergent finance capitalism, its dilating stock-exchange and a burgeoning money-market, were creating enormous and foundational opportunities for enrichment and development, by the time of Pope's death, he had left the capacities of his favourite form virtually exhausted. It is a telling disjunction. At the precise historical moment of a revolutionary proliferation of socio-economic activity, the encapsulatory pretensions of the couplet must come to seem a partially redundant imposition. The epigrammatic containment to which, as literary form, the couplet aspires, necessarily fractures. Due to Pope's mastery, the couplet does not disintegrate altogether. What happens instead is that in the decade and a half of its incremental composition and textual complication, *The Dunciad* contrives itself as a satire on the very notion of the book as a means of communication. In its pages the couplet, staggering under the weight of an endlessly fertile cross-breeding of joke and explication, of editorial ironies and obfuscations, seems to form something of an imaginative continuity with Pope's strategic perception of an economics where 'money upon money increases, copulates, and multiplies . . . in saecular saeculorum'. As we try to pursue these continuities and discontinuities we realise that a clear sense of origins is being confounded, the construction and transmission of meaning itself at times jeopardised by the addictive machinery which conglomerates the real with the unreal. An age of reason, as articulated in *The Dunciad* is germinally enriched and corrupted by a magnetic irrationalism.

This crisis of form and meaning might register now as a crisis in Pope's natural inheritance, the discourse of civic humanism. Throughout the seventeenth century, the recognisable tones of English civic humanism had been framing the discussion of political conduct in ethical terms, imposing a moral hierarchy upon the world of its utterance. But the entry into history of a new accounting system for a radically expanded acquisitive individualism heralded the demise of civic humanism's classical ethos, leaving the conventions of its literacy stranded. Those conventions had not yet developed a vocabulary with which to analyse the revolutionary developments in economic relations. Mandeville had seen this and, though its whole drift seems to contradict the perception, in his *Essay on Man*, in many ways an elegiac, if somewhat strident hymning of the paradise lost of landed stability, Pope had allowed his own God to glimpse (I, 89–90):

> Atoms or systems into ruin hurl'd,
> And now a bubble burst, and now a world.

NOTES

1 James Sutherland (ed), *The Dunciad*(B), 1, p 79, in *The Twickenham Edition of the Poems of Alexander Pope*, John Butt (ed). All quotations from the poem are from the (B) version: all quotations from the poetry are from the relevant volume of the Twickenham edition, to which line and page numbers refer.
2 For the facts and technicalities concerning the advent of the new dispositions of personal and national finance, I rely throughout on Dickson (1967).
3 Karl Marx, *Early Writings*, Penguin Books, Harmondsworth (1967), p 265.
4 Ibid, p 264.

References

Aden, J *Pope's Once and Future Kings: Satire and Politics in the Early Career* (Knoxville: Univ of Tennessee Press, 1978)

Blanchard, R (ed) Sir Richard Steele, *Tracts and Pamphlets* (Baltimore: Johns Hopkins UP, 1944)

Davis, H (ed) *The Prose Works of Jonathan Swift* (London: Basil Blackwell, 1965, rpt)

Defoe, D *An Essay Upon Projects* (London, 1697)

—— *The Villainy of Stock-Jobbers Detected* (London, 1701)

—— *An Essay Upon the Public Credit* (London, 1710)

Dickson, P G M *The Financial Revolution in England: A Study in the Development of Public Credit* (London: Macmillan, 1967)

Habakkuk, H J 'English Landownership 1680–1740', *EHR* 3 (1939–40) 2–17

Kramnick, I *Bolingbroke and his Circle: The Politics of Nostalgia in the Age of Walpole* (Cambridge: Univ of Massachusetts Press, 1968)

Mack, M *The Garden and the City: Retirement and Politics in the Later Poetry of Pope, 1731–1743* (London: Oxford UP, 1969)

Pocock, J G A *The Machiavellian Moment: Florentine Political Thought and the Atlantic Republican Tradition* (Princeton: Princeton UP, 1975)

Sherburn, G *The Correspondence of Alexander Pope*, 3 vols (London: Oxford UP, 1956)

Ward, A 'The Tory View of Roman History', *SEL* 4 (1964) 413–53.

> *Apollo* check'd my Pride; and bade me feed
> My fatning Flocks, nor dare beyond the Reed.[8]

In the 1744 text, Phoebus, kings and wars are removed and immortal Rome restored along with Maro's boundless mind (though he remains *young* Maro, not great: it had clearly been a *faux pas* to imply that the noblest poet of them all could be fallible in his maturity). However, a footnote still refers to the Eclogue's *reges et proelia*, and Pope adds:

> It is a tradition preserved by *Servius*, that *Virgil* began with writing a poem of the *Alban* and *Roman* affairs; which he found above his years, and descended first to imitate *Theocritus* on rural subjects, and afterwards to copy *Homer* in Heroic poetry.

What Servius in fact says is that the *reges et proelia* verse refers perhaps to a false start on the *Aeneid* and perhaps to a poem on the kings of Alba Longa which Vergil later abandoned because of the harshness of their names. (One sympathises: the Alban part of Livy's *History of Rome* includes, among other discordant monarchs, Cluilius, Proca and Fufetius.) Servius's colleague Donatus adds that, as a young man, Vergil had written about *res Romanae*—the phrase seems to imply the doings of Romulus and his successors rather than those of the pious Aeneas—but that, finding himself unhappy with the material, he turned to eclogues instead.[9]

All this is re-ordered by Pope to suit his own book. His strategy, it seems, is to take the hypothetical false start on the *Aeneid* and to inject into it the suggestion that Vergil was at the time interested in a realistic, documentary chronicling style such as might well be appropriate to such things as Livian verse-histories of Alban/Roman affairs. The likelihood that such chronicling is in Pope's mind as a contrast to the eventual techniques of the *Aeneid* is supported by a remark made by his admired Réné Rapin in the *Comparison of Homer and Virgil* which was put into English by Basil Kennett in 1706. Rapin takes up the Horatian distinction between the 'cyclic' chroniclers (who foolishly start their poems *ab ovo*) and the true epic writers (who begin *in medias res*), declaring that Horace is right to 'inveigh with so much Vehemency against those Poets he calls *Cyclick*, by reason of the purely Natural and Historical Representation they gave of things.'[10] Such pure naturalness chimes well with young Maro's plan to draw only from nature's fountains.

Pope's fable, then, has a tolerable scholarly pedigree. It is also quite scrupulous not to make firm assertions about the Vergil of history which are unseemly or unknowable. '*Perhaps* he seemed above the critic's law' is a carefully hedged speculation, and '*As if* the Stagyrite o'erlooked each line' wisely leaves it an open question whether Vergil read Aristotle's *Poetics* closely—or indeed read it at all. (Pope is more prudent here than Charles Gildon, who seven years later insists that '*Virgil, that supreme Genius*, was . . .

as well acquainted with the *Fountain* of *Criticism*, as *Horace* himself; nay, and has visibly observed the Rules of *Aristotle*, in his *Aeneis*'.[11]) But once Pope has rendered unto scholarship that which is scholarship's, he can use the mere speculative possibility that Vergil was once a tearaway young Turk to create a myth-figure with strong resonances for the seventeenth and early eighteenth centuries. Did Young Maro's boundless mind drive him to dispense at first with tradition? Then he was a forerunner of Sir William Davenant, who hints in the 1650 preface to his singular epic *Gondibert* that he will not be following Homer, that 'eminent Sea-mark' by which previous poets have steered, because 'Sea-marks are chiefly useful to Coasters, and serve not those who have the ambition of Discoverers, that love to sail in untry'd Seas'.[12] Was Vergil '*above* the Critick's Law'? If so, he foreshadowed John Milton, as Addison and Dennis saw him around 1700. Indeed, the Milton of Dennis's 1704 account could have been part-model for Pope's Young Maro. Dennis's Milton 'had a desire to give the World something like an Epick Poem; but he resolv'd at the same time to break thro' the Rules of *Aristotle*'. Not wanting the reputation of a mere copyist of Homer, 'he was resolved to write a Poem, that, by vertue of its extraordinary Subject, cannot so properly be said to be against the Rules, as it may be affirmed to be above them all'.[13] Again, did Young Maro scorn to draw but from nature's fountains? Milton himself had flirted with the same idea, debating, while he was pondering an epic of his own in the 1640s, 'whether the rules of *Aristotle* herein are strictly to be kept, or nature to be follow'd, which in them that know art, and use judgement is no transgression, but an inriching of art;'[14] and less judicious followers of nature were vocal enough in 1710, the year before Pope's *Essay* appeared, to draw a rebuke from Gildon:

> *Nature, Nature*, is the great Cry against the Rules. We must be judg'd by *Nature*, say they, not at all considering that *Nature* is an equivocal Word, whose Sense is too various and Extensive ever to be able to appeal to.[15]

As for Young Maro's choosing to draw from a fountain, this would have resonances too. True, there might be something of a *frisson* when the fountain he chose was declared to be nature's (even though Pope *had* declared nature to be the 'source' of art a few lines earlier[16]). After all, it was a commonplace, backed by such distinguished ancients as Ovid, Pliny, Quintilian and Longinus, that Homer was the fountain of all poetry and high speech. As Manilius phrases it in Thomas Creech's translation of 1697, Homer was the great original

> from whose abundant Spring
> Succeeding *Poets* draw the Songs they sing;
> From *Him* they take, from *Him* adorn their Themes,
> And into little Channels cut his Streams,

which chimes with the implication elsewhere in the *Essay on Criticism* that, if a critic should 'trace the Muses *upward* to their *Spring*', he would find

Homeric headwaters.[17] In the visual arts things were similar. The surviving Graeco-Roman marbles and bronzes were widely held to be 'the true fountains of science, out of which both painters and statuaries are bound to draw for their own use, without amusing themselves with dipping in streams which are often muddy'. The words are Roger de Piles', as Dryden translated him in 1695. The muddy streams signify the styles of the artists' immediate mentors. To lead the artists away from these to the proper antique fountains, de Piles cites Cicero's *De Oratore*: 'It belongs only to heavy minds to spend their time on streams, without searching for the springs, from whence their materials flow in all manner of abundance.'[18] This was a wise saying which by the Renaissance had become proverbial: Leonardo da Vinci's version of it was 'He who can go to the fountain does not go to the water-jar';[19] and Young Maro's strategy is, so to speak, to raise the stakes on de Piles' use of the proverb, casting Homer as a mere muddy stream flowing from the pure springs of the goddess *Natura*. In the sixteenth century, *Natura Dea* had been several times sculpted as a fountain (at Fontainebleau and Tivoli, for example) in her manifestation as Diana of the Ephesians, the many-breasted fertility-goddess. The same Diana was engraved in seventeenth-century treatises on the arts with abundant milk springing from her several breasts. In de Piles' *Lives of the Painters*, as put into English in 1706, nature is described as 'the fountain of variety'; and in 1709, two years before Pope's *Essay* was published, Pierce Tempest issued an English version of Ripa's *Iconologia* in which the Venus-figure who usually stands in for *Natura* in Ripa-adaptations is depicted by Isaac Fuller as towering over the earthly globe and fructifying it with great streams from her two breasts [Plate 1].[20] So Young Maro could meaningfully reject Homer's fountains for hers in 1711. (He would have for company at least one artist of the previous century, the Bolognese painter Alessandro Tiarini, who is said to have dismissed the ancients as models with the question: 'Why go to draw water from the rivulets of imitation when you can take it abundantly from the primal, authentic fountain of nature?'[21])

Lastly, when Young Maro in Pope's fable receives, through a thorough scrutiny of Homer, the revelation which leads him to confine his epic within strict rules, he foreshadows those turn-of-the-*grand-siècle* poets convinced that classical epic was a needful and viable model through examining Le Bossu's *Traité du poëme épique* of 1675. That amazing systematisation of Homer (and of the reformed Vergil himself) was held, by the Earl of Mulgrave for instance, to be the first full disclosure of the heroic genre's 'sacred Mysteries', showing 'where all the mighty Magick lyes.'[22] Indeed, the fable in the *Essay on Criticism* might almost be called On Looking Into Le Bossu's Homer. It was presumably Le Bossu's ambition to create such well-regulated poets as the ineffable Richard Blackmore, author of *Prince Arthur*, as praised in 1695 by Le Bossu's translator, one W.J.: 'Throughout the whole [poem] he seems in a great Measure to have confin'd himself to the Rules of *Aristotle* and *Horace*, *Which may be one great Argument to prove that the writing according to the Rules of* Aristotle *and* Horace *is no such Clog to a Poet's Fancy as some pretend*'. Similarly, in the previous year the historian and translator Laurence Echard had claimed that the rules were not arbitrary, 'but pure Nature only Methodiz'd: They never hamper a *Poet*'s Fancy or clip his Wings, but adorn their Thoughts, and regulate their Flights so as to give 'em a clearer insight into *Nature*'. With which Charles Gildon was to agree in 1710: 'the Business of Poetry is to copy Nature truely and observe *Probability* and *Verisimilitude* justly, and the Rules of Art are to show us what Nature is and how to distinguish its lineaments from the unruly and preposterous Sallies and Flights of an irregular and uninstructed Fancy.'[23] To follow such rules is to follow essential nature.

Pope says much the same in his fable: much the same but not precisely the same. As we have seen, Charles Batteux was to argue in 1746 that antiquity became a kind of nature to the Renaissance because it provided both 'useful examples diligently set to view' and 'rules properly established'. Le Bossu had mentioned this duality in 1675. Insisting that the principles of epic poetry should be drawn only from those with 'the glory of having either practis'd with the most Success, or collected and prescrib'd Rules with the greatest Judgement', he declares that Homer and Vergil are the 'perfect Models' and Aristotle and Horace the 'perfect Masters'.[24] It is the latter strand in all this that Gildon and Echard stress, emphasising rules and rule-givers. Elsewhere in his *Essay* Pope is able to synthesise both strands in the figure of Longinus,

> Whose *own Example* strengthens all his Laws,
> And *Is himself* that great Sublime he draws.

But in his fable he emphasises the former strand, the practitioners and poetic models. This is hardly surprising, since by 1711 Pope had himself attempted one epic (*Alcander*), would eventually attempt another (*Brutus*), was soon to work on the first of two major mock-epics, and had already (though he may not have known it) taken the first steps towards his complete Homer translation. Of course he agrees with Gildon and Echard, among many others, that the classical rules are to be followed: but *his* way of arguing the case is to declare that the rules are natural, that their first formulator Aristotle did not so much devise as discover them, that it was in Homer's work that he did so, and that it was valid for him to go to Homer because Homer and nature are 'the same'. The *Iliad* and *Odyssey*, then, rather than any abstract critical system, form the bottom line of Pope's account; Homer, the fountain of natural poetry, is his matrix, not Aristotle, Gildon's 'fountain of criticism'.[25] (That an attitude to poetry rather than to system-building is his central concern is perhaps further shown by that oddly phrased assertion apropos the rules: 'To copy *Nature* is to copy *Them*.' One does not normally *copy* a rule, one follows it; it is an original or model that one copies—the word recurring in the 1744 footnote, where the mature Vergil is said 'to copy *Homer* in Heroic poetry'.)

There is a telling contrast between this emphasis of Pope's and that of his contemporary the elder Jonathan Richardson when he is discussing the proper training for painters. Pope and Richardson became friends; Richardson painted a fine portrait of a laurel-crowned Pope as something of a latter-day Vergil; and Richardson's drift and terminology here are close to Pope's—yet with a significant difference. Give painters proper aristocratic patronage, Richardson argues, and they

> would thus learn not to attach themselves Meanly, and Servilely to the Imitation of This, or That particular Manner, or Master, and those perhaps none of the Best, but to have more Noble, Open, and Extensive Views; to go to the Fountain Head from whence the Greatest Men have drawn That which has made their Works the Wonder of succeeding Ages; They would thus learn to go to Nature, and to the Reason of things. Let them receive all the Warmth, and Light they can from Drawings, Pictures, and Antiques, but let them not stop there, but endeavour to discover what Rules the Great Masters went by, what Principles they built upon, or might have built upon, and let them do the same; not because They did so, or were Supposed to have done so, but because 'twas Reasonable.[26]

Richardson stresses 'the Reason of things' as central to life and to the proper acquisition of art, while Pope stresses the imitable incarnation of such things in the Homer-that-is-true-nature.

Pope's equation of Homer with nature is boldly a-prioristic: a necessary truth not subject to argument, the equivalent in criticism to a first cause in theology. (One can speculate that it owes something to Pope's Catholicism and something to his adoring absorption in Homer from the precocious age of eight.) It is not surprising, then, that he should forget all his scholarly scrupulousness about the historical Vergil when revealing it, that the revelation itself should have something of a road-to-Damascus effect on Young Maro (who is as amazed by it as he is convinced), and that the formula revealed should so strongly resist simple paraphrase. It is not greatly elucidated when Pope recurs to it in the Postscript to his *Odyssey* translation fifteen years later, where he warns that

> Whoever expects here the same pomp of verse, and the same ornaments of diction, as in the Iliad; he will, and he ought to be disappointed. Were the original otherwise, it had been an offence against nature; and were the translation so, it were an offence against *Homer*, which is the same thing.

And Samuel Johnson's use of Pope's formula to illustrate his tenth definition of 'nature'—'sentiments or images adapted to nature and conformable to Truth and Reality'—points one in the right direction but does not get one very far.[27] However, that resistance to paraphrase does not prove, as Dennis would have it, that Pope's equation is without any manner of meaning. Homer and nature are the same. He is himself the *rerum natura* he draws. A great Omnium descends on Pope out of the classic eloquence. The formidable artistic achievements of the ancients become indistinguishable from nature, define and reveal nature, make nature artistically digestible, draw nature up to her proper height, replace nature. We can perhaps find useful ways through this maze of meanings by following the clues contained in those foreshadowings of Pope's equation which occur in the four major critical verse-essays written in the *Ars Poetica* tradition in the two centuries before Pope: Marco Girolamo Vida's *De Arte Poetica*, Charles du Fresnoy's *De Arte Graphica*, Nicolas Boileau's *L'Art poétique* and the Earl of Mulgrave's *Essay Upon Poetry*.

One can glimpse the idea of antiquity as nature in Boileau's advice on effective comic realism in his *Art poétique* of 1674. 'You, then, that would the comic laurels wear,' he exhorts in the Soame-Dryden translation, 'To study nature be your only care.' After expanding on how this should be done and stressing the evils of straying from nature after false lights, he produces a classical corrective to such folly:

> Observe how Terence does this error shun:
> A careful father chides his amorous son;
> Then see that son, whom no advice can move,
> Forget those orders, and pursue his love!
> 'Tis not a well-drawn picture we discover;
> 'Tis a true son, a father, and a lover.[28]

Terence and nature come close here, through Boileau's endorsement of Terence's method and his praise for Terentian verisimilitude. However, though Boileau must have been aware of the remarkably tenacious traditions of structuring and characterisation that bound 'new comedy' together from Menander, through Plautus and Terence and the sixteenth-century *commedia*, to his contemporary Molière, it is not patent that he sees the sole inference of his argument to be that we must draw on the substance of Terentian comedy if we are to have any hope of copying nature properly.

Terence himself, on the other hand, did feel that *his* only hope of copying nature (or rather 'life', since the word 'nature' seems never to have been used in the classical world to stand for the object of dramatic *mimesis*) was to draw on the substance of Menander. Menandrian comedy, in the classic definition of Cicero, was 'an imitation of life, mirror of custom and reflection of reality', though its life, custom and reality were formalised, as Dryden puts it in the *Essay of Dramatic Poesy*, into 'the general characters of men and manners; as old men, lovers, serving-men, courtesans, parasites, and such other persons as we see in their comedies; all which they made alike: that is, one old man or father, one lover, one courtesan, so like another, as if the first of them had begot the rest of every sort.'[29] Yet Menandrian comedy was widely held to be supremely, almost definitively, vivid—as one Alexandrian enthusiast, Aristophanes of Byzantium, put it: 'O Menander, O Life, which of you imitated which?'[30]—and Roman comedy leant heavily on it. This made for complex relations between the 'joint' Greek and Latin authors, and between the imitation of life and the imitation of art. It was while attempting to harmonise all these things in the prologue to his *Eunuch* that Terence comes close to a concept of antiquity as nature. The play, he says, is a version of Menander's *Eunuch*, with a couple of characters—a parasite and *miles gloriosus*—added from Menander's *Flatterer*. Some troublemaker at rehearsal accused him of stealing the soldier and parasite from an old Plautine piece, but this Terence denies:

> Our playwright does not deny that he has transferred these characters to his play out of the Greek original; he denies any knowledge of the Greek play's having been used as a foundation for Latin plays. But if our playwright is not allowed to introduce the same characters, how can it be more legitimate to introduce a servant on the run or good old gentlewomen or unprincipled cour-tesans or a greedy parasite or a braggart soldier or a supposititious child or an old gentleman tricked by a servant or love or hate or jealousy? In fact nothing is said that has not been said before. So you should recognize facts and pardon new playwrights if they present what their predecessors presented before them.[31]

The last line concentrates the ambiguity of the whole: 'Quae veteres fac-titarunt si faciunt novi.' Does it defend a *mimesis* of the same world our predecessors imitated, or a copying of their *mimesis* of that world? Away from its context, Terence's argument seems to lean to the former: there is nothing new under the sun, so it will not be surprising to an intelligent audience if the characters in my plays resemble those in Menander or Plautus or anyone else. But *in* Terence's context, this seems an odd way to account for taking two characters from Menander's *Flatterer* to improve one's version of Menander's *Eunuch*, and the other reading seems more apt: everything has been said by the Greeks; they have articulated comic life as a perfect system of courtesans, slaves, parasites, soldiers, trickery, love, hate and jealousy; to hold the mirror up to Menander is to hold it (as 'twere) up to comic life itself.

Renaissance writers pondered Terence's line 'Nullumst iam dictum'—'nothing is said that has not been said before'—soft-pedalling it when they wanted to stress originality and inventiveness as literary strengths, as Pierre de Deimier did in his *Académie de l'art poëtique* of 1610, and trumpeting it when they were concerned to justify elaborate re-orderings of existent material, as Robert Burton was eleven years later in his *Anatomy of Melan-choly*.[32] It is, Burton claims, the artful arrangement of things, not the creation of fresh substance, that characterises worthwhile latterday authors, poets included: 'Our poets steal from Homer; he spews, saith Aelian, they lick it up.' How far Vergil was independently original and how far he licked up Homer's spewings were preoccupations of Dryden a generation later in several of his critical prefaces. One impulse led him to argue that 'Descrip-tions, Figures, Fables, and the rest, must be in all Heroick Poems; they are the Common Materials of Poetry, furnish'd from the Magazine of Nature: Every Poet hath as much right to them, as every Man hath to Air or Water', and that '*Virgil* cannot be said to copy *Homer*: The *Grecian* had only the advantage of writing first'. But another impulse counter-argued that 'if Homer had not led the way, it was not in Virgil to have begun heroic poetry', and that Vergil wisely 'endeavoured not to introduce or innovate any thing in a design already perfected, but imitated the plan of the inventor; and [they] are only so far true heroic poets as they have built on the foundations of Homer'.[33]

If epic resources were both the invention of Homer and part of 'the Magazine of Nature', a young Alexander Pope reading Dryden would be forgiven for wondering whether Homer and nature were perhaps the same, and whether borrowing from previous art could be separated from *mimesis*. He was certainly concerned enough in his late 'teens with the question of literary borrowing to write to his mentor William Walsh about it. Walsh replied:

> As for what you ask of the *Liberty* of *Borrowing*; 'tis very evident the best *Latin* Poets have extended this very far; and none so far as *Virgil*, who is the best of them. As for the *Greek* Poets, if we cannot trace them so plainly, 'tis perhaps because we have none before them; 'tis evident that most of them borrow'd from *Homer*, and *Homer* has been accus'd of burning those that wrote before him, that his Thefts might not be discover'd. The best of the modern Poets in all Languages, are those that have the nearest copied the Ancients. Indeed in all the common Subjects of Poetry, the Thoughts are so obvious (at least if they are natural) that whoever writes last, must write things like what have been said before: But they may as well applaud the Ancients for the Arts of eating and drinking, and accuse the Moderns of having stol'n those Inventions from them; it being evident in all such cases, that whoever live first, must first find them out.[34]

Plagiarism, adaptation and simple resemblance chase each other's tails in Walsh's letter (which, to do him justice, he allows may be 'Nonsense' since there is 'Company round me while I write this'); but at least the letter supplies a meeting place for the *Eunuch* prologue, which haunts the latter part of Walsh's argument, and ideas later expressed by Pope, both in the preface to his 1717 collection ('All that is left us is to recommend our productions by the imitation of the Ancients . . .') and in the fable of Young Maro itself: Maro too comes to acknowledge the necessity of copying one particular ancient if his thoughts are to be truly natural.

Sorting out the various strands of borrowing, resembling and plagiarising was left to Samuel Johnson in *The Rambler* and, as we have seen, to Richard Hurd in his 'Discourse on Poetical Imitation'. In *Rambler* No. 143, Johnson, meditating on the famous allusion to the *Eunuch* prologue which opens the *Caractères* of La Bruyère ('Tout est dit, et l'on vient trop tard . . .'), concludes that, 'as not every Instance of Similitude can be considered as a Proof of Imitation, so not every Imitation ought to be stigmatized as Plagiarism'. For his 'Discourse', Hurd naturally chooses as his epigraph

> Nullum est jam dictum, quod non dictum sit prius.
> Quaere aequm est vos cognoscere atq. ignoscere
> Quae veteres factitarunt, si faciunt novi

and the terms of Terence's prologue are at the back of his mind throughout. He can make capital out of its ambiguity, for it allows him to treat both the necessary, accidental coincidences between works of art whose subject is the same aspect of an unchanging reality, and also quite conscious borrowings:

> When the greater provinces of poetry have been already occupied, and its most interesting scenes exhausted; or, rather, their application to the uses of poetry determined by great masters, it becomes thenceforward unavoidable for succeeding writers to draw from their sources. The law of probability exacts this at their hands; and one may almost affirm, that to *copy* them closely is to paint after *nature*.

To copy nature is to copy them. To avoid copying them is to court perversity, as with Davenant's *Gondibert*: that 'perpetual monument of the mischiefs which must ever arise from this affectation of originality in lettered and polite poets'. The threads of Pope's and Terence's arguments are drawn even closer in Hurd's account of the similarity of the *Aeneid*'s funeral games to those in Homer:

> The *subject-matter* admitted not any material variation: I mean, in the hands of so judicious a copier of Nature as Virgil. For,
>
> > 'Homer and Nature were, he found, the same.'
>
> . . . The very *contexture* of a work, designed to evidence [characters] in *action* will, under the management of different writers, be, frequently, much the same. A *conclusion*, which indeed is neither mine nor any novel one, but was long ago insisted on by a discerning antient, and applied to the comic drama, in these words,
>
> > —— *Si personis isdem huic uti aliis non licet,*
> > *Qui magis licet currentis servos scribere . . .*

And so on through Terence's catalogue of Menandrian life.[35]

However, if we are right in seeing Pope's Vergil confronted with an external master's great Omnium of *heightened* nature, Terence's low comic world can only account for half of what is revealed to him. The law of probability might, as Hurd says, convince him that to copy the ancients is to paint after nature, and that to avoid them is to risk unnatural perversity; but it would scarcely amaze him or compel him to check his bold design. Terence delivers a brazen world, but Young Maro needs to perceive a golden if he is to pattern the *Aeneid* after it.

The existence of such an ideally beautiful second nature for the modern to imitate it is hinted at in Vida's verse-essay *De Arte Poetica* of 1527. Vida is concerned, as were many of his near-contemporaries,[36] that modern poets should follow in the footsteps of Mother Nature:

> The noblest poets own her sov'reign way,
> And always follow where she leads the way,

as Christopher Pitt translates in 1725. But Vida is even more concerned that they should gather a store of words, ideas and examples from the ancients, and most particularly from Vergil, whose work he celebrates as impeccably eloquent and opulently beautiful. Accidentally perhaps, but revealingly, Vida uses the same image—*sequere vestigia*—for our reverently following Vergil as for our wisely following nature. This does not mean that Vergil and nature are the same, of course; but it does install them as twin poetic gods; and at the end of the poem it is Vergil who is adored as the fructifying presence without whom poetry would have no beauty. 'Te sine, nil nobis pulchrum.'[37]

The idea of an ancient author providing a super-reality of heightened beauty for his successors to render is in fact more rigorously presented in antiquity itself (albeit very late antiquity) as part of that corpus of writings on ideal visual art which collected around the third wonder of the ancient world, the colossal statue of Zeus at Olympia which was carved by Phidias out of gold and ivory.[38] In the first book of the *Iliad*, Zeus is petitioned by Thetis to give victory to the Trojans, so that the Greeks may know what comes of rousing the wrath of her son, Achilles. Zeus assents, in Pope's translation, with 'the Nod that ratifies the Will Divine':

> He spoke, and awful, bends his sable Brows;
> Shakes his Ambrosial Curls, and gives the Nod;
> The Stamp of Fate, and Sanction of the God:
> High Heav'n with trembling the dread Signal took,
> And all *Olympus* to the Centre shook.

Pope's note to this passage reads:

> This Description of the Majesty of *Jupiter* has something exceedingly grand and venerable. *Macrobius* reports, that *Phidias* having made his *Olympian Jupiter* which past for one of the greatest Miracles of Art, he was ask'd from what Pattern he fram'd so divine a Figure, and answer'd, it was from that Archetype which he found in these Lines of *Homer*.[39]

The story that the Olympian Zeus was in some sense an imitation of the *Iliad* is some centuries older than Macrobius and was often told in antiquity: Plutarch says it was on every tongue. In Valerius Maximus' version, Homer is literally an external master of knowledge; Phidias uses his verses 'quasi magistro'.[40] But one allusion to the tale is especially apropos for the way the teller, the late neo-Platonist Diadochus Proclus, marries its Homeric theory of the Zeus's creation to a quite distinct, un-Homeric theory also current at the time.

The basic quarrel of Plato himself with the arts had been with their unreality. In the tenth book of *The Republic*, painting and poetry are proscribed as *mimesis* of a generated world of appearances which is itself no more than *mimesis*. Not that Plato flatly denies the possibility of a noble art which imitates the unchanging world of forms. The opportunity of achieving this is offered to the Demiurge of his *Timaeus*. 'Whenever the maker of anything looks to that which is always unchanging and uses a model of that description in fashioning the form and quality of his work,' says Plato, 'all that he thus accomplishes must be good. If he looks to something that has come to be and uses a generated model, it will not be good.'[41] Plato of course felt that all the art around him in the Athens of his day was given over to mere generated appearances; it was left to his later followers to discover an idealising art of the unchanging. The symbol of their discovery was the Olympian Zeus, in making which, they held, Phidias had copied not mere appearances but his own transcendent imagination. Even Plotinus gave the Zeus his blessing.[42] Hence Proclus, writing his ambitious commentary on the *Timaeus*, had good reason to mention the neo-Platonic interpretation of the Zeus when he came to the passage in Plato about the choice before the Demiurge. Phidias can conveniently stand as its human counterpart, looking to that which is always unchanging. But it so happens that Proclus was almost as great a devotee of Homer as he was of Plato, and spent much time trying to reconcile the two; so he introduces the Homeric account of the Olympian Zeus as well. The relevant gloss on Plato's text in his *Commentary* was translated into Latin in that influential mosaic of classic documents on classic art produced in 1637 by Francis Junius, *De Pictura Veterum*. Junius put his mosaic into English the following year as *The Painting of the Ancients*:

> He that maketh any thing after intelligible things [i.e. things of the *mundus intelligibilis*, the world of the unchanging], must needs make it like the conceived things, or else unlike: if he doth make it like by imitation, so is it that the imitation of necessitie shall be faire; seeing there is in the conceived things a principall beautie. . . . Likewise he that maketh any thing after the example of things generated, shall never, as long namely as he doth fix his eyes upon them, attaine to what is perfectly beautifull; seeing the things generated are full of deformed disproportions, and far remoted [*sic*] from the principall true beautie. Hence it is that *Phidias*, when he made *Jupiter*, did not cast his eyes upon any thing generated, but he fetched the patterne of his worke out of a *Jupiter* conceived after *Homers* description.[43]

It is arguable that when Pope's convinced, amazed Vergil imitated nature in the *Aeneid*, he did not cast his eyes upon anything generated, but fetched the pattern of his work out of a nature conceived after Homer's description. (It is even arguable that something like Proclus's idea is part of the scenario of the enigmatic portrait of Pope painted by Charles Gervas as Pope was getting deep into his *Iliad* project [see Frontispiece]. There the poet is presented as turned away from an energetic physical young woman and withdrawn into his own imaginings, over which hovers the shadowy presence of Homer as a classical bust.[44])

Proclus's gloss is rarely cited by writers in the classic-idealist tradition of Renaissance art criticism, with the notable exception of Sir Joshua Reynolds, using it to bolster a plea for heightened *mimesis* at the end of that tradition.[45] But several other retellings of the story of Phidias's Homeric inspiration take on a Proclan cast: for instance, Francesco Bocchi's citing of it in 1584 to supply a precedent for Michelangelo's use of lines from Dante's *Inferno* as the model for his figure of Charon in the *Last Judgement*, and René Rapin's in some sentences of 1674 which may well have influenced Pope's *Essay* directly. Rapin refers to the account of the Zeus in the Homeric commentary of Eustathius, links it with another anecdote from the same source and uses both to support a call for imitation of Homer in literature rather than in sculpture or painting. If we want to frame great ideas, he says in his *Reflections on Aristotle's Treatise of Poesie* (as translated by Thomas Rymer), we must go to Homer and Vergil:

> It is in these great *Originals* that our modern Poets ought to consult *Nature*, to learn how to raise their Wits, and be Lofty. . . . Never Person in any Language possess'd all these Qualities in such eminent Degree, as *Homer*; he is the first Model a Poet must propose to himself to write as he ought. . . . It was formerly on this Original, that *Euphranor* form'd his Idea for drawing the Image of *Jupiter*. . . . The same hapnd to *Phidias* in that admirable Statue of *Jupiter* he made, after the Model he found in the same Place in *Homer*, as *Eustathius* affirms. . . . Nothing Noble and Sublime can be made without consulting the *Ancients*.[46]

These Terentian and Proclan traditions are partial evidence that, when Pope declared Homer and nature to be the same, he was not uttering a private nonsense. Admittedly John Dennis's nineteenth-century representative, Whitwell Elwin, thought that he was:

> The argument of Pope is sophistical and inconsistent. It is inconsistent, because if Virgil found Homer and nature the same, his work would not have been confined within stricter rules when he copied Homer than when he copied nature. It is sophistical, because though Homer may always be natural, all nature is not contained in his works.[47]

To the charge of inconsistency, Proclus could reply that the ideal world for which Homer stands (what French Classicism was to call *la belle nature*) is more rigorous in its demands on the artist than the world of appearances; hence strictness is in order. To the charge of sophistry, Terence could counter that everything sound and apropos has been said in previous art; hence echoing of that art is inevitable. Still, partly because neither tradition concerned itself originally with *nature* as such—the term is very rare as the object of *mimesis* in poetry or the fine arts before the Renaissance[49]—neither can supply Pope with a strict precedent for the formula Antiquity = Nature. However, when the Earl of Mulgrave saluted classical epic in his *Essay upon Poetry* of 1682—

> *Homer* and *Virgil*: with what awfull sound
> Each of those names the trembling Air does wound! . . .
> Nature's whole strength united! endless fame,
> And universal shouts attend their name!

—he may have nudged Pope (who admired the lines) in the direction of thinking of classic art as an imitable microcosmic union of all that is most worthwhile in the *rerum natura*, and so linked him to another slender tradition of ideas going back to the end of the Roman Empire.[49]

In the early centuries AD, rhetoricians and philosophers were becoming interested in the *concordia discors*, the variety-within-unity, of big literary works. Thus in the first century Quintilian praises Homer because stylistically he is 'at once luxuriant and concise, sprightly and serious, remarkable at once for his fullness and his brevity'; and in the sixth, Olympiodorus of Alexandria (developing an idea from Plato's *Phaedrus*) announces that 'the best-constructed composition must resemble the noblest of living things; and the noblest of living things is the cosmos'.[50] Around AD 400 such notions merge strikingly in the *Saturnalia* of Macrobius. The *Saturnalia* is much concerned with Vergil: his erudition, relation to poetic tradition, stylistic variety and rhetorical force; and in Book V there is a discussion of the relative merits of Vergil and Cicero as writers from whom the student of rhetoric can learn. Cicero is naturally praised for his great expertise, but this is felt to be all in one key, whereas Vergil is 'multiplex et multiformis'. Having illustrated that multiplicity, Macrobius is moved to compare the poet to the creating god of the Stoic cosmologists, *Natura*, the benign craftsman who orders and sustains the universe providentially:

> As I see it, Vergil was at pains to combine every mode of eloquence, being possessed of a certain intuition that his work should serve as universal model. Such foresight was the result of divine—not mortal—genius. So it was that, following the lead of none but the mother of all things, Nature herself, he wove all eloquence together, as music weaves harmony from dissonance. Indeed, if you look closely at the world we live in, you will find a great similarity between that divine work and the work of our poet. For just as Vergil's eloquence is well adapted to every mood—now succinct and now copious, now dry and now florid, now mild and now overflowing—so the earth itself is rich in part with crops and meadows, in part wild with forests and crags, in part arid with deserts, in part watered with streams, in part washed by the immense sea. So forgive me, and do not accuse me of exaggerating, if I compare Vergil with nature [*naturae rerum Vergilium comparavi*].[51]

Vergil and nature are, Macrobius finds, if not the same then at least comparable, and in a context of subsequent literary imitation. But the imitation will be of Vergil's rhetoric by public speakers, not of his aesthetic, narrative techniques and substance by other poets; so Macrobius only provides a partial analogy to Pope's equation.

However, sixteenth-century poetics in the hands of the formidable Italian polymath Julius Caesar Scaliger bring the Macrobian idea mush closer to Pope. In the *Poetices Libri Septem*, published in 1561 three years after his death, Scaliger is concerned, unlike Macrobius, with forming good neo-Latin poets. These will need to be expert in the imitation both of nature and of previous literature. From some of the more adventurous Italian thinkers of the earlier Renaissance[52] Scaliger inherits the idea that, if a poet or painter has genius and practises his art skilfully, he can become almost a second god, surpassing or vanquishing mundane nature in the process of copying it, and creating in his work of art a more opulent, excellent and concentrated second nature, the *altera natura* of an *alter Deus*. But Scaliger develops this concept rather idiosyncratically. For one thing, though he holds in principle that, where literature is concerned, any gifted writer can achieve this creativity, in practice he maintains that the only one to have done so is the one by whom he is as obsessed as Macrobius and Vida were: Vergil. It is uniquely Vergil who has 'not only triumphed over all human wits but raised himself, so to speak, to an equality with nature'.[53] Again, Scaliger's minute knowledge of the *Aeneid*, his reverence for its variety-within-unity and his penchant for making long lists of things ensure that his ideas about the poem as an *altera natura* are not just vague speculations. In the *Aeneid* he perceives, and then tabulates at length, a Vergilian cosmos having vivid beauty and ordered plenitude as its chief characteristics. It is in this that he seems to be adapting the cosmological analogy from the fifth book of the *Saturnalia* (a book he knew well, though he does not quote the critical passage), substituting for the multiformity of rhetorical modes which make up the Macrobian *rerum natura* a compendious multiplicity of events, descriptions, speeches and actions.[54] Finally and crucially, since Vergil has uniquely become a superior second nature, Scaliger deduces that aspiring poets can derive the material they need more easily and more rewardingly from his work than they can from day-to-day exterior nature:

> All these things that you will imitate you have in the second nature that is Vergil. . . . We could not take from any one work of nature herself the examples which we have borrowed from the work of Vergil. . . . More could be added, but we thought that these were sufficient for the practice of imitation: the example, rule, principle and end of which must for us be Vergil.[55]

Scaliger has no time for Homer; his reaction to the manifest similarities between the Homeric epics and Vergil's is to adapt Ovid's account of the creation of the world in the *Metamorphoses*: Homer stands in for Ovid's 'rough undigested lump' of primal matter, while Vergil is the 'God or better nature' calling it to lucid order.[56] But a shift in taste is all that is needed to transfer the idea of a poetical second nature from Vergil to Homer. Pierre de Ronsard in fact effects the transfer nearly a century and a half before Pope, in the very practical context of how the French are to write their epics. 'The whole essence of heroic poetry', he declares in the Third Preface to his *Franciade* of 1587, 'lies in the painting, or rather imitation, of nature'; and it is with this *peinture ou plutost imitation* that you should 'copy the effects of nature in all your descriptions following Homer'. *Suyvant Homere* here is ambiguous. It could merely imply a vague empathetic imitation of the master: Homer always copied nature, so we should do the same. But the likelihood that Ronsard is actually recommending an objective imitation and that Homer's poetry is seen as a superior alternative to *les effets de la nature* is increased by a teasing sentence in the earlier *Abbregé de l'Art Poëtique*, which came out four years after Scaliger's *Poetices*:

> And you must not neglect comparisons and descriptions of places, rivers, forests, mountains, night, dawn, noon, the winds, the sea, and the gods and goddesses with their appropriate functions, manners, dresses, chariots and horses— fashioning yourself for all this in imitation of Homer, whom you shall observe as a divine model, taking the most perfect outlines of your picture from the life in him.

To suggest making one's poem perfect by taking its features *au vif sur le divin exemple d'Homere* seems to imply a belief that Homer is perfect imitable life. To follow Homer, then, in copying the effects of nature in all your descriptions is to use his work as an objective *altera natura*.[57]

Ronsard could well have read Scaliger's treatise hot from the press. But did young Pope read it in his 'teens nearly 150 years later? Certainly he knew it, at least in part, by his later twenties: Scaliger's is one of the learned folios that 'whelm'd me under a Fit of the Head Ach' while working on the *Iliad* project. Indeed, Pope's contention in his *Iliad* preface that there are 'such different Kinds of Deaths' in the poem 'that no two Heroes are wounded in the same manner' reads like an adaptation of the observation about deaths in the *Aeneid* which appears in the same paragraph of Scaliger as his most striking naturising of Vergil: 'Haec omnia quae imiteris, habes apud alteram naturam, id est Virgilium.'[58] When Pope was six, however, another of those naturisings had become easily available in English. It appeared in 1694 in the anthology of criticism *De Re Poetica: or, Remarks upon Poetry With Characters and Censures of the Most Considerable Poets*. The anthologist was Sir Thomas Pope Blount. Though he was not a close relation of Pope's own family or of that of his friends Martha and Teresa, the anthologist's name could well have drawn Pope to the book, and in its chapter on Vergil he would have found:

> *Julius Scaliger*, in his Sixth Book *De Poetica, pag.* 765. says, That *Virgil* not only excells all *Humane* Wit; but has rais'd himself to a kind of equality with Nature it self. And in another place he tells us, That *Virgil* ought to be the Pattern, Rule, Beginning and End of all *Poetical* Imitation.[59]

As with many of his more recondite selections, these Scaliger citations are not necessarily the result of encyclopaedic reading on Blount's part. The reference to Scaliger's Sixth Book is probably taken silently from the work of a genuine encyclopaedist Blount often quarried: Adrien Baillet, in his *Jugemens des scavans sur les principaux ouvrages des auteurs* of 1685–6.[60] Still, it may have been the contraband of one Pope that enabled another to equate antiquity with nature so memorably.

If Pope in later life could have been persuaded to provide an extended note on his Homer and nature line, he might have done worse than transcribe a paragraph from an essay of 1734 by his humble but intelligent contemporary, Hildebrand Jacob:

> If *Poets*, and *Painters* are to propose the *Idea* of *perfect* Nature for their *Imitation*, it is absolutely necessary that they attain to that *Idea*; and how is that *Idea* to be acquir'd, but by studying the *Perfections* both of the *Body*, and the *Mind*? And where are these *Perfections* found in such Excellence, and Abundance as in the Works of the *Ancients*? In the Statues, Bas-relieves and precious *Relicts* of the great Masters of old, and in the *Writings* of those learned Philosophers, Poets, and Historians, who have drawn the *Manners* and *Sentiments* of Mankind with the same Majesty, and Justness, as these great *Painters* did their *exterior* Forms, and the *visible* Beauties of *Nature*? But why, say some People, must we have recourse to *Antiquity*? Have we not our *Organs* as perfect as the *Ancients* had? And is it unreasonable to suppose, that we may have *Ideas* as great, as beautiful, as just, and surprizing as they had? . . . [Yet] that Majesty, that Truth, or Justness, that beautiful Simplicity, and natural Grace, so peculiar to the *Ancients*, are rarely to be met with in any Degree amongst the *Moderns*, and never but amongst such of them, as have imitated *Antiquity*; for it has been the *Fate* of these *latter* Ages, to *refine* so much upon *Nature*, that they have quite *lost Sight* of her, and that not only in Relation to these *Arts* in Question; but in almost *every* Thing else. The *Ancients* endeavour'd to *improve Nature*; we seem, on the contrary, to strive to *hide her* as much as is possible; they consulted *Nature* in her self, and considering, in general, what she *could*, and *ought* to do, they copy'd her *Perfections*; nor was this so beautiful *Simplicity* of the *Ancients* confin'd to these *Arts*; but diffus'd it self thro' their *Manners*; nor should we, perhaps, have had any *Idea* of it at all; but from what Remains we have found of it in their Works.[61]

The statues and bas-reliefs of antiquity are to the Augustan painter what the manners, sentiments, ideas and techniques of classical poetry are to the Augustan poet. Jacob's parallellism would not be lost on Pope. From boyhood he had been interested in the visual arts; a drawing of his showing a classical bard with a parchment ('Vergil Convinced by Homer' perhaps?) survives from around the time of the *Essay on Criticism*; and by 1716 he was closely enough involved with the classic-idealist painting tradition to urge his painter-friend Charles Jervas to persevere with his 'noble design' of writing a book on the characteristics of ancient sculpture.[62] Of course he also wrote an epistle on friendship and the sister-arts at that time in connection with Jervas's 'corrected and enlarged' edition of the Dryden version of du Fresnoy's Latin verse-essay *De Arte Graphica*, a poem which had first appeared in Paris in 1668 with a commentary by Roger de Piles. So it is not surprising that the Franco-Italian art-theorising tradition of which *De Arte Graphica* is a significant part should produce, from among its profusion of approaches and attitudes, some vivid parallells with Pope's equation.

Dryden's du Fresnoy announces that 'our business is to imitate the beauties of nature, as the ancients have done before us [*juxta antiquos naturam imitabere pulchram*], and as the object and nature of the thing require from

Poussin . . . knew that in order to make the most graceful, beauteous and well proportioned Bodies, there were no better Models to be studied and imitated than the Statues and Bas-reliefs of antient Artists, those Master-pieces of Workmanship, which have ever been so highly admired by all the Intelligent; and which, ever since the Art was at such a Degree of Perfection as to have been capable of producing them, all Artists have thought it the best thing they could do to copy after them, and endeavour to come as near to their Excellence as possibly they could.[70]

The great Omnium descends on Félibien's Poussin, and Félibien demonstrates the descent in Poussin's painting of *The Israelites Gathering Manna in the Desert* [Plate 3]. In a letter to Jacques Stella, the painter himself claimed to have found for the picture 'certain natural attitudes which make manifest the misery and famine to which the Jewish people were reduced, and also their joy and delight, the astonishment that seized them, and their respect and reverence for their law-giver'. As part of Félibien's many-levelled analysis of the painting (derived from another 1667 meeting of the Académie Royale during which it was monumentally discussed under the leadership of Charles Le Brun), he points out that the proportions of one of Poussin's old men are taken from the Borghese *Seneca*; that those of a youth bending over him derive from the Belvedere *Antinous*; that a kneeling girl bears a resemblance to the Louvre *Diana*; that one of a pair of quarrelling boys is based on one of the antique *Wrestlers* and the other on one of the sons in the *Laocoön*, and so on. Of the fifteen or so antique sculptures most celebrated in the seventeenth century, nine are declared to have lent proportions to figures in the *Manna*. The whole picture becomes a cento of ancient art (rather as Pope, in his early, abandoned epic *Alcander* 'endeavoured . . . to collect all the beauties of the great epic writers into one piece'); but since ancient art is perfect nature, such a cento is perfect *mimesis*.[71] Poussin, says Félibien,

> knew, that it was impossible to find any where such perfect Bodies of Men and Women as Art had formed by the Hands of those excellent Masters, to whom the Manners and Customs of their Country had furnished all the most advantageous and favourable Means of making a fine Choice of Nature: And that therefore, without studying and following these Models, a Painter would undoubtedly fall into many Faults; as indeed all those have done, who studying Nature alone, took indifferently for their Models all Sorts of Persons, as they chanced to present themselves to them, without once thinking of shunning what was defective, ill proportioned, imperfect or unbeauteous.[72]

The most notorious 'student of nature alone' in seventeenth-century Franco-Italian art-criticism was Michelangelo Merisi da Caravaggio. According to G. P. Bellori's 1672 account—one among many—he

> not only ignored the most excellent marbles of the ancients and the famous paintings of Raphael, but he despised them, and nature alone became the object of his brush. Thus when the most famous statues of Phidias and Glycon were pointed out to him as models for his painting, he gave no other reply than to extend his hand toward a crowd of men, indicating that nature had provided

him sufficiently with teachers. . . . Moreover, he followed his model so slavishly that he did not take credit for even one brush stroke, but said that it was the work of nature. He repudiated every other precept and considered it the highest achievement in art not to be bound to the rules of art. . . . Many were those who imitated his manner of painting from nature, and for that reason they were called 'naturalists'.[73]

If Poussin (a mind 'naturalized in antiquity', as Sir Joshua Reynolds was to call him) is the equivalent of the regenerate Vergil in Pope's fable, Caravaggio represents the extremest dangers of borrowing only from nature's fountains, and is an awful warning to all Young Maros. In the tradition of seventeenth-century poetic theory he is comparable with those who, as Rymer puts it in *The Tragedies of the Last Age*, 'mistake *use* for *nature*', which is an aberration because 'a Poet is not to be an Historiographer, but a Philosopher, he is not to take *Nature* at the *second hand*, soyl'd and deform'd as it passes in the customes of the unthinking vulgar.'[74]

As we have seen, it was arguably the first impulse of Pope's Vergil to be a historiographer rather than a philosopher, until scrutinising Homer set him right. Similarly Pope was to urge Charles Jervas to desert his trade of portrait-painting—'be not confined, like the rest, to draw only such silly stories as our own faces tell of us'—for more ambitious and imaginative *mimesis* which would do justice in practice as well as theory to 'those Statues from which you learned your beautiful and noble Ideas'. And one imagines that Pope would have been posthumously pleased when, in 1762, Francesco Algarotti bracketed together the material treated by mere naturalistic painters and fact-grubbing historians, contrasting it with the proper subject of high idealistic art: ''Tis nature all (says an English writer about poetry, and the same is to be said of painting), but nature perfected and methodized.'[75]

The theorists' fascinated horror at Caravaggio's naturalism comes partly from their awareness that he is—or at least can be made to seem—the reincarnation of that provocative ancient painter Eupompus, whom Pliny described as replying to a question about which of his predecessors he took for a model by 'pointing at a crowd of people and saying it was nature herself, not an artist, one ought to imitate'. Guido Reni's pointing at a group of ancient heads in plaster is almost certainly a pious inversion of the Eupompan creed. The force, allure and iconoclastic danger of the creed itself, given an exponent with Caravaggio's gifts (to say nothing of a Christian name shared with an artist of very different aesthetic persuasions), is clear from the *Dialogues on Painting* of 1633 by the Spaniard Vincencio Carducho:

Did anyone ever paint, and with as much success, as this monster of genius and talent, almost without rules, without theory, without learning and meditation, solely by the power of his genius and the model in front of him which he simply copied so admirably? . . . This Anti-Michelangelo with his showy and external copying of nature . . . has been able to persuade such a large number of all kinds of people that his is good painting . . . that they have turned their backs on the true manner of perpetuating themselves.[76]

By Carducho's time the English literary tradition had found—or was in the process of manufacturing—a seemingly very similar figure: the William Shakespeare who is fancy's child, who does not borrow 'one phrase from Greekes, nor Latines imitate' (as Leonard Digges put it), and who is a notable demonstration (as Francis Beaumont pointed out) of

> how farre sometimes a mortall man may goe
> by the dimme light of Nature.[77]

By Pope's time, Shakespeare's great intimacy with nature (for all that he had small Latin and less Greek) had come to seem both amazingly fruitful in itself and anarchically dangerous in the bad influence it was bound to have on other writers. In a prologue written the year after the *Essay on Criticism* appeared, Richard Steele is teased by the duality:

> Since Fancy of it self is loose and vain,
> The Wise by Rules, that airy Power restrain . . .
> But *Shakespear's* self transgress'd; and shall each Elf,
> Each Pigmy Genius, quote Great *Shakespear's* self!

Two decades later, Judith Cowper can echo Pope's fable while setting up what seems to be the definitive *anti*-Maro:

> EXALTED SHAKESPEARE, with a boundless mind,
> Rang'd far and wide; a genius unconfin'd![78]

The paradoxes multiply when Pope himself, in the preface to his Shakespeare edition of 1725, appears to be joining the naturalists against the drift of his own fable and pre-empting the anti-classicism of Young's *Conjectures on Original Composition*:

> If ever any Author deserved the name of an *Original*, it was *Shakespear*. *Homer* himself drew not his art so immediately from the fountains of Nature, it proceeded thro' *Ægyptian* strainers and channels, and came to him not without some tincture of the learning, or some cast of the models, of those before him. The Poetry of *Shakespear* was Inspiration indeed: he is not so much an Imitator, as an Instrument, of Nature.[79]

However, the paradox here is more apparent than real. The clue to this is in the comparison with Homer. Shakespeare is not really being presented as a tearaway Young Maro who refuses ever to reform and conform, or as a Caravaggio spitting in the faces of Phidias and Glycon. Vergil and Caravaggio were both born to a sophisticated artistic heritage, with high art all around them and the presence of a pervasive tradition of adapting it. Shakespeare, in Pope's view, was not. In fact, though he is sixteen centuries younger than

Young Maro and a contemporary of Caravaggio's, Pope's Shakespeare is poetically a primitive ancient, a Homer-figure: less a *doctus poeta* in the Renaissance-humanist tradition than blessed with what Dryden had called a *natural* learnedness. Pope's Vergil in comparison is a Queen Anne modern— even briefly a Fontenellian modernist.

It is Dryden's forethoughts on the subject which make it likely that Pope was aware of a Homer-Shakespeare connection even when he was writing the *Essay on Criticism* itself. In the *Essay of Dramatic Poesy*, Dryden gives Neander some pertinent reflections on Shakespeare, Beaumont, Fletcher and Jonson. Shakespeare is characterised by Neander as 'the Homer, or father of our dramatic poets': one to whom 'all the images of nature were still present' and who was 'naturally learned; he needed not the spectacles of books to read nature; he looked inwards, and found her there'; while Beaumont and Fletcher are said to have benefited from 'Shakespeare's wit, which was their precedent', and Jonson is described as 'the Virgil, the pattern of elaborate writing' to Shakespeare's Homer.[80] Within a few months of writing his *Essay*, while supplying a prologue for the adaptation of *The Tempest* on which he collaborated with Davenant, Dryden sharpens this view of Shakespeare and his school (possibly adding to it a dash of the 'Haec omnia quae imiteris, habes apud alteram naturam' from Scaliger's *Poetices*, a book he knew quite well). It was Shakespeare, the prologue announces,

> who (taught by none) did first impart
> To *Fletcher* Wit, to labouring *Johnson* Art.
> He Monarch-like gave those his subjects law,
> And is that Nature which they paint and draw.
> *Fletcher* reach'd that which on his heights did grow,
> Whilst *Johnson* crept and gather'd all below . . .
> If they have since out-writ all other men,
> 'Tis with the drops which fell from *Shakespear*'s Pen.[81]

The teasing ambiguity of 'And is that Nature . . .' recalls similar things we have seen in Terence and Ronsard; and it looks forward to the pregnancy of Pope's fable. Indeed, taken with Neander's remarks, Dryden's couplets here provide Pope the fabulist with quite a full resource. Shakespeare (who is Shakespeare-Homer) has all of nature within him, which he externalises into *a* nature; indeed he becomes a sort of landscape, with heights and depths. He gives other writers 'law', if not quite rules. He is a fountain, if only of ink. And in his train, Jonson (who is Jonson-Vergil) sedulously creeps, gathers and labours. It is hardly possible that Pope did not recall Dryden's verses when writing his own: even the *law/draw* rhyme of the couplet in which Dryden naturises Shakespeare recurs in the couplet in which Young Maro cleaves to nature's fountains (and indeed recurs again in the related couplet about Longinus being his own 'sublime').

Two years before Pope published his fable, Nicholas Rowe reflected on the providential ignorance of Shakespeare, living as he had done 'under a kind of mere Light of Nature'. Clearly he had not read the poetic classics of Greece and Rome. That much is obvious

> from his Works themselves, where we find no traces of any thing that looks like an Imitation of 'em; the Delicacy of his Taste, and the natural Bent of his own Great *Genius*, equal, if not superior to some of the best of theirs, would certainly have led him to Read and Study 'em with so much Pleasure, that some of their fine Images would naturally have insinuated themselves into, and been mix'd with his own Writings; so that his not copying at least something from them, may be an Argument of his never having read 'em.

Rowe speculates as to what a conventionally learned Shakespeare would have given us: 'the most beautiful Passages out of the *Greek* and *Latin* Poets, and that in the most agreeable manner that it was possible for a Master of the *English* Language to deliver 'em.' Yet, faced with this as an elegant alternative, are we not happier with the Shakespeare we have?

> Whether his Ignorance of the Antients were a disadvantage to him or no, may admit of a Dispute: For tho' the knowledge of 'em might have made him more Correct, yet it is not improbable but that the Regularity and Deference for them, which would have attended that Correctness, might have restrain'd some of that Fire, Impetuosity, and even beautiful Extravagance which we admire in *Shakespear*: And I believe we are better pleas'd with those Thoughts, altogether New and Uncommon, which his own Imagination supplied him so abundantly with . . .[82]

than with any cento, however brilliant, that he could have compiled with the help of a classical education. To borrow from Richard Hurd's 'Discourse' of 1751 at its most speculative, the Augustan forms of learning would have proved '*rather injurious to the true poet, than really assisting to him*': as they proved injurious, Hurd believed, in the case of Addison, whose poetry was 'restrained and disabled by his constant and superstitious study of the old classics'. (The 1758 *Literary Magazine* aptly said of Addison that 'his Cato, like the pictures of Poussin, is faultless in the drawing, because copied after whatever is most graceful in the antique. But though the figures have *motion*, they are destitute of *life*; they have *beauty*, but are void of *nature*.'[83])

As we have seen, Batteux and Wordsworth as well as Hurd had cause to be concerned about the way deferential regularity and the insinuation of fine classical images created 'a nature to the heart' which constrained true poetic fire and imagination. And indeed if nature and *Shakespeare* were to be generally deemed 'the same' in the later eighteenth century, their amalgam was not to be one which demanded objective imitation—at least by poets. For the poets it was a matter of once constrained, twice shy; though, as the age of *neo*classicism approached, other arts might still bow to a great Omnium, as William Mason does in *The English Garden* of 1772, encouraging the landed gentry to 'transplant again on nature' the ideal landscapes of Claude, much as Raphael had transplanted Greek sculptures into his religious paintings. This, Mason says, is not a matter of forgetting 'great Nature's fount', since

> Beauty best is taught
> By those, the favor'd few, whom Heav'n has lent
> The power to seize, select, and reunite
> Her loveliest features; and from these to form
> One Archetype compleat of sovereign Grace.
> Here Nature sees her fairest forms more fair:
> Owns them her own, yet owns herself excell'd
> By what herself produc'd. Here Art and she
> Embrace; connubial Juno smiles benign,
> And from the warm embrace perfection springs.[84]

So it is significant that when, in that great age of Shakespeare performance, painting, celebration and quotation, the revelation of the Bard's identity with nature in a context of subsequent imitation is eventually set down in as definitive a way as Pope's fable had set down Homer's nature-identity, this is done by a *painter* depicting an *actor*. The actor was David Garrick, the English Roscius and high priest of Bardolatry. To recall his benevolent establishment of the actors' pension fund at Drury Lane, his grateful company presented him in 1777 with a medal especially designed by Giovanni Battista Cipriani [Plate 4]. On it, young Roscius throws back a curtain to reveal a 'term': an ancient pillar of the kind which could be expected to support the lone figure of the many-breasted Diana of the Ephesians. On this particular term, however, *Natura Dea* is Siamese-twinned with a *penseroso* Shakespeare. Goddess and bard are one. The unveiling has a certain bizarre hermetic splendour; but for the later eighteenth century the equation it celebrated was far from hermetic, as is shown by the tone of a contribution (mercifully anonymous) to the *Universal Magazine* of six years before:

> When Nature to Athens and Rome bid adieu
> To Britain the Goddess, with extasy flew . . .
> On Avon's fair banks, now the subject of Fame
> She brought forth a boy, and Will Shakespeare his name;
> Not egg was to egg more alike, than in feature,
> The smiling young rogue to his Parent, dame Nature.[85]

Pope's Maro could be forgiven for wincing.

NOTES

1 *The Prelude* (1850 text), VI, 109–14; cf. 1805 text, VI, 127–34.

2 *Q. Horatii Flacci Epistolae . . . to which are added Critical Dissertations*, 5th edn (1776), III, 119, 122; cf. S Johnson, Preface to Shakespeare (1765): *Eighteenth Century Essays on Shakespeare*, D N Smith (ed), 2nd edn (Oxford, 1963), pp 129–30.

3 *Les Beaux arts* (1746), pp 55, 73–4; trans in J Miller, *A Course of the Belles Lettres* (1761), I, 36, 48–9.

4   *Il Cortegiano* (1528), I, xxx.

5   *Ars Poetica*, verses 268–9, 317–18; 'To Mr Lemuel Gulliver', verse 8; *Essay on Man*, III, 317–18.

6   *Essay on Criticism*, verses 130–40. For the textual variants etc discussed here, see Twickenham Edition, I, 254–5.

7   *Critical Works*, E N Hooker (ed) (Baltimore, 1939), I, 402.

8   *Eclogues*, VI, 3–5; *The Poems of John Dryden*, J Kinsley (ed) (Oxford, 1958), II, 894.

9   Livy, I, iii and xxiii. For Servius & Donatus, see R Coleman's edition of the *Eclogues* (Cambridge, 1977), pp 175–6; cf. W F Jackson Knight, *Roman Vergil* (London, 1944), pp 67–9.

10   *Ars Poetica*, verses 147–8; *Whole Critical Works of Monsier Rapin* (1706), I, 176.

11   *The Complete Art of Poetry* (1718), I, 121.

12   *Critical Essays of the Seventeenth Century*, J E Springarn (ed) (Oxford, 1908), II, 1–2.

13   Addison, *Account of the Greatest English Poets* (1694), as cited in Twickenham Edition, I, 254; Dennis, *The Grounds of Criticism in Poetry: Critical Works* (edn cit., note 7 above), I, 333.

14   *Reason of Church-Government* (1641), pref. to Bk II; *Works* (Columbia Edition: New York, 1931–8), III.i, 237. Cf. Eugenius in Dryden's *Essay of Dramatic Poesy: Of Dramatic Poesy & Other Critical Essays*, G Watson (ed) (London, 1962), I, 32.

15   Essay on the Art, Rise, & Progress of the Stage' (1710), in *Shakespeare: The Critical Heritage*, B Vickers (ed), II: 1693–1733 (London, 1974), p 220.

16   *Essay on Criticism*, verse 73. For a subtle treatment of Pope's metaphoric play with the word 'source', see D B Park, ' "At Once the *Source*, and *End*": Nature's Designing Pattern in *An Essay on Criticism*', *PMLA*, 90 (1975), 861–73.

17   Ovid, *Amores*, III, ix, 25; Pliny, *Natural History*, XVII, 5; Quintilian, *Institutes*, X, i, 46; Longinus, *On the Sublime*, XIII, 3; Manilius, *Astronomicon*, II, 8–11; Creech, *Five Books of M. Manilius* (1697), p 49; *Essay on Criticism*, verse 127.

18   De Piles, Commentary on du Fresnoy's *De Arte Graphica: Works of John Dryden*, W Scott (ed) (London, 1808), XVII, 402; Cicero, *De Oratore*, II, xxvii, 117.

19   *Codex Atlanticus* 199ᵛ, clinching a discussion of artistic apprenticeship: *Literary Works of Leonardo da Vinci*, J P Richter (ed & trans), 2nd edn (London, 1939), no. 490.

20   For Fontainebleau and Tivoli, see B H Wiles, *The Fountains of the Florentine Sculptors* (Cambridge [Mass], 1933), pp 84, 129–30, and D R Coffin, *The Villa d'Este at Tivoli* (Princeton, 1960), pp 17–18, 188–9; for engravings, see G P Bellori, *Vite de' Pittori* (1672), E Borea (ed) (Turin, 1976), p 377, and R Blome, *The Gentleman's Recreation* (1686), p 214; De Piles, *The Art of Painting & the Lives of the Painters* (1706), p 352; Ripa/Tempest, *Iconologia or Morall Emblems* (1709), fig. 222.

21   C C Malvasia, *Felesina Pittrice* (1678), II, 205 (trans. mine).

22   *An Essay upon Poetry* (1682); Spingarn, *Critical Essays* (edn cit., note 12 above), II, 296.

23   W J, *Monsieur Bossu's Treatise of the Epick Poem*, Preface, fo. a4; Echard, *Terence's Comedies Made English*, Preface, p xiv (italic and Roman reversed); Gildon, op. and edn cit. (note 15 above), p 220. For Gildon's use of the phrase 'nature methodised' half-way between Echard and Pope, see D M Vieth, *Notes & Queries*, 222 (1977), 233.

24   *Traité du poëme épique*, trans cit. (note 23 above), pp 1–2.

25   For Gildon, see above, note 11. For a vivid account of the relation of precept to

example here, see C Rawson, *Order from Confusion Sprung* (London, 1985), pp 238–40.

26 *Two Discourses . . . A Discourse on the Science of a Connoisseur* (1719), p 60.

27 Pope, Twickenham Edition, X, 389; Johnson, *Dictionary* (1755), II, s.v. 'Nature'. For two valuable modern meditations on the line (albeit not in a history-of-ideas context), see H A Mason, *To Homer Through Pope* (London, 1972), p 42 *et passim*, and N Frye, *Fables of Identity* (New York, 1963), pp 39–51.

28 *L'Art poétique*, III, 359–60, 415–20; S Elledge and D Schier (eds), *The Continental Model*, rev. edn (Ithaca, 1970), pp 251, 255.

29 For Cicero, see pp 102 and 126 of A P McMahon, 'Seven Questions on Aristotelian Definitions of Tragedy & Comedy', *Harvard Studies in Classical Philology*, 40 (1929), 97–198; Dryden, *Essay*, edn cit. (note 14 above), I, 73.

30 McMahon, op. cit. (note 29 above), p 106.

31 *Eunuchus*, Prologue, verses 31–43, trans J Sargeaunt, *Terence* (London, 1912), I, 239. See W Ludwig, 'The Originality of Terence & His Greek Models', *Greek, Roman & Byzantine Studies*, 9 (1968), 169–82.

32 Deimier, *Académie*, pp 209–12; Burton, *Anatomy*, Everyman edn (London, 1932), I, 25.

33 Kinsley, edn cit. (note 8 above), III, 1033–4, 1035; Watson, edn cit. (note 14 above), II, 274, 36.

34 20 July, 1706: *The Correspondence of Alexander Pope*, G Sherburn (ed) (Oxford, 1956), I, 20–1. Cf. *Guardian* no. 12 (March, 1713), and see Lecture II ('The Neoclassic Dilemma') of W Jackson Bate, *The Burden of the Past and the English Poet* (London, 1971).

35 Op. and edn cit. (note 2 above), III, 129, 139, 88, 92–3. (The *Eunuch* epigraph is omitted in Hurd's 5th edn, though it appears, e.g., in his 2nd.)

36 See H S Wilson, 'Some Meanings of "Nature" in Renaissance Literary Theory', *Journal of the History of Ideas*, 2 (1941), 430–48.

37 Vida, II, 456–8, trans Pitt, p 69; Vida, III, 570.

38 The corpus—except for Proclus' contribution (see note 43 below)—is assembled between nos. 692 and 743 of J Overbeck, *Die Antiken Schriftquellen zur Geschichte der Bildenden Künste* (Leipzig, 1868/*R* 1959).

39 Pope, *Iliad*, I, 680, 683–7; Twickenham Edition, VII, 119.

40 Macrobius, *Saturnalia*, V, xiii, 23; Plutarch, *Life of Aemilius Paulus*, xxviii, 2; Valerius Maximus, *Memorabilia*, III, vii, ext. 4. (Lessing, cap. 22 of *Laokoon* [1766], cites the Valerius Maximus as a case of ancient artists being accustomed 'to copy nature through Homer'.)

41 *Timaeus* 28a–b, trans F M Cornford, *Plato's Cosmology* (London, 1937), p 22.

42 Plotinus, *Enneads*, V, viii, 1; cf. Cicero, *Orator*, II, 9. See E Panofsky, *Idea: A Concept in Art Theory*, trans J Peake (Columbia, 1968), esp. cap. 2.

43 Proclus, *Commentary*, II, 81c–d (= 265.18–22); Junius, *The Painting of the Ancients*, p 19 (italic and Roman reversed). For a modern trans, see W Tatarkiewicz, *History of Aesthetics* (The Hague, 1970–4), I, 297.

44 For other possible readings, see D B Morris, *Alexander Pope: The Genius of Sense* (Cambridge [Mass], 1984), pp 305–10, and M Mack, *Alexander Pope: A Life* (New Haven, 1985), pp 341–3.

45 Discourse III (citing Junius), *Discourses on Art*, R R Wark (ed) (San Marino, 1959), p 42.

46 Bocchi, *Eccellenza del San Giorgio di Donatello*: (ed) P Barocchi, *Trattati d'Arte del Cinquecento* (Bari, 1960), III, 150; Rapin, *Réflexions*, E T Dubois (ed) (Geneva, 1970), pp 45, 49, 56: trans Rymer, in *The Whole Critical Works of Monsieur Rapin* (1706), II, 162, 164–5, 170. Cf. Lessing in note 40 above.

47 *The Works of Alexander Pope*, W Elwin and W J Courthope (eds) (London, 1871–89), II, 42.

48 It is not, of course, rare in the Aristotelian/Stoic sense of a spirit (*natura naturans*) emulated by human crafts in general. See A J Close's two essays on 'Theories of Art & Nature in Classical Antiquity', *Journal of the History of Ideas*, 30 (1969), 467–86 (esp. pp 471–2); 32 (1971), 163–84 (esp. pp 169–70).

49 Mulgrave, op. and edn cit. (notes 12 and 22 above), II, 295. Cf. Pope's *Iliad* Preface, Twickenham Edition, VII, 24.

50 Quintilian, *Institutes*, X, i, 46, trans H E Butler, *Quintilian* (London, 1922), IV, 29; Plato, *Phaedrus*, 264c; Olympiodorus, *Commentary on Alcibiades* (105c). See J A Coulter, *The Literary Microcosm* (Leiden, 1976), p 95 *et passim*.

51 *Saturnalia*, V, ii, 1 (trans mine). See E R Curtius, *European Literature & the Latin Middle Ages*, trans W R Trask (New York, 1953), pp 443–5.

52 See, e.g., F Lancilotti, *Tractato di Pictura* (1509), F. Raffaelli (ed) (Ancona, 1885), p 3 ('Un altro Iddio e un'altra natura'), and F Francia, Sonnet to Raphael (*c*. 1510) in V Golzio, *Raffaello nei Documenti* (Rome, 1936), p 333 ('Vinta sarà Natura').

53 *Poetices*, VI, i, p 295 (trans mine); see B Weinberg, 'Scaliger versus Aristotle on Poetics', *Modern Philology*, 39 (1942), 337–60 (esp. 348–9).

54 For a similar possible Macrobian adaptation, see Tasso, *Discorsi del Poema Eroico* (1594), trans M Cavalchini and I Samuel (Oxford, 1973), pp 77–8.

55 *Poetices*, III, iv, p 86; III, xxv, p 113; V, iii, p 245 (trans mine).

56 *Metamorphoses*, I, 5–25; *Poetices*, V, iii, p 225.

57 *Critical Prefaces of the French Renaissance*, B Wienberg (ed) (Evanston, 1950), pp 263, 201 (trans mine). See I Silver, *Ronsard & the Greek Epic* (St Louis, 1961), pp 150–3, and *Ronsard's General Theory of Poetry* (St Louis, 1973), pp 138–48.

58 *The Correspondence of Alexander Pope*, edn cit. (note 34 above), I, 225; *Iliad* Preface, Twickenham Edition, VII, 9; *Poetices*, III, iv, p 86. The first modern scholar to connect the Scaliger and Pope *loci* seems to have been I Babbitt, *The New Laokoon* (London, 1910), p 12n.

59 *De Re Poetica* (1694), 'Characters & Censures', pp 238–9.

60 *Jugemens*, IV, ii, 139, 243. For Blount's reliance on Baillet, compare, e.g., their treatment of Callimachus: 'Characters & Censures', pp 37–8; *Jugemens*, IV, i, 253, 254.

61 *Of the Sister Arts; an Essay*, pp 30–2. Cf. Hogarth's *Antinous* & Dancing Master in Plate 2.

62 Drawing rep. in M B Brownell, *Alexander Pope & the Arts of Georgian England* (Oxford, 1978), p 11; *Correspondence of Alexander Pope*, ed. cit. (note 34 above), I, 377.

63 Du Fresnoy, verses 185–8; Dryden, edn cit. (note 18 above), XVII, 355; de Piles, *Art of Painting*, p 2. See Pt III.i 'La Nature comme concept esthétique' of B Tocanne, *L'Idée de nature en France dans le seconde moitié du XVII* siècle (Paris, 1978), esp. pp 339–46.

64 *Seven Conferences Held in the King of France's Cabinet of Paintings*, trans anon. (1740), pp 31, 40. For Michelangelo's *Torso*, see F Haskell and N Penny, *Taste & the Antique* (New Haven, 1981), pp 311–14. For Polycletus' Canon, see (e.g.) Pliny, *Natural History*, XXXIV, 55; G della Casa, *Galateo* (1558), cap. 25; W Aglionby, *Painting Illustrated* (1685), p 12.

65 Félibien, *Entretiens sur les . . . plus excellens peintres anciens et modernes*, 2nd edn (1685–88), II, 59–63 (trans mine).

66 Aglionby, *Painting Illustrated*, p 105; de Piles in Dryden, op. and edn cit. (note 18 above), XVII, 400.

67 *Dialogo . . . intitolato l'Aretino* (1557), pp 61–2; trans M W Roskill, *Dolce's "Aretino"* (New York, 1968), pp 205, 207. Cf. Dolce, pp 28, 46; Roskill, pp 139, 175. See R W Lee, *Ut Pictura Poesis: The Humanistic Theory of Painting* (New York, 1967), esp. pp 9–16.

68 Mantegna: Vasari, *Lives of the Artists*, trans G Bull (Harmondsworth, 1965), p 242; Reni: Passeri, *Künstlerbiographien* [= *Vite de' Pittori*, 1772], J Hess (ed) (Leipzig, 1934), p 81, trans R Goldwater and M Treves, *Artists on Art* (London, 1947), p 126; Poussin: Rapin, *Réflexions*, edn cit. (note 46 above), p 49, & de Piles, *Art of Painting*, pp 344–5.

69 De Piles, op. cit. (note 68 above), pp 349, 352.

70 Félibien, op. & edn cit. (note 65 above), II, 385; trans G Turnbull, in his *Treatise on Ancient Painting* (1740), p 166.

71 Poussin, *Lettres et propos sur l'art*, A Blunt (ed) (Paris, 1964), p 27 (trans mine); Félibien, op. and edn cit. (note 65 above), II, 411–13; Pope, in J Spence, *Observations, Anecdotes, & Characters*, J M Osborn (ed) (Oxford, 1966), I, 18.

72 Félibien, op. and edn cit. (note 65 above), II, 385–6; trans Turnbull, loc. cit. (note 70 above).

73 Bellori, op. and edn cit. (note 20 above), pp 214–33; trans W Friedlaender, *Caravaggio Studies* (Princeton, 1955), pp 246–54.

74 Reynolds, op. and edn cit. (note 45 above), p 256; Rymer, *Critical Works*, C A Zimansky (ed) (New Haven, 1956), p 62.

75 Pope, *Correspondence*, edn cit. (note 34 above), I, 377; Algarotti, 'Saggio sopra la Pittura', *Saggi*, G da Pozzo (ed) (Bari, 1963), p 96 (trans mine). Cf. Gay's fable, 'The Painter who pleased No body and Every body', *Poetry and Prose*, V A Dearing (ed) (Oxford, 1974), II, 325–7.

76 Pliny, *Natural History*, XXXIV, xix, 61; Carducho, Dialogue VI, trans M S Soria in E G Holt (ed), *A Documentary History of Art* (New York, 1958), II, 209–10. For the Eupompus 'topos', see E Kris and O Kurz, *Legend, Myth & Magic in the Image of the Artist* (New Haven, 1979), pp 14–20.

77 C M Ingleby *et al.*, *The Shakespere Allusion-Book* (London, 1932 edn), I, 455, xi.

78 Steele, Prologue to *The Distrest Mother*, verses 1–2, 9–10: *Occasional Verse*, R Blanchard (ed) (Oxford, 1952), p 46; Cowper, 'The Progress of Poetry', in *The Flower-Piece*, M Concanen (ed) (1731), p 134.

79 *Eighteenth Century Essays on Shakespeare*, edn cit. (note 2 above), p 44.

80 *Essay*, ed. cit. (note 14 above), I, 67–70.

81 Vv. 5–10 & 13–14: *The Works of John Dryden*, gen. ed. H. T. Swedenberg, X (Berkeley, 1970), 6 (italic & Roman reversed); see Commentary, ibid., pp. 346–8.

82 *Eighteenth Century Essays on Shakespeare*, ed. cit. (note 2 above), pp. 15 & 2.

83 Hurd, op. & ed. cit. (note 2 above), III, 122–3; *Works of Goldsmith*, ed. J. W. M. Gibbs (London, 1884–6), IV, 426—a dubious attribution to Goldsmith.

84 *The English Garden*, I, 290–99. The 'Claude-glass' of the genteel late 18th-century connoisseur recalls William Warburton's account of the Maro of Pope's fable learning to contemplate nature 'collected in all her charms in the clear mirror of Homer': Commentary on *An Essay on Criticism* (1743), p. 13.

85 *Univ. Magazine*, 48 (1771), 97–8. For the context of the Cipriani medal, see [National Portrait Gallery], *'O Sweet Mr. Shakespeare, I'll Have His Picture'* (London, 1964), esp. pp. 32–3.

7

The French Pope

PETER FRANCE

Pope is hardly a name to conjure with in twentieth-century France. His works are studied by specialists, but unlike those of Chaucer and Coleridge, or even Tennyson and Dryden, they are not currently available in French translation, and have not been so for many years. E Audra, writing more than fifty years ago of the decline of his reputation after about 1825, noted that Taine's brutal portrait of him was 'à peu près tout ce que connaissent de lui la plupart des lecteurs français, si même ils ont rencontré son nom' (Audra 1931, p x). It may well be the case that in Britain Pope's reputation among academics is not matched by any real popularity with common readers (and the same is very likely true of Boileau in France), but even so his eclipse in France is striking, for things were once very different there.

In the age of Louis XIV English literature was of little interest to the French. Shakespeare and Milton were virtually unknown. *Paradise Lost*, for instance, was not translated into French until 1729—and few French people were capable of reading it in the original. Pope was the first English poet to become widely known across the Channel. If England provided first and foremost models of philosophy (Bacon, Newton, Locke), Pope inaugurated the line of British literary figures (including Richardson and 'Ossian') who were capable of generating enthusiasm and imitation. His reputation, from about 1735 onwards, was immense. The most tangible sign of this is to be found in the numerous editions of his works in French translation. Audra, in his invaluable bibliography, *Les Traductions françaises de Pope (1717–1825)*, lists a total of 240 editions, including not only versions by several different hands of the more popular works, but also numerous multi-volume selections and indeed complete collections. It is not at all common at any period for all the works of a poet to be made available in translation, least of all when these make up eight sizeable volumes.

In the introduction to his bibliography, Audra writes that this phenomenon constitutes 'un des chapîtres les plus intéressants de l'histoire des rapports intellectuels entre la France et l'Angleterre' and deserves a full-scale study.

This would cover: the gradual establishment of his reputation, his influence on philosophical poetry, the 'héroïde' and the descriptive poetry of Delille and his school, the value of the various translations and what they tell us the tastes of two neighbouring countries, and more generally, the modification of the image of Pope the man. Audra himself gives a brief but well-informed sketch for such a study, and subsequent scholars have filled in some of the outline, most notably R G Knapp in his *The Fortunes of Pope's 'Essay on Man' in Eighteenth-Century France* (Knapp 1971). In this essay I shall concentrate on only one of the fields mentioned by Audra, that of translation, since a consideration of the translators and their problems (as well as raising some interesting general issues) helps one to understand how Pope's poetic system was perceived in another culture. Such a 'view from outside' can sometimes prove enlightening for those living within a tradition.

But first, to set the scene, a brief account of Pope's acceptance on the French literary stage. The key figure here was Voltaire. It is true that even before Voltaire took refuge in England in 1726, Pope's name had reached France; his *Essay on Criticism* was first translated in 1717 and his Preface to the *Iliad* had been taken up in the final phase of the Quarrel of the Ancients and the Moderns (Knight 1980). But it was Voltaire who raised the stakes by declaring him one of the great poets and encouraging the French to translate him. He did this first in private letters and then in his *Lettres philosophiques* of 1734 (first published in English the previous year under the title *Letters concerning the English Nation*). Chapter 22, 'Sur M. Pope et quelques autres poètes fameux', is the *locus classicus*, and is worth citing here as an indication of the way the English poet was to be received in France:

> C'est, je crois, le poète le plus élégant, le plus correct et, ce qui est encore beaucoup, le plus harmonieux qu'ait eu l'Angleterre. Il a réduit les sifflements aigres de la trompette anglaise aux sons doux de la flûte. On peut le traduire, parce qu'il est extrêmement clair, et que ses sujets, pour la plupart, sont généraux et du ressort de toutes les nations.
>
> (Voltaire 1915, vol II, p 136)

The adjectives conspire to suggest a Pope who will fit well into a polite French tradition, while the final sentence stresses the translatability of universally valid ideas; the whole passage tends therefore to underplay the concise force and the imaginative richness which several translators emphasised. It may indeed seem that this is somewhat faint praise, implying as it does that Pope's virtue is to have shaken off the barbarity of the English and come nearer to the norms of French classicism. In a subsequent edition, however, we find the much more unequivocal praise of the *Essay on Man* as 'le plus beau poème didactique, le plus utile, le plus sublime qu'on ait jamais fait en aucune langue' (p 139)—and this in spite of the hostility to 'Whatever is, is right' which is so memorably expressed in *Candide*. In later life Voltaire also made strong (if somewhat hypocritical) criticisms of the brutality of Pope's satire, but all in all he was still the English poet's most important champion in France.

Influenced (and probably aided) by Voltaire, Abbé Du Resnel published a new translation of the *Essay on Criticism* in 1730, and this was duly noted in the literary periodicals, which throughout the century were to play their part in keeping Pope's name in the public eye (La Harpe 1933). But it was the *Essay on Man* that set the seal on his reputation—or his notoriety. Three different translations followed one another in quick succession between 1736 and 1739; two of these, by Silhouette and Du Resnel, went into many editions. The reason for this popularity is partly to be found in the polemic the work generated. Since its supposed unorthodoxy provoked refutations by French catholics and protestants alike, the *Essay* became a rallying point for 'philosophical' readers. This was no doubt what attracted the young Diderot to write a long commentary on one of the French translations of the work.

The *Essay on Man* retained its popularity throughout the century—and several new translations were done over the next fifty years. In its wake all of Pope's poetry was gradually made available to French readers. It is interesting to see which poems appealed most to translators (though of course this does not prove that they were the most attractive to readers). To judge from Audra's bibliography, five texts lead the field (not counting the brief 'Universal Prayer', which shared some of the notoriety of the *Essay on Man* (Van Tieghem 1923)). Although less popular than its sister, the *Essay on Criticism* was often printed with the *Essay on Man*; it was easily assimilated into the French tradition alongside Boileau's *Art poétique*. In the same way, the *Rape of the Lock* owed some of its favour to the possibility of comparing it with Boileau's *Lutrin*; it attracted eight translators, including Marmontel. The fourth poem, *Eloisa to Abelard*, is a different case; it remained untranslated until 1751, but thereafter was probably Pope's most popular poem, being translated or adapted by some fifteen writers, imitated by many more, and included in a composite publication entitled *Les Lettres et Épîtres amoureuses d'Héloïse avec les responses d'Abeilard*, which went into many editions between 1776 and 1825 (we may recall that one of the great fictional successes of the century was Rousseau's *La Nouvelle Héloïse*). And finally the later years of the century saw many versions of the *Pastorals* at a time when descriptive or seasonal poetry was in vogue in France.

The Pope of the French translations is, therefore, above all the thinker and the poet of feeling and imagination. The satirist is much less in evidence. True, the *Dunciad* was translated (and even found itself mentioned in the unlikely context of *La Nouvelle Héloïse*, in the hero's comic description of the Paris opera), but it is hardly surprising if a work so dependent on local allusion did not cross the Channel easily. What is more, French opinion was rather dismayed by the vicious personal abuse (and the disorderly composition) of such works as the *Epistle to Arbuthnot* (La Harpe 1933, pp 187–8). On the other hand, such works could provide models for imitation—just as Pope himself had imitated Horace. Thus we find Palissot writing a *Dunciade* as part of his satirical campaign against the *philosophes*. And it has been persuasively argued that Voltaire, for all his fastidious remarks about the vulgarity of Pope's satires, did in fact draw inspiration from them for his own not very clean polemics (Gunny 1979, pp 208–34). But the broad and difficult subject of Pope's influence on French writers goes beyond my present more limited subject, translation.

The best single place to study French translations of Pope is the eight-volume *Œuvres complètes* of 1779, reprinted in 1780 (Pope, 1780). This uses with only very slight modification the text of the *Œuvres diverses* produced by Arkstée and Merkus in Amsterdam and Leipzig in 1767, the last and most complete of a series of collections published by the same firm. The 1779/1780 edition differs from the *Œuvres diverses*, however, in printing the English text for the most important works—an indication, one presumes, of a growing interest in learning English. Like its predecessor, it also includes alternative translations for such poems as the two *Essays*, the *Rape of the Lock* and *Eloisa to Abelard*. The most striking thing, however, is that the greater part of this edition is in prose. Indeed almost all the poems apart from the four just mentioned are given in prose only. Nor should it be thought that where both prose and verse translations existed, the former was regarded simply as a crib. The translation of poetry in prose was quite normal in eighteenth-century France, and the example of Pope gives us a chance to look at some of the theoretical disputes this involved (on this subject see Knapp 1971, pp 35–52).

In 1743 Abbé Desfontaines, who had been responsible for the first (prose) version of the *Rape of the Lock*, published the first volume of a French translation of the works of Virgil. He notes in his preface that there are six French translations of Virgil, five of them in prose. A new one is needed, however, and in a 'discours sur la traduction des poètes' Desfontaines outlines his own theory of translation. Uttering familiar warnings against the Scylla of excessive literalism and the Charybdis of paraphrase, he declares himself in favour of prose versions which remain as faithful as possible to the figures of the original. Metre is less essential, since poetry resides essentially 'dans les images hardiment dessinées, dans les couleurs vives, dans les expressions vigoureuses, dans les tours serrés et expressifs, dans un langage doux, coulant et mélodieux, sans faiblesse, sans langueur, sans prolixité' (Virgile 1743, p xxx). Verse poetry may be superior to prose poetry since it has an additional 'ornament', but in translation it inevitably leads to infidelity. What is more, long translations in verse (and even most long poems) are wearing.

In writing all this, Desfontaines knows he will meet formidable opposition. He notes, interestingly, that the English always translate verse by verse and tells us that he has argued with English people about the excessive freedom of Dryden's Virgil (Roscommon, in his poem on the translation of poetry had provided a vigorous defence of the English tradition (Roscommon, 1684)). In France, prose translation of poetry was the norm, and it had been advocated most notably by Madame Dacier in her famous quarrel with La Motte about Homer, but this practice had been attacked by Bouhier (among others) in the preface to his verse translation of *Aeneid* 4. And it was the Bouhier line that was consistently defended by Voltaire. In his 'Essai sur la poésie épique' (which Desfontaines attempts to refute in his 'Discours'), Voltaire compares translations of poetry to engravings of paintings, which preserve the line, but lose the colour: 'les traductions augmentent les fautes d'un ouvrage, et en gâtent les beautés' (Voltaire 1877, vol viii, p 319). These are sadly familiar notes for the poor translator. However, Voltaire does not conclude that poetry should not be translated, but simply that it must be translated in verse, by a great poet, and freely. This was how he himself worked when in the *Lettres philosophiques* he rendered into French fragments of Shakespeare, Rochester, Waller and, as we shall see, some lines from the *Rape of the Lock*.

Abbé Du Resnel, who made verse translations of Pope's two *Essays*, and whom Voltaire claimed to have helped with the *Essay on Criticism* (Knapp 1971, pp 23–32), is the leading exponent of free poetic translation in the Pope *Œuvres complètes*. His *Essay on Criticism* (1730) was followed by a rendering of the *Essay on Man* in 1737, and the two works were thereafter issued together as *Les Principes de la morale et du goût*. To judge from the periodical press of the time, his work seems to have been widely admired (La Harpe 1933), although in 1782 his *Essay on Man* was sufficiently outmoded for Fontanes to feel another verse translation was needed. This is how Du Resnel's version begins:

> Sors de l'enchantement, Milord; laisse au vulgaire
> Le séduisant espoir d'un bien imaginaire:
> Fuis le faste des cours, les honneurs, les plaisirs;
> Ils ne méritent point de fixer tes desirs.
> Est-ce à toi de grandir cette foule importune,
> Qui court auprès des rois encenser la fortune?
> Viens; un plus grand objet, des soins plus importants,
> Doivent de notre vie occuper les instants.
> Ce grand objet, c'est l'homme, étonnant labyrinthe
> Ou d'un plan regulier l'œil reconnaît l'empreinte;
> Champ fécond, mais sauvage, où par de sages lois
> La rose et le chardon fleurissent à la fois.
> (Pope 1780, vol III, pp 167–8)

Twelve lines out of seven, and of course the French alexandrines are two syllables longer than Pope's line. The main addition is the amplification of Pope's 'all meaner things'. Du Resnel's phrases ('bien imaginaire', 'faste des cours', 'foule importune', 'encenser la fortune') are the stock-in-trade of French moralising verse, and they totally obscure Pope's brutal dismissal of the 'pride of Kings'. All the English poet's urgency has been lost. Look for instance at what has happened to the 'wild where weeds and flow'rs promiscuous shoot'—Du Resnel's 'sages lois' preside over a reassuring balance (rather than a perplexing 'promiscuity') of fertility and wildness, rose and thistle, and the violent verb 'shoot' has given way to a decorative 'fleurissent'. Pope throws a challenge at his readers, Du Resnel soothes them with the bland discourse of the comfortable moralist. What is more, he completely omits line 8, with its allusion to the Garden of Eden.

Such fairly obvious criticisms were made in 1737 by Du Resnel's rival Étienne de Silhouette, who was later to become more famous as the French finance minister. Silhouette, who was living in England, had produced his own (prose) translation of the *Essay on Man* in 1736. In a new edition of 1737 he published his 'Réflexions preliminaires du traducteur sur le goût des traductions' in which he remarks of Du Resnel's version that 'le sublime ainsi que le sens et la concision de l'original me paraissent noyés dans la paraphrase' (Pope 1737, p 14). The three nouns are important: the word 'sens' declares Silhouette's belief that translation must be accurate, whereas 'sublime' and 'concision' refer to the poetic qualities which he admires in Pope and hopes to render in his own text. It is worth looking in a little more detail at what he has to say on this subject.

Silhouette defends prose translation of poetry for the same sort of reasons as Desfontaines—that too much of the original is inevitably lost and diluted in verse. He too favours a faithful and figurative poetic prose. Indeed he goes further than Desfontaines, whose translation of *Gulliver's Travels* he accuses of being excessively prettified. Desfontaines believed that foreign authors could be improved and in his review in the *Observations sur les écrits modernes* he, like others, criticised Silhouette's *Essay on Man* as being unnecessarily obscure. Silhouette for his part is full of respect for his original. In his 'Réflexions preliminaires' and in the preface to his 1736 edition of the *Essay on Man*, later reprinted in the *Œuvres complètes*, he repeatedly stresses the English poet's power and richness, admitting that he cannot match Pope's expressive harmonies (in the *Essay on Criticism* for instance), but hoping that his accurate translation will render something of the vigour of the original. Pope's concision is such, he says, that 'la moindre paraphrase énerve sa vigueur, lâche et dissout pour ainsi dire un corps entièrement solide et serré' (Pope 1737, p 13).

This emphasis on Pope's strength and density is some way removed from the praise of his elegance and clarity in Voltaire's *Lettres philosophiques*. It appears to indicate a greater willingness to admire English poetry in its own right, rather than as a worthy copy of the French. In his 1736 preface Silhouette declares that the greater freedom, force and subtlety of English verse makes it far more suitable than French verse as a medium of translation. Indeed he goes further, saying: 'C'est ce qui fait que leurs poésies sont fort supérieures aux nôtres' (something Voltaire would never have allowed). He adopts in fact the position so memorably expressed in the often-quoted lines of Roscommon:

> But who did ever in French authors see
> The comprehensive English energy?
> The weighty bullion of one sterling line
> Drawn to French wire would through whole pages shine.

Interestingly, these lines are also quoted by Du Resnel in his 'Discours préliminaire du traducteur' (written in 1737, partly in answer to Silhouette's criticisms). He too notes the general 'hardiesse' of English poetry and Pope's incomparable brevity, imaginative richness and intellectual sublimity. He concludes, however, firstly that only a verse translation can 'répondre en quelque sorte à cette brièveté', and secondly that French taste cannot accept

Costard des Ifs is more faithful (at least to Desfontaines) and more like normal French verse, but his alexandrines remain flat.

Both of these translations were soon ousted by that of Jean-François Marmontel, which was to be the standard version used in the collected editions. Much later in his life, in his *Éléments de littérature*, Marmontel wrote about the theory of translation, attempting to steer a middle course between the schools represented by Silhouette and Du Resnel. His *Boucle de cheveux enlevée* is an early work, published in 1746 at the age of twenty-two, when he was still the young protégé of Voltaire. For the passage that concerns us, however, he does not try to use his master's version, but produces his own free translation. This was based on Desfontaines's version, since Marmontel had no English. When compared with Pope's text, its most noticeable characteristic is its length:

> Aux côtés de son lit paraissent deux Vestales:
> Leurs traits fort différents, leurs dignités égales,
> L'une, vieille Sibylle, au teint noir et plombé,
> Y traîne un corps mourant sous cent lustres courbé;
> C'est la Malignité. Sur ses membres arides,
> S'étend un cuir tanné que sillonnent les rides.
> Les yeux pleins de douceur, le cœur rempli de fiel,
> Déchirant les humains, elle bénit le Ciel,
> Et flattant avec art le mérite modeste,
> A ses embrassements mele un poison funeste.
> (Pope 1780, vol II, p 120)

It appears that Desfontaines is responsible for the misreading of 'in black and white arrayed'. Generally Marmontel's translation is free rather than inaccurate. It is not without energy (for instance in the syntax and choice of words of the fifth and sixth lines), but the amplification of the portrait of Ill-Nature tends to reduce its immediacy. The physicality of the hand filled 'with store of prayers, for mornings, nights and noons', and the bosom filled with lampoons has given way to the conventionally metaphorical 'fiel', 'dechirer', and 'poison', and once again Pope's powerfully asymmetrical chiasmus has been lost. French commentators tended to assimilate the *Rape of the Lock* to Boileau's *Le Lutrin*, but Marmontel's language here is more akin to the French satirist's moral epistles than to his mock-heroic poem, which shares some of the unexpected transformational powers we associate with Pope (Edwards 1985).

Not surprisingly, it is Voltaire, the advocate of free poetic translation, who gets closest to the feel of the *Rape of the Lock*. Unlike Marmontel, Voltaire knew English, and knew it well. For some of the extract he too expands and embroiders on the original, but he also allows himself to cut. Thus in the passage that concerns us, he omits lines 25 and 26 (which are less interesting than the lines which surround them), while altering the rest to suit his own preoccupations:

> La médisante Envie est assise auprès d'elle,
> Vieux spectre féminin, décrépite pucelle,

> Avec un air dévot déchirant son prochain,
> Et chansonnant les gens l'Evangile à la main.
> (Voltaire 1915, vol II, p 137)

With his 'air dévot' and his 'Évangile', Voltaire has seized the chance of satirising religious hypocrisy in the manner of *Tartuffe*, but the 'black and white' and the prayers in the original fully justify this. The heavily loaded second line catches the grotesque quality of Pope's picture, and above all the final line echoes Pope's down-to-earth brutality with its unexpectedly familiar verb and the precise image of the hand clutching the Bible. Here, for once, Pope has not been doctored to suit French decorum.

One can only regret then, that Voltaire translated no more than eighteen lines of the *Rape of the Lock*. I have no space here to examine other translations of Pope's poetry (such as those published by Abbé Yart in his voluminous *Idée de la poésie anglaise*, or the various versions, more or less free, of *Eloisa to Abelard*), but I do not think it unfair to say that Voltaire was the only gifted poet to tackle him. We have seen how translators such as Du Resnel and Silhouette acknowledged the freedom and richness of English poetry. As Roscommon had suggested, this could hardly be matched in the French literary language of the day—and it may be true that such is still the case in the twentieth century. Unfortunately, no modern poet has felt moved to translate Pope. As for contemporary translators, they were fully aware— in theory if not in practice—of the striking concision and imaginative force of his writing. To a French ear he could seem jagged, dense and obscure. In the work of mediocre translators this was lost, so it was naturally as thinker and moralist that he was perceived by most French readers. Of course there were those, such as Diderot, who learned to read and appreciate him in the original—and it appears that their number grew as the century progressed. But his huge popularity was essentially based on translations, and here it must be said that the French have never had a Pope who was like Pope.

References

Audra, E *Les Traductions françaises de Pope (1717–1825): Étude de bibliographie* (Paris: Champion, 1931)

Diderot, D *Observations sur la traduction de 'An Essay on Man' de Pope par Silhouette*, A Seznec and J Varloot (eds). In H Dieckmann, J Proust and J Varloot (eds) *Œuvres complètes*, vol I (Paris: Hermann, 1975)

Diderot, D *Lettres sur les sourds et muets*, J Chouillet (ed). In *Œuvres complètes*, vol IV (Paris: Hermann, 1978)

Edwards, M 'A Meaning for Mock-Heroic', *Yearbook of English Studies*, 15 (1985), 48–63

Goujet, Abbé C-P *Bibliothèque française*, new edition, vol VIII (Paris: Mariette, 1755)

Gunny, A *Voltaire and the English. Studies on Voltaire and the Eighteenth Century*, 177 (Oxford: The Voltaire Foundation, 1979)

Knapp, R G *The Fortunes of Pope's 'Essay on Man' in Eighteenth-Century France. Studies on Voltaire and the Eighteenth Century*, 82 (Geneva: Institut Voltaire, 1971)

Knight, R C 'Anne Dacier and Gardens: Ancient and Modern', *Studies on Voltaire and the Eighteenth Century*, 185 (1980) 119–29

La Harpe, J de (1933) 'Le Journal des Savants et la renommée de Pope en France au dix-huitième siècle', *University of California Publications in Modern Philology*, 16 (1983) 173–215

Pope, A (1737) *Essais sur la critique et sur l'homme*, trans É de Silhouette (London: G Smith, 1737)

Pope, A (1780) *Œuvres complètes*, 8 vols (Paris: Durand, 1780)

Roscommon, Earl of *An Essay on Translated Verse* (London: Tonson, 1684)

Van Tieghem, P 'La "Prière Universelle" de Pope et le déisme français au XVIIIe siècle', *Revue de littérature comparée*, 3 (1923) 190–212

Virgile *Œuvres complètes*, trans Abbé P-F G Desfontaines, vol I (Paris: Quillau, 1743)

Voltaire, F M Arouet de *Œuvres complètes*, L Moland (ed) (Paris: Garnier, 1877)

Voltaire, F M Arouet de *Lettres philosophiques*, G Lanson (ed) (Paris: Hachette, 1915)

8

Belinda's Bibles

GEOFFREY CARNALL

'Puffs, Powders, Patches, Bibles, Billet-doux'
(*The Rape of the Lock*, 1714, I, 138)

What were the Bibles doing on Belinda's dressing-table? In the Twickenham edition, Geoffrey Tillotson sees them as chubby duodecimo volumes, about 120 mm by 50 mm, ornamentally bound, with clasps, affording a choice as to colour or style.

> Two or three of these small books on the crowded, if not untidy dressing-table of an unthinking Belinda would bulk no more inconveniently than two or three pretty prayer books on a modern dressing-table. She might, moreover, find them useful for keeping ribbons straight.[1]

But there is another possibility, suggested by an incident in Act 1 Scene 2 of *The Rivals* by R B Sheridan. Lydia Languish and her maid Lucy are hastily making the room presentable while Mrs Malaprop and Sir Anthony Absolute are coming upstairs. *Peregrine Pickle* is flung under the toilet, *Roderick Random* thrown into the closet, *Lord Aimworth* thrust under the sofa, and so on. Among the books substituted is Fordyce's *Sermons*. Lydia instructs Lucy to leave it open on the table.

> *Lucy.* O burn it, ma'am! the hairdresser has torn away as far as *Proper Pride*.
> *Lydia.* Never mind—open at *Sobriety*.

Pages from the Bible would serve the purpose of curling hair quite as well as pages from Fordyce; better, indeed, because much of it is more poetical.[2] 'I never pin up my hair with prose', says Millamant in Congreve's *Way of the World* (Act 2 Scene 5). 'I think I tried once, Mincing.'

> *Mincing.* O mem, I shall never foret it.
> *Millamant.* Ay, poor Mincing tift and tift all the morning,

Mincing. Till I had the cramp in my fingers, I'll vow, mem. And all to no purpose. But when your laship pins it up with poetry, it sits so pleasant the next day as any thing, and is so pure and so crips.

This interpretation occurred to me in 1962, and I made haste to write it up for *Notes and Queries.* The then editor, J C Maxwell, returned my 300-word note with a courteous refutation. He suggested that there would have been more room on a dressing-table for the small volumes mentioned by Tillotson than for the larger ones needed by a hairdresser.

I feel, too, that it doesn't really work poetically. I think it would be a disturbance to have bibles mentioned with an oblique, unexpressed reference to their being used for an extraneous purpose, in the middle of a catalogue of articles figuring in their own right. It seems to me to be sacrificing a deliberate incongruity to a laboured under-the-surface uniformity.[3]

I showed Maxwell's letter to John Butt, who was kind enough to say that he didn't find it altogether convincing, and that he thought my conjecture deserved some consideration. Even so, my interest in the matter wasn't strong enough to inspire me to re-write the note in a longer and more contentious form for a rival journal. Over the years it has simply served to enliven my Pope tutorials, where I have found that it still has a curious power to shock. It is not only conservative evangelicals who find the use of the Bible as waste paper grossly indecent. But that does not mean that Pope would have rejected the idea, and when contributions were invited for the present volume of essays, it seemed a good opportunity to look at the matter again.

In a sense, the issue is altogether unimportant, hardly worth a Query, let alone a Note. Belinda is a priestess of the religion of vanity. It is appropriate that she should have the scriptures of the true religion as some mere miscellaneous adjunct among the puffs and powders, patches and billets-doux. However she is doing it, she is clearly denying the traditional authority of the Bible in a quite radical way, if not altogether with the vehemence and deliberation with which William Blake was later to denounce 'sacred codes'.

That stony law I stamp to dust, and scatter religion abroad
To the four winds as a torn book, and none shall gather the leaves.[4]

So Orc declaims in *America*, straining every muscle. Belinda's iconoclasm is achieved with a mere twitch of the eyebrow. Nor is 'iconoclasm' too strong a word to use in the context of readers' sensitivities in 1714. As we shall see, this was a period of animated religious activity, finding expression in organisations like the newly-founded Societies for the Promotion of Christian Knowledge and for the Propagation of the Gospel, and in the hundred thousand prosecutions instigated by the London Society for the Reformation of Manners.[5] Belinda is serenely at odds with this ethos, and it might hardly seem to matter whether her Bibles were for adornment or for use in curling the hair.

None the less, the association with hair is genuinely significant. Elaborately dressed hair often serves as an indication of estrangement from the religion of the Bible. The first Epistle to Timothy urges women to adorn themselves modestly, 'not with braided hair, or gold or pearls or costly attire' (I Timothy 2.9). Similarly, in the first Epistle of Peter, wives are reminded that their adorning should not be with 'braiding of hair, decoration of gold, and wearing of robes', but rather 'with the imperishable jewel of a gentle and quiet spirit' [I Peter 3. 3–4). The wicked Queen Jezebel 'painted her eyes and tired her head' with a view to making an enticing impression on the ferocious Jehu (II Kings 9.30). To use holy scripture as curl-paper would underline this association of hairdressing with apostasy, the more so as such curl-papers could be used also to protect the hair from damage by heated curling-irons. The process is described by James Stewart in *Plocacosmos; or the Whole Art of Hairdressing* (1782). The irons, says Stewart, should take hold of the whole paper, but not touch the hair itself, and keep in position 'till the paper smoaks'.[6] As Simon Patrick pointed out in *Search the Scriptures* (1685), referring to persecutions under the Roman Empire,

> It was the very mark and character of a Christian to have a Bible; and of an apostate, to deliver his Bible to be burnt, when the inquisitors came to search for it in times of persecution.[7]

While Belinda didn't exactly give up her Bibles to be burnt, she may have allowed them to be scorched.

Simon Patrick, Bishop of Ely at the turn of the seventeenth and eighteenth centuries, was a distinguished scholar and controversialist, a dedicated parish priest who remained at his post throughout the Great Plague of London in 1665. *Search the Scriptures* forms part of a great debate on the claims of the Roman Catholic Church which generated so much publication in the latter part of the reign of Charles II and the whole of James II's reign.[8] It is a fine piece of polemic on behalf of the Protestant view that all should read the Bible freely. Patrick finds a particularly venerable authority to support his case in St John Chrysostom, Patriarch of Constantinople at the beginning of the fifth century AD. Chrysostom himself was unrivalled as an interpreter of the scriptures, and loses no opportunity of commending their study to his congregations. Patrick quotes at length from his third sermon on Lazarus, where we are reminded that lay people need to read the Bible more than do those who are dedicated to a religious life. The Ethiopian eunuch reading the book of the prophet Isaiah while travelling in his chariot (Acts 8.27–39) shows that 'no time should be thought unfit to the reading of the holy oracles'—going to market, on journeys, in company, in business. Lay people have to cope with so many occasions of anger or sorrow,

> and many also of vainglory and senseless pride: straits and difficulties encompass us on every side, and a thousand darts from all sides come flying at us. And therefore we have perpetual need of that panoply (complete armour) which is to be fetched out of the Scriptures.[9]

good word from Gibbon.[30] John Henry Newman celebrated Chrysostom's 'discriminating affectionateness', his willingness to accept people, not losing one fibre or vibration of 'the complicated whole of human sentiment and affection'.[31] The discriminating affectionateness of this particular poem has often been remarked on. It's a pity that there's no evidence that the poet ever read the patriarch at all—unless, indeed, Simon Patrick's *Search the Scriptures* was included in old Mr Pope's collection.

NOTES

1   *The Rape of the Lock*, G Tillotson (ed) *Twickenham Edition of the Poems of Alexander Pope*, vol 2 (3rd edn 1962) p 402.

2   See John Dennis, *The Grounds of Criticism in Poetry*, 1704: 'Almost all but the Ceremonial and Historical part of the old Testament, was deliver'd in Poetry and that is almost Half of it. And a considerable part of the Doctrine of the Gospel was deliver'd in Parables, which . . . are a kind of Divine Poesy.' (John Dennis, *Critical Works*, E N Hooker (ed) Baltimore 1937, vol 1 p 325).

3   5 June 1962.

4   William Blake, *America*, ll. 63–4.

5   *Report* of the London Society for the Reformation of Manners, 1736. Cited in F W Wilson, *The Importance of the Reign of Queen Anne in English Church History* (Oxford 1911), p 45.

6   Quoted by R Corson, *Fashions in Hair* (1965), p 366.

7   S Patrick, *Works*, A Taylor (ed) (Oxford 1858), vol 6 pp 542–3.

8   Francis Peck compiled *A Complete Catalogue of all the Discourses written, both for and against Popery, in the time of King James II*, 1735. Peck makes clear that collections of such tracts were common. One has found its way into the Chetham Library in Manchester, and there is a revised and augmented reissue of Peck, edited by Thomas Jones, in *Publications of the Chetham Society*, vols 48 and 64 (1859, 1865).

9   S Patrick, *Works*, vol 6 p 540. The Sermons on Lazarus are printed in J P Migne, *Patrologiae*, ser. Graeca, vol 48 cols 963–1054. See esp. cols 992–5.

10 S Patrick, *Works*, vol 6 p 531.

11 St John Chrysostom, *Homilies on St Matthew. Select Library of the Nicene and Post-Nicene Fathers*, P Schaff (ed) (Grand Rapids 1956), vol 10 p 437.

12 *St John Chrysostom's Picture of his Age* (S.P.C.K. 1875), p 175.

13 Simon Patrick gives few details of the works he is opposing, and one could be forgiven for thinking that much of his acquaintance with Catholic doctrine is derived from fellow-Anglicans. But he does mention a certain *Abridger of Controversies* when discussing the eunuch in Acts, and the reproach of Jesus to his disciples on their failure to understand the prophecies (Luke 24.25). The identity of the Abridger is indicated in a book which Patrick had actually read, Richard Montagu's *A Gagg for the new Gospell? . . . An Answere to a late Abridger of Controversies, and Belyar of the Protestant Doctrine, 1626*. The actual title of the work answered appears to have been *A Briefe Abridgment of the Errors of the Protestants of our Times*, but I have not been able to find a copy, and I doubt whether Patrick had either.

14   Matthew Kellison, *A Survey of the New Religion* (Douai 1603), pp 35–6.

15   Ibid, pp 44–53.

16   J Evelyn, *Diary*, W Bray and H B Wheatley (eds), 1879, vol 3 p 411. Letter to the Bishop of Oxford (Dr Fell), 19 March 1682.

17   J Dryden, *Religio Laici*, ll. 297–300. Dryden's response to Simon is thoroughly examined by Phillip Harth, *Contexts of Dryden's Thought* (Chicago 1968).

18   J Dryden, *The Hind and the Panther*, part 2 ll. 340–8.

19   H Turberville, *A Manuel of Controversies* (Douai 1654), p 104; see also p 117. Turberville's place in English Catholic thought is considered by G H Tavard, *The Seventeenth Century Tradition* (Leyden 1978), pp 198–200. I am indebted to Miss Elisabeth Poyser for drawing my attention to Turberville's work.

20   H Turberville, *Manuel*, p 111. The reference is to Homily 4, on 2 Thessalonians 2, *Select Library of the Nicene and Post-Nicene Fathers*, P Schaff (ed) (Grand Rapids 1956), vol 13 p 390.

21   *Select Library of the Nicene and Post-Nicene Fathers*, vol 10 p 1.

22   J Dryden, *Religio Laici*, ll. 419–20.

23   *The Clergies Honour; or, the Lives of St Basil the Great and St Chrysostom*, 1681.

24   See E McClure, *A Chapter in English Church History: being the Minutes of the Society for Promoting Christian Knowledge for 1698–1704* (1888).

25   Ibid, pp 101–3, 23 Dec 1700.

26   Francis Atterbury, *Epistolary Correspondence, Visitation Charges, Speeches and Miscellanies*, vol 2 (1783) p 324.

27   Ibid, p 252.

28   Ibid, p 248. William Dansey's *Horae Decanicae Rurales*, 2 vols. 1835, second edn 1844, is a copious source of information about rural deans from the Synod of Laodicea (AD 364) down to his own time. Dansey's suggestion about the distribution of Bibles may be found in part 5 sect. 4.

29   *Correspondence of Alexander Pope*, G Sherburn (ed) (Oxford 1956), vol 1 pp 453–4.

30   See *History of the Decline and Fall of the Roman Empire*, chap. 32.

31   J H Newman, *Essays and Sketches*, C F Harrold (ed) (New York 1948) vol 3 p 218.

9

Parts and Wholes: Pope and Poetic Structure

COLIN MANLOVE

Perhaps not enough critical attention has been paid to the structure of Pope's poetry—how far a given poem holds together in terms of argument, relevance or consistency; and how far any formal organisation or shape is latent in the material. Yet Pope's 'list'-type work, in common with much of that of his contemporaries, peculiarly invites this investigation.

In *An Essay on Criticism* Pope sets forth a consistent neo-classical view of the work of literature as a whole made of subordinated parts, none of which juts out. He sees aesthetic incongruity in the same terms that he sees the attention of a critic to the minute parts of a work rather than to the totality: and both are made at least analogous with the moral vice of pride. This aesthetic grace and harmony, where 'No single Parts unequally surprize;/All comes *united* to th'admiring Eyes', he equates with nature itself, a seamless robe of being. But when Pope talks about parts becoming subordinate to wholes, it is not so much the wholes themselves he is interested in, but the contribution of the parts. What he is talking about is a process of arrangement, a kind of internal harmony, rather than the fusing of a series of items into a unity that transcends them:

> In Wit, as Nature, what affects our Hearts
> Is not th'Exactness of peculiar Parts;
> 'Tis not a *Lip*, or *Eye*, we Beauty call,
> But the joint Force and full *Result* of all.
> (243–6)

Pope does not talk of a governing idea for a work, a 'fore-conceit' as the Renaissance would have put it, or an after-realisation as might the Romantics, but simply the harmonising of separate constituents, like different items of a painting into a unity whose only effect is one of 'beauty' or 'nature'. Nature Pope sees as the informing principle of creativity, but it is not so much an idea in itself as an invisible plastic power which is the essential ground of all right being:

> *Unerring Nature*, still divinely bright,
> One *clear, unchang'd,* and *Universal* Light,
> Life, Force, and Beauty, must to all impart,
> At once the *Source,* and *End,* and *Test* of *Art.*
> *Art* from that Fund each *just Supply* provides,
> Works *without Show,* and *without Pomp* presides:
> In some fair Body thus th'informing Soul
> With Spirits feeds, with Vigour fills the whole,
> Each Motion guides, and ev'ry Nerve sustains;
> *It self unseen,* but in th'*Effects,* remains.
>
> (70–9)

The artistic principle of unity for Pope is one, as he puts it elsewhere, in which 'Parts answ'ring parts shall slide into a whole' (*To Burlington*, 66).

A fine instance of Pope's notion of unity at work is his *An Epistle to Miss Blount, On Her Leaving the Town, After the Coronation.* Pope opens by describing 'some fair virgin', whom he goes on to name 'Zephalinda', who must leave the town and its delights for the country. He describes the boredom of the girl amid the dullness of rusticity, and her dreams of the lost pleasures of the city. The poem has no ruling idea: Pope is not even portraying pride rightly being taken down a peg in her going to the country; nor does he value the city any more than the country. There is no significance either way in the parting Zephalinda's 'She sigh'd not that They stay'd, but that She went'. Pope is sympathetic to and amused at her plight, and explores the tedium in all its varieties, from dull aunts, morning walks and prayers three hours a day, to solitary teas and intrusive visits by coarse squires. But then, having talked of how she dreams of the town, he goes on to speak of someone in the town thinking of her:

> So when your slave, at some dear, idle time,
> (Not plagu'd with headachs, or the want of rhime)
> Stands in the streets, abstracted from the crew,
> And while he seems to study, thinks of you . . .

By now the poem seems to be turning from a straight description of the girl's experience to the romantic thoughts of some 'slave' of hers still in town. And then there is a further change—this 'slave' turns out to be an 'I'—the slave-lover of this Zephalinda becomes revealed as the apparently impartial narrator of the poem who till now has simply been recording her experience.

> Just when his fancy points your sprightly eyes,
> Or sees the blush of soft *Parthenia* rise,
> *Gay* pats my shoulder, and you vanish quite;
> Streets, chairs, and coxcombs rush upon my sight;
> Vext to be still in town, I knit my brow,
> Look sow'r, and hum a tune—as you may now.

So we seem to have moved from a plain account of a gay belle's miseries on being forced to quit the town, to the point where the poet who has so objectively been describing her turns out to be partly enamoured of her—and we are jerked back to the town and to him thinking about her. The whole poem thus seems to have a series of parts ill at ease with one another. Even the image with which Pope starts the poem,

> As some fond virgin, whom her mother's care
> Drags from the town to wholsom country air,

prepares us for an enforced separation in some other context than that of mothers and daughters, but in fact the analogy describes the literal—it likens a girl dragged from town by her mother to a girl dragged from town by her mother: and thus glares by being anticlimactic.

But if we look closely we find more harmony among the parts of the poem than we might have supposed. As Pope put it in the *Essay on Criticism*,

> Some Figures *monstrous* and *mis-shap'd* appear,
> Consider'd *singly*, or beheld too *near*,
> Which, but *proportion'd* to their *Light*, or *Place*,
> Due Distance *reconciles* to Form and Grace.
>   (171–4)

We seem to approach the girl gradually, first through the indirection of 'some fond virgin'; then she is Zephalinda; then plain 'she' ('She sigh'd not that They stay'd, but that She went'); by the time we have got to line 23 she is 'you' ('Some Squire, perhaps, you take delight to rack'). This in itself might make a sort of graded approach to the direct address: but Pope goes even further by making the shifts between one stage and the next imperceptible. The best instance of this is the way he moves from prepositional phrases to infinitive verbs and thence to imperative verbs in mid-poem:

> She went, to plain-work, and to purling brooks,
> Old-fashion'd halls, dull aunts, and croaking rooks,
> She went from Op'ra, park, assembly, play,
> To morning walks, and pray'rs three hours a day;
> To pass her time 'twixt reading and Bohea,
> To muse, and spill her solitary Tea,
> Or o'er cold coffee trifle with the spoon,
> Count the slow clock, and dine exact at noon;
> Divert her eyes with pictures in the fire,
> Hum half a tune, tell stories to the squire;
> Up to her godly garret after sev'n,
> There starve and pray, for that's the way to heav'n.
>   Some Squire, perhaps, you take delight to rack . . .

She goes to plain-work, to purling brooks, to morning walks; but then almost without our noticing, the 'to's become attached to verbs, 'to pass', 'to muse'.

Then the 'to' is dropped from before the infinitive verbs 'trifle', 'count', 'dine', 'divert', 'hum', 'tell'; and as this happens, and these implicitly indicative verbs are placed at the beginning of their little phrases, they take on more and more of a prompting and commanding tinge until the imperative is three-quarters assumed by the last line, 'There starve and pray, for that's the way to heav'n'. This eases the shift in the next line from 'she' to 'you', 'Some Squire, perhaps, you take delight to rack', so that the poet is now addressing her directly and has entered into something of a relationship with her well before the actual fondness, on his side at least, is introduced. But more than this, the move through the 'neutral' of the infinitive has allowed a shift of tense. What started as past (Zephalinda 'flew' and 'went' from the town) is now present and personal, 'you take delight', 'you dream'. We are not only getting nearer her, we are also getting nearer a 'now'. The present tense still refers to a continuous present—'Some Squire, perhaps [some time], you take delight to rack', 'In some fair evening, on your elbow laid'; the poet thinking of her in the town still does so 'at some dear, idle time'; but then as the relationship is thrown more into relief, so is the time, and we arrive at a punctual spot: '*Gay* pats my shoulder, and you vanish quite', 'I knit my brow,/Look sow'r, and hum a tune—as you may now'. With that 'now' the movement of increasing approach is concluded. It does not assert a full relationship—she does not think of him but of the town, and what they share will be at best a tune hummed just possibly at the same time: but what proximity has been created has as it were been established by the decorous approach of the poem.

It is a poem of which it could be said, in Pope's own characterisation of artistic unity, 'The *Whole* at once is *Bold*, and *Regular* (*Essay on Criticism*, 252). The parts do surprise, but considered more carefully in relation to 'their *Light*, or *Place*,/Due Distance *reconciles* to Form and Grace' (ibid, 173–4). The unity of the poem is directly analogous to that of the chain of being which is so central to Pope's thought—a linear movement from rung to rung accomplished through a gracious continuity of movement, or 'just gradation', between one position and the next (*Essay on Man*, I, 207–32). But we should be aware of the kind of unity we are talking about. It is not one with an informing idea. The 'chain of being' was not instinct with spiritual meaning: it was a way of talking about the make-up of the universe as a great tower of being from infinite to nothing, a tower which by its very existence made it cosmic folly for any one being in the chain to attempt to alter its position: sequence, linear subordination of parts, was all. Pope is not celebrating or contemplating grace in the poem: he is showing it in action; it exists through its self-effacement. The skills are poetical, not moral.

Arguably *An Epistle to Miss Blount* . . . , which others have found one of Pope's finest poems, is one of the most unified according to his own prescriptions that he ever wrote. Nearest to it is perhaps *The Rape of the Lock*, but here we begin to see a lifelong fascination of Pope's that works against any settled unity—a delight in change and volatility. It is curious to have to say this of a poet often best known for his resistance to all change, his attempts to hold the line of old values, his refusal of the 'novel' and the independent mind; yet actually his poetry is shot through with a sense of plasticity, of evanescence, of metamorphosis. The *Epistle* we have just looked at is itself as much a portrayal of change and metamorphosis as anything else: a 'fond virgin' turning to a Zephalinda, then to a 'she' and last a 'you'; an impartial poet becoming a 'slave' and an 'I'; a past tense mutating towards the present, and the country changing back to the town. The whole of *The Rape of the Lock* is in constant movement. One of its motifs might be the name of Belinda's dog, Shock. It begins with Belinda being woken up; then the sylphs are shocked by her behaviour, she by the Baron's and he finally by hers. The poem is crammed with images of metamorphosis, from Belinda's combs, the transformations of elephant and tortoise, to her bodkin, whose metal has served so many purposes to her ancestors, to the changed shapes of women in the Cave of Spleen, the cards become people, and men and women reduced to wigs, sword-knots, whalebones and locks. At the end the severed lock becomes, via poetic compliment, a constellation. Imagery of movement is pervasive, especially of rising and falling—hopes rise and are dashed, prayers ascend, sylphs descend to their tasks, Umbriel goes down to the Cave of Spleen, sylphic coquetry sinks to gnomish dumps before arising in fire once more. The mock heroic analogies used throughout keep us constantly swerving between the sublime and the ridiculous.

Meanwhile what unity the poem has partly depends on change. At the evident level Belinda simply goes to Hampton Court and is despoiled of the lock. But the five-canto structure of the poem is suggestive. Early in Canto I we are told that there are four orders of spright (as in the Rosicrucian scheme): the sylph, associated with coquetry and the element of air, the yielding nymph creature of water, the gnome of prudish rejection and of earth, the salamander of fiery rage (I, 57–66). Through all the poem Belinda's progress can be seen emotionally as a progress from one spright to another: first she is coquette and sylphid, preparing herself before the glass and flirting with the gazers outside; then in Canto II she takes to the water of the Thames, and in Canto III the lock is severed while she is *bending* over tea; Canto IV sees a descent by a gnome to the Cave of Spleen and Belinda in sorrowing tears; Canto V portrays the salamandrine anger awakened by Thalestris, and the subsequent battle. Through all these stages we also move through the elements, from air to water to earth to fire; and finally to that which transcends the elements, the poetic metamorphosis of the lock to a constellation beyond the province of the moon and subjection to mortality.

At the same time Pope has refused us any settled valuation of Belinda. Sometimes the mock-heroic element belittles her, pointing out that her fault lies in placing disproportionate worth on trivia. But equally the technique can serve sometimes partly to elevate: Belinda may be blamed for her lack of discrimination with the Bibles at her dressing table but she is still a wondrous creation paid homage to by the various offerings of the world, however curiously culled . . . It is a case of awful Beauty putting on its arms as much as the sacred rites of Pride; and similarly at the beginning of Canto II, in that description of her as she takes to her craft on the silver Thames, her gaze may be vacuously impartial, but it is also universal, with her as the sun-like cynosure ('ev'ry Eye was fix'd on her alone'):

> Bright as the Sun, her Eyes the Gazers strike,
> And, like the Sun, they shine on all alike.

She may have faults, but 'Look on her Face, and you'll forget 'em all'. Similarly, at her lament at the loss of her lock, we may be meant to feel amused disdain for such misplaced grief, yet equally the fullness of the psychological portrait invites our sympathy, asks us whether we ourselves have not often mourned the loss of trivia with the passion of bereavement.

> What mov'd my Mind with youthful Lords to rome?
> O had I stay'd, and said my Pray'rs at home!

That prayers would hardly have been the first of her occupations at home does not alter the plangency that co-exists with the ridicule in this portrait to produce mobility of judgement.

Perhaps the most telling instance in the poem of this involvement with change is Clarissa's speech on female beauty and its transience (V, 9–34). Here we seem to have someone who offers a clear moral judgement on Belinda, and the footnote by Pope telling us that the speech of Clarissa was designed '*to open more clearly the* Moral *of the Poem*' seems to confirm this. But considered closely Clarissa's speech will not bear inspection in these terms. It begins by apparently proposing moral judgement on the excess attention paid to beauty instead of other more worthy moral values:

> Say, why are Beauties prais'd and honour'd most,
> The wise Man's Passion, and the vain Man's Toast?
> Why deck'd with all that Land and Sea afford,
> Why Angels call'd, and Angel-like ador'd?
> Why round our Coaches crowd the white-glov'd Beaus,
> Why bows the Side-box from its inmost Rows?
> How vain are all these Glories, all our Pains . . .

It seems a straightforward condemnation of misplaced value. But then the whole speech turns round. We think that 'vain' means 'guilty of vanity'; but in the next line we find that it means 'in vain', 'impractical': all these things will be lost

> Unless good Sense preserve what Beauty gains.

All the praises of side-box, Beaus, and wise and foolish men are no longer the absurdities they appeared, but the sort of praise one desires and should keep. Clarissa is caught up in Belinda's world herself—after all it was she who gave the Baron the scissors with which to sever the lock. But then she shifts back to moral terminology in her next lines: the object of this preservation of Beauty's gains is

> That Men may say, when we the Front-box grace,
> Behold the first in Virtue, as in Face!

Throughout her speech Clarissa is torn by her complicity in the world where
beauty is the supreme value, and her sense of 'real' virtues. The only defect
of beauty, she goes on, is that it fades (19–30). But by the end she has reverted
to a moral view of beauty as inefficacious, which contradicts her earlier view
of its gains:

> Beauties in vain their pretty Eyes may roll;
> Charms strike the Sight, but Merit wins the Soul.

In her way Clarissa is as changeable as Belinda and as the whole idiom of
the poem of which she is a part. One might almost argue that Pope's introduction of her '*to open more clearly the* Moral *of the Poem*' opens more
clearly quite another 'moral' from the one we expect (and perhaps, with an
only impressionistic reading of the speech, receive). The whole poem seems
to make its own elusive life and character its supreme value.

The *Essay on Man*, Pope's poetical philosophy, as eclectic as that of the
Romans to whom he looked, is also full of change, though of a less deliberate
order. Several commentators, particularly Elwin and Nuttall, have pointed
out some of the inconsistencies and philosophic problems in the poem. For
instance, Pope tells men they are fools to try to inquire into the nature of the
universe, but then has to do the same himself in order to tell them why they
should not: the poet who tells his reader that the proper study of mankind is
man spends much of the first epistle among the constellations and well above
or beneath the sphere of human existence on the great chain of being. Then
there is difficulty with Pope's conception of the governing spring of human
conduct—the 'Ruling Passion', a force conferred by the deity working
through nature: where is there to be human choice in such a deterministic
arrangement? In Epistles II and III of the poem Pope shifts from one to
another view of the power of human reason to control and direct the ruling
passion: now he sees reason as dominant, now as a guide, now as helpless.
There is another major discrepancy one might point out. Throughout the
first epistle Pope invokes the great chain of being as a reason for man keeping
his station: he tells us that the chain is so made that every possible form of
life has been realised and each has its place on the ladder. But the man he
describes on the ladder is a halfway creature—between a god and a beast,
'Created half to rise, and half to fall'—and Pope expands on this picture
of inherent human uneasiness within the chain at the beginning of Epistle
II. It follows that man's aspiring nature, the very faculty attacked and
prohibited by Pope, is an inherent part of his character as placed on that
rung of the great chain—God gave him his inquisitive and restless reason.
Pope's later insistence on the 'ruling passion' itself is an admission of divine
excess into a fabric where he has previously insisted on human submission
and self-control; that very ruling passion is what drives some men to the
speculation that Pope forbids. There is a larger split here across the whole
poem.

Many more inconsistencies and unanswered questions could be found.
Obviously Pope was no real philosopher; nor, basically, could he argue. But

this is not the real point. The primary poetic force of the poem lies in the first two epistles, and it comes not from argument but from shifts of mood—Pope taking the course his fancy directs, as he indicated at the outset, 'Together let us beat this ample field,/Try what the open, what the covert yield.' He will take what comes; he bumps into his thoughts; he takes small account of the wider context but simply lets his poetic powers loose on the present observation. Now we are on the glories of the universe; now man is being told he is a fool to explore them; now we are on entirely fictive accounts of human behaviour—how many men have claimed the whole universe was made to serve them (I, 131ff), and how many have desired the attributes of the beasts (175ff)? Now the universe is a wondrous fabric with which we interfere at our peril; now it is the dealer out of earthquakes, tempests, pestilences, or evil men. One can see how Pope happens upon these various observations, but they do not agree with one another. But the primary force behind this diversity is his own changeability: for him the world is too various for his dancing spirit to alight for long or with consistency on any one point. He himself is as much a creature of shifting moods as man whom he mocks. Now Pope condemns human pride in its rebellion against the *status quo* (I, 123–30), now he sees it as 'Pride bestow'd on all, a common friend' to keep men stupidly content with their condition (II, 272, 286). In his renunciation of pride Pope finds himself temporarily on the side of the humble Indian and primitivism (I, 99–112); yet he later portrays self-love and the ruling passion as engines by which man rises above his brutal lot and becomes social and civilised. Furthermore, any notion that polite is better than savage man—and it is an oft-repeated maxim of Pope's—supposes that aspiration upwards within the chain of being is legitimate. But of course it is all rhetorical forces of the moment: one instant Pope drives one way, the next the multifarious and ill-consorting data of his argument drive him another. In Epistle I man is a fool, scarce separate from the beasts, best fulfilling his creator's wish when he submits in ignorant trust; by Epistle IV, with or without his reason directing, man's ruling passion has made him the architect of a potential utopia of happiness, civility and social concord. Gone is the sense of human mortality, of pain, gone is the idea that no justice or bliss is to be found on this earth but only in another sphere: now it can be realised, even *has* been realised (in Augustan England), by man with the divine ruling passion working through him, here and now.

There is a broad procedure in the poem—first cut man down to size and show how helpless he is on his own, then show how God and nature look after him if he will only cooperate. But it is continually being undercut by the one-sidedness and localism of the stance taken at one part of the poem, which does not allow for reconciliation with others in a larger view. There was a moment, in the celebrated speech on the creature placed on this isthmus of a middle state at the beginning of Epistle II, when Pope might have reconciled the two views of man as 'created half to rise, and half to fall', but the drive of that speech—and it shows how feeling, indeed Popean (ruling) passion, is behind it—is towards one side only, emphasis on man's folly, 'Born but to die, and reas'ning but to err';

> Chaos of Thought and Passion, all confus'd;
> Still by himself abus'd, or disabus'd;
> Created half to rise, and half to fall;
> Great lord of all things, yet a prey to all;
> Sole judge of Truth, in endless Error hurl'd:
> The glory, jest, and riddle of the world!

The weight of each line ends on the belittling; and the whole tone is mockery far more than wonder.

To some extent the shift in the poem from mockery to sympathy and even praise of man results from the fact that in the later epistles Pope is no longer so much comparing men to other levels of being, but dealing with man on his own: he has turned from the potentially satiric perspective of detachment to more sympathetic involvement. A significant change in the poem is from a vertical to a horizontal conception of being. The prepositions 'above' and 'below' become fewer, and we deal with a passion that pervades, a social impulse that spreads. This is already happening in that beautiful passage on the activity of God at the end of Epistle I—He is an immanent force that 'spreads' through all being and 'extends thro' all extent'; His presence in all things removes hierarchic distinctions, levelling all created things in equal importance: 'To him no high, no low, no great, no small;/He fills, he bounds, connects, and equals all.' The ladder of all being in which mankind is reduced to a mere point in space, is later in the poem transformed to the surface of a lake over which like a dropped pebble the loving action of one man ripples out to embrace all being: just as the vertical has shifted to the horizontal, so has shrinkage to expansion:

> Self-love but serves the virtuous mind to wake,
> As the small pebble stirs the peaceful lake;
> The centre mov'd, a circle strait succeeds,
> Another still, and still another spreads,
> Friend, parent, neighbour, first it will embrace,
> His country next, and next all human race,
> Wide and more wide, th'o'erflowings of the mind
> Take ev'ry creature in, of ev'ry kind;
> Earth smiles around, with boundless bounty blest,
> And Heav'n beholds its image in his breast.
>
> (IV, 363–72)

If the *Essay on Man* could at least pretend to a single line of argument, Pope's accompanying *Epistles to Several Persons* (or *Moral Essays*) are evidently without any but the loosest unity. Ostensibly a portrayal of the ruling passion at work in certain areas of human experience—among women, in the lust for wealth and the urge for self-display through one's property—the *Epistles* are 'several' both among and within themselves, settling down to a brilliant portrait gallery of usually absurd individuals whose illustration of a ruling passion is at best only a 'given', at worst ignored for local satire. So far as discussion of the ruling passion itself is concerned, Pope devotes one hundred and seventy lines of the first epistle, *To Cobham*, to telling us how totally elusive of classification human character is, before suddenly turning round to tell us in six lines that we should 'Search then the Ruling Passion' to unravel human nature. This is a clear enough illustration of how the baffling multiplicity of human nature and individuality means far more to Pope in this poem than any unifying feature; even though his 'eighteenth-century' desire for some universal key to human nature is also present. In *To a Lady: Of the Characters of Women* Pope tells us, after a series of portraits, which only occasionally seem to touch on a ruling passion, that two passions guide womankind—'The Love of Pleasure, and the Love of Sway' (II, 210): yet a little later he is to admit that 'Woman's at best a Contradiction still' (270). The poem does have a measure of unintended unity which is at variance with its official concern: every one of the satiric portraits is of some disproportion—the ludicrous persistences of the gluttonous, the avaricious or the vain in the face of death, the excessive reactions of women to trivia and their general inability to match their behaviour to the world, the amassing of wealth by those who starve themselves of its benefits, the gap between man's tiny frame and the gross monuments he erects to express his discordant pride. Here it is not harmony and unity that fire Pope's imagination, but those things which work against them. There is, in this poem once again, a split between 'unity' and 'variety', sense and sensibility, announced theme and actual material.

In the *Moral Essays* we arguably reach a point where the continual tension between unity and diversity in Pope's poetry is at its greatest. In the *Epistle to Miss Blount . . .* the two worked together; in *The Rape of the Lock* the ethical and imaginative drives began to be at variance; in the *Essay on Man* the aim of finding a key to human character is played against by numerous inconsistencies born out of Pope's preference for local poetic and emotional positions. Here unity of comprehension seems to have largely disappeared.

But after this the whole character of Pope's poetry changes. It becomes more exclusively satiric, and the poet is 'committed'. As a public poet, Pope had certainly been involved in the grand analysis of God's plan and human nature in the *Essay on Man* and the *Moral Essays*, but this analysis had not involved him immediately at a personal level. He was still, as he was in the earlier poems, the detached poet pointing out human folly, but with his own withers unwrung. In *An Epistle to Dr Arbuthnot* all that has changed. Here we have the poet speaking in his own person as someone attacked and used by others; here we have him actively committing himself to one role, that of the satirist of hacks and libellers.

An Epistle to Dr Arbuthnot has a central theme and unity which is all the more potent for not being overtly stated. The theme is that of personal integrity. For much of the poem Pope is defending his own integrity. His first act is to try to establish a place for himself to exist: 'Shut, shut the door', the poem begins. He writes an *apologia pro vita sua*, explaining how he has been led to change from a poet of 'pure Description' to one of satire, and how he has done this not out of malevolence but because he was forced to if his friends and family were to continue to live in peace and honour. The poem,

in part at least, describes a process of personal development on Pope's part.
In that sense its unity is 'organic' or 'mobile', because it shows the growth of
a satirist. Earlier poems were more 'static', defining the nature of a thing—
the true character of poetry and criticism, the exact dimension of Belinda's
misfortune, the fixed constitution of the universe and human nature, the
character of a Wharton, a Cloe, the house of Timon. But here Pope is dealing
with 'becoming', with process. Instead of being an assemblage of varied parts,
the poem is a plastic whole, expressive of its central theme of personal
integrity. Pope keeps his integrity by portraying himself as not being mal-
evolently motivated in his becoming a satirist. Those hacks who pursue him
to his home have no regard for his privacy, nor really for their own true
natures, since most of them in becoming poets have violated their true callings
(1–26). So Pope continues, beyond those who seek to use him to further
their work to those who madly attack him, while he stands back in mild
astonishment; and so eventually to the point where he can stand back no
more (173–92). At the core of the poem are three satiric portaits, of Atticus,
Bufo and Sporus—though here the portraits do not stand alone but encapsulate the surrounding material. Those portraits develop in intensity. Atticus
is a talented writer like Pope himself, but desperate for praise, and envious
of rivals: he has given away an identity of which he is not certain to the
dubious keeping of others of lesser merit (even Pope calls him 'One' and
pretends not to be certain that he is Atticus). Bufo is an empty-headed, vain
patron who has hardly any self left: his bust of Pindar is appropriately
headless, and it is his library rather than he that admits his poetic dependants;
he has no knowledge of literary worth, and exists only for flattery. Sporus,
the last, is a nothing; but a dangerous one. Unlike the two others, who are
described as sitting and being passively 'fed', Sporus is actively mobile. In
him we have descended from 'One' to a 'Toad' to a 'Bug': but we have also
moved to the present tense, suggestive of his menace. These three portraits
serve as developing antitypes to Pope. Atticus has concerned himself with
what the world thinks of him as Pope never will; Bufo is a picture of someone
who feeds on others while caring nothing for them; Sporus is a picture of the
corrupt satirist-turned-scandalmonger Pope will never be, 'spitting' himself
abroad in aimless malignity; so little a self that he acts 'either Part,/The
trifling Head, or the corrupted Heart' (326–7). All these figures depend on
the public world: Pope ends the poem with a picture of the self-dependent
poet and moral teacher, surrounded only by the private world of people dear
to him, his few honest friends and his family. The poem closes rather as it
began, with return to the home, but now no longer in desperate flight but in
calm assurance that here alone is where true value and self exist:

> Me, let the tender Office long engage
> To rock the Cradle of reposing Age,
> With lenient Arts extend a Mother's breath,
> Make Languor smile, and smooth the Bed of Death . . .
>   (408–11)

Clearly with this poem the concept of unity outlined in the *Essay on*

Criticism has altered. Now we are dealing with a whole not just made up of parts, but one that is more than the sum of its parts. And that is what we find again in *The Dunciad*. Here, though, the dominant source of unity is a ruling idea rather than a process. There is a *translatio stultitiae*, parodying the cultural transfer from Greece to Rome described in Virgil's *Aeneid*, as the goddess Dulness extends her empire from the City of London to the Court; there is an expansion of the range of the poem until by Book IV Dulness takes in every form of learning; and there is a form of transition from First to Last Things, as the birth and growth of dull poems is described in Book I and the eclipse of all the productions of mind in Book IV. But the pervasive unifying force of the poem is Dulness itself: so real here as to be given separate existence in the form of a ruling goddess. Here there are as many and varied portraits as those in the *Moral Essays*, from Cibber himself to the foppish 'young Aeneas' of the grand tour, or from Oldmixon the Fleet Ditch diver to Busby the headmaster or the butterfly-collector, yet we know and feel as we read that each of those portraits is simply a form of Dulness; where in the *Moral Essays* each portrait amasses life to itself in virtual separation from the governing idea. But this relation to a presiding concept goes even further in *The Dunciad*: the figures portrayed not only illustrate Dulness, they are reducible to it, are indeed reduced to it literally in the vortex of being at the end of the poem, where 'Universal Darkness buries All'. The poem follows a strange process of expansion and contraction: Pope gives amazing and grotesque life to an immense range of dunces, all antipathetic to one another, yet even as he does so that life shrivels down to one dead level shared by all, and in the end one in which all are absorbed.

What we have seen then is how the structural principle behind Pope's poetry changes, from what might be called an 'eighteenth-century' to a 'pre-Romantic' one involving process and the integration of ruling idea with material, as his involvement with his subjects becomes more personal and committed. Obviously the price is a narrowing of focus: we cease to range over all being as in the *Essay on Man* and becomes confined to one particular concern, however universal Pope may have felt its ultimate implications; but the gain is in intensity and consistency. Strangely enough there is a kind of organic unity behind Pope's poetic output considered as a whole: he starts with single individuals and localities—Miss Blount, Belinda, the unfortunate lady, Eloisa and Abelard, Windsor Forest, Hampton Court—and then expands to the whole world of man, considered both in the abstract and in all his 'concrete' variety; then again his subjects become more local, and now personal, until all identity is finally lost at the close of *The Dunciad*. But through all his poetry one thing remains constant, even where he seeks to resist it: his delight in change and variety, energising and adding grace to his earlier work, producing inconsistencies and disunities in his middle poems, and at the last joined even to its own cessation, as the metamorphoses and absurdities of the Dunces serve at once to vitalise and to nullify them.

10

The Paradoxical Machinery of *The Rape of the Lock*

ALASTAIR FOWLER

The two-canto *The Rape of the Locke* of 1712 had mythological machinery of an ordinary epic (or mock-heroic) sort—'Now Jove suspends his golden Scales in Air'.[1] But in the five-canto 1714 version Pope greatly enlarged and individualised the machinery. Indeed, much of the poem's effect is due to its Rosicrucian mythology. Yet John Dennis, the Critic himself, called it contemptible, in his *Remarks on Mr Pope's The Rape of the Lock*, the final dud missile of his poetomachia. As often with Dennis's admirably detailed criticism, even his formidable failures, compounded as they are by irascibility, help more than many other critics' successes to define the context of Pope's intentions.

All machineries and none

Dennis objects that Pope's machines

> are not taken from one System, but are double, nay treble or quadruple. In the first Canto we hear of nothing but Sylphs, and Gnomes, and Salamanders, which are Rosycrucian Visions. In the second we meet with Fairies, Genii, and Daemons . . . Spleen and the Phantoms about, are deriv'd from the Powers of Nature, and are of a separate System. And Fate and Jove . . . in the fifth Canto, belong to the Heathen Religion.[2]

What Dennis took for indecorum is a complexity that eluded his inelegant mind. For Pope's machinery stylishly subsumes a whole library of Renaissance and seventeenth-century controversies about Christian epic. These debated whether epic should have a Christian machinery of angels, like the *Gerusalemme Liberata*; or Olympian deities; or allegorical powers like Discord, whose employment 'always excites conviction of its own absurdity';[3] or all of these, like *The Faerie Queene*; or none.[4] Pope has represented

151

all these possibilities—and the whole pre-Enlightenment pneumatology—
within his elegant miniature epic. Already 1712 hints at something more than
poetic religion in 'So when bold Homer makes the Gods engage,/And heav'nly
Breasts with human Passions rage'; (2.104–5), where the Olympians with their
destructive rages are contained in a simile and effectively euhemerised. But
the 1714 *The Rape of the Lock* is far more complex, assimilating as it does
'Fays, Fairies, Genii, Elves and Daemons' (2.74) reminiscent of Spenser;[5]
allegorical powers of nature; guardian angels and devilish *succubi* hidden
under the Sylphs; and the 'Rosicrucian' spirits themselves, suggested by *The
Count of Gabalis*, but as Johnson says, original with Pope—'A race of aerial
people never heard of before . . . presented to us in a manner so clear and
easy, that the reader seeks for no further information' (3.233).

Could the sylphs be taken seriously enough to work as real machinery?
The serious Dennis thought not, since Pope 'has not taken his Machines . . .
from any Religion, nor from Morality' (p 337). Dennis is not blinkered by a
circumscribed idea of mock-heroic: as his objection shows, he senses that
more than mock-heroic has been attempted. Indeed, Pope himself evidently
feels the need to defend a machinery incredible to 'Learned Pride' (1.37).
Ariel solicits belief in what the superstitious instruction of nurse and priest
instil (visions of 'airy Elves' or 'Angel-Pow'rs') almost as audiences of *Peter
Pan* will be asked to remain immature and save Tinker Bell. Pope's admission
that his 'unnumber'd Spirits', are beneath the credit of 'doubting Wits', and
such as 'Fair and Innocent' young girls believe despite them, may seem to
discount in advance Dennis's objection (p 339). Society gets the machinery it
deserves.

But this is not to say that Pope shared Dennis's and Butler's contempt for
the Rosicrucians, 'the most ridiculous Sots of all Mankind'.[6] The sylphs had
once been part of a serious philosophical magic, hardly to be judged by the
popularisations of *The Count of Gabalis*. *The Rape of the Lock* accurately
reflects this decline of the spirits: although Ariel still relates them to the
spirits moving the planets,[7] their circumstances are clearly much reduced.
Dennis finds inconsistency in Ariel's choosing to be 'Guard of Shock' (2.116):
the leader of the aerial spirits is only 'Keeper of a vile Iseland Cur' (338), while
Crispissa, presumably his junior, tends the fatal lock (2.80). Earl Wasserman
explains that Ariel observes in this the right order of importance (lock—
Shock—petticoat); since Belinda's lapdog is a theriomorphic husband-substitute. Pope makes here through machinery the same point about disordered
values as he makes through zeugma in 'When Husbands or when Lapdogs breathe their last'. However, the name Shock was generic for lapdogs
(originally for Icelandic 'shock-dogs') because they consisted mainly of a
'shock of hair'.[8] Shock is not only a husband-substitute but a symbol of
Belinda's own pudendal 'Hairs less in sight'. Ariel is himself a former
coquette, and the libido 'he' encourages need not be orientated to anything
outside Belinda's narcissism.

Pope's machinery has the originality of being thoroughly interiorised. His
spirits are not supernatural at all, but natural female types after death, or
abstraction. Dr Johnson has no answer (p 235) to Dennis's objections that

'There is no Opposition of the Machines to one another' (p 337), and that the machinery does not work, 'that by all the bustle of preternatural operation the main event is neither hastened nor retarded'. Both critics conceived the action in so rationalistic and external a way that they failed to see how Pope's spirits exerted a continual leverage psychologically. For, in his attempt to capture the elusive, Pope had fallen back on an older set of thought forms. His machinery does not belong entirely to Dennis's Enlightenment world of conscious decisions and mechanical operation, but in part to an older, more animistic one, operating as a drama of spirits.[9] Emrys Jones hints at something like this when he writes:

> 'Melting Maids' are not held in check by anything corresponding to sound moral principles; they are checked only by something as insubstantial, or as unreal, as their 'Sylph'. Mere female caprice or whim prevents a young girl from surrendering her honour to the importunity of rakes. Pope is working on a double standard: as readers of the poem we enjoy the fiction of the sylphs, but the satire can only work if we are also men and women of good sense who do not confuse fiction with fact—so that we do not 'believe in' the sylphs any more than we 'believe in' fairies.[10]

The principles of female conduct were not rational, but 'mystic' or psychological. And Pope extends the same treatment to all his machines. Dennis (p 340) ridicules the opening because the Muse is replaced by Belinda herself—'If she inspire'.[11] He is determined not to see the decorum whereby Pope methodically replaces supernatural machinery by internal 'spirits'—not Dennisian allegorical 'powers of nature', but ones rather more elusive. Even the Cave of Spleen, that hell of nightmare disorders, is presided over not by a supernatural being, but by a psychological power.

The Olympian machinery is comparably interiorised, as the gods engage 'with human Passions' (5.45). Most obviously, Apollo is humanised in Belinda, 'Rival of his Beams' (2.3). But she manifests other Olympians too: just after Jove's judgement, there is 'Lightning in her eyes' (5.76); and at 5.82 the 'wily Virgin' is probably Athene, when, in a Homeric strife of the gods (''Gainst Pallas, Mars', 5.47) she encounters the Baron. And, of course, she is (or ought to be) a Venus all the time.

Rather less obviously, Sir Plume naturalises the messenger god, when he is sent (not by Jupiter but by the fulminating Thalestris) to moderate the dispute and request the return of the lock.[12] His name comes from the feathers of Mercury's *petasus* or winged cap;[13] and for caduceus he has a 'clouded Cane'. This richly condensed but beautifully natural image refers to a fashionable type of cane, variegated with dark veins. But 'clouded' glances, in a general way, at the god's power to control clouds by the conduct of his magic staff; while, more particularly, variegated colours were assigned to Mercury as planetary deity.[14] The feathers of the *petasus* and the *talaria* were to show the speed of the god's words;[15] and we are soon given a specimen of Sir Plume's swift eloquence: 'My Lord, why, what the Devil? . . .' (4.127–30). Even the Baron acknowledges the power of this brilliant rhetoric—'It grieves me much . . . Who speaks so well shou'd ever speak in vain' (131–2). How little has Pope's Renaissance reading been allowed for, when a joke so good as the 'unthinking' Sir Plume's miscasting as Mercury could be missed.

Psychological machinery

Without making Pope into a post-Jungian and Ariel into an *animus* figure, one can regard *The Rape of the Lock* as working out ideas of feminine psychology in terms of 'irrational' mythologies. Dennis calls *The Count of Gabalis* 'fantastick' (p 328), and Locke treats all talk of aerial vehicles as 'gibberish';[16] Pope's interiorising of machinery might suggest he agreed. But the matter is not so simple—any more than it would be, to decide how far Pope embraced Enlightenment ideals. After all, the Rosicrucian movement was itself an enlightenment, in its reformism and insistence on new illumination.[17] As a moderate Catholic and a Freemason, Pope would find the ecumenical ideals of the Rosicrucians congenial—indeed, the Freemasons traced their origins to the Rosicrucian Fraternity.[18] The doubtfully rational, 'fantastic' character of the Rosicrucian system—by turns above and below reason—would be attractive to any poet who felt Enlightenment rationalism constricting. Its alchemic element retained lingering associations with philosophical magic, while having become a psychological disipline of inner illumination.[19]

Even aerial spirits and fairies could be seriously credited in Pope's time. (One might compare attitudes to spiritualism around 1900.) Shaftesbury, in his 'Letter Concerning Enthusiasm', wrote of 'an Eminent, Learned and truly Christian Prelate' who was 'so great a Volunteer in Faith, as beyond the ordinary Prescription of the Catholick Church, to believe in *Fairys*';[20] and the life of Goodwin Wharton shows that a Restoration courtier might be prepared to stake good money—repeatedly—on their existence.[21] For the more sophisticated, fairy lore, half-real and potentially meaningful, offered a convenient non-moralistic language for broaching unconventional matters. Political and sexual taboos in particular were addressed in this way, as the long tradition of fairy poetry strikingly demonstrates. To this tradition Pope's sylphs stand in some close relation still to be determined. But the answer to Ariel's question 'What guards the purity of melting Maids?' may be a little more than the 'Nothing' Emrys Jones proposes.

If the machinery has psychological functions, what are they? A widely accepted view is outlined in Maynard Mack's Life of Pope.[22] The sylphs ('maidenly coquetries') guard Belinda, until she falls in love and Ariel leaves her; whereupon 'the lock of maidenliness is forfeit'. (Here the account becomes a little unclear.) Belinda objects, a little prudishly; being afflicted by Umbriel's furies of affectation. She then learns from Thalestris to confuse the name and reality of honour: '*Honour* forbid! at whose unrival'd shrine/Ease, Pleasure, Virtue, All, our Sex resign' (4.105–6). The account is well enough; but its narrative leaves the problematic side of Belinda's character alone. Yet it seems a little bland about the Baron's enormity too: is it mere affectation to be affronted at losing half one's hair style?[23]

On a different tack, Gary Boire valuably relates the poem to Burton's *The Anatomy of Melancholy*, and sees Belinda's experience in terms of seventeenth-century medical concepts.[24] On Boire's view, she suffers throughout from 'maid's melancholy', a splenetic disorder. Love melancholy underlies her initial changeableness no less than her 'dotage' on the 'light' occasion of losing a lock of hair. Developing an emphasis of Wasserman's, Boire sees Ariel as a Burtonian *incubus* desiring aery copulation with Belinda, and therefore encouraging her in 'an unnatural, aggressive virginity' (p 13). Belinda becomes a love melancholic in the special sense that she takes pride in making men enamoured only to scorn them. At the crisis, Boire's Ariel leaves in melancholic depression, while Belinda herself suffers melancholy with an equally sexual basis, as the description of forms of spleen indicates (4.54: 'Maids turned Bottels, call aloud for Corks').

There can be no doubt of Pope's interest in the medical tradition, or of the intertextuality with Burtonian subtexts. Yet melancholy can hardly be sole mover of the action—even taking into account the many varieties of it distinguished by seventeenth-century psychologists (some of them could write in all seriousness of 'sanguine melancholy'), as well as Burton's generalisation of the disease into *la condition humaine*.[25] For *The Rape of the Lock* is solidly built on a scheme of four complexions, all of them functional:

element	*temperament*	*spirit*	*character*
fire	choleric	salamander	Thalestris
air	sanguine	sylph	Ariel
water	phlegmatic	nymph	
earth	melancholic	gnome	Umbriel

Besides using the four elements implicitly throughout as a rhetorical topos,[26] Pope makes the scheme explicit:

> For when the Fair in all their Pride expire,
> To their first Elements their Souls retire:
> The Sprights of fiery Termagants in Flame
> Mount up, and take a Salamander's Name.
> Soft yielding Minds to Water glide away,
> And sip with Nymphs, their Elemental Tea.
> The graver Prude sinks downward to a Gnome,
> In search of Mischief still on Earth to roam.
> The light Coquettes in Sylphs aloft repair,
> And sport and flutter in the Fields of Air.
>
> (1.57–66)

The various individual nymphs exemplify the same typology. Thus 'fierce' Thalestris, who 'fans the rising Fire' of Belinda's anger (4.99)—'raging' (4.121) 'enrag'd Thalestris' (5.57) the 'fierce Virago' (5.37)—displays the influence of choleric salamanders, spirits of 'fiery Termagants'. And 'grave' Clarissa (5.7), whom 'Thalestris call'd . . . Prude' (5.36), is melancholic, influenced by an erstwhile 'graver Prude' and given to gnomic speeches.

Moral machinery

Clarissa carries great authority, as most agree. Her important speech (5.7–36), added for the first time in 1717, seems to represent the poet's own moral. Indeed, Pope's annotation in his copy of Dennis's *Remarks* has been taken to imply as much.[27] Are we, then, to prefer the melancholic perspective? Is that what the poem's machinery implies? For, as Dennis says (p 337), it would be a fault if the machinery were to 'give no instruction'.

Here again it may help to glance at the older moral psychologies Pope inherited. In medieval thought, pervasively imbued as it was by Christian ideals, cheerful sanguine was regarded as the best complexion, melancholy as the worst. Gradually, however, and especially after the Florentine Renaissance, an alternative tradition developed: melancholy came to be thought of as a creative mood rather than merely a disease. Despite its pathological tendencies, it came to be valued as the source of contemplation and imagination—none other than Spleen, in fact, gave the 'poetic Fit' (4.60).[28] These two opposed traditions coexisted up to Pope's time; so that occasions would easily arise for choice—or ambivalence—between a sanguine ethic and a melancholic. Given the age's rationalism, the choice might present itself as one between a cheerful, reasonable, sanguine ideal ('Sense') and a gloomy, fantastic melancholy ('Sensibility').—Or, of course, as between a serious, imaginative, reasonable melancholy, and a frivolous, fantastic, sanguine vanity. Some such intellectual history as this appears to underlie Pope's contrast of sylphs and gnomes. It is one reason why his sylphs and gnomes bulk larger than the salamanders and nymphs.

As Johnson says, the reader seeks no further information about the Rosicrucian spirits, 'but immediately mingles with his new acquaintance, adopts their interests and attends their pursuits, loves a sylph and detests a gnome' (pp 233–4). Nonetheless, the perspicacious Dennis—who like most critics takes the side of gravity and the gnomes—detects ambivalence in Pope's machinery:

> The Spirits, which he intends for benign ones, are malignant, and those, which he designs for malignant, are beneficent to Mankind. The Gnomes he intends for malignant, and the Sylphs for beneficent Spirits. Now the Sylphs in this Poem promote that Female Vanity which the Gnomes mortify. And Vanity is . . . the Cause of most of the Misfortunes which are incident to Humanity.
>
> (p 339)

It will not do to suppose that Dennis missed all the ironies criticising Belinda, any more than Johnson did. Nor can it be said that Pope has done much to make the gnomes attractive. It almost looks as if the confusion Dennis seized on was real—and as if Pope, when he added Clarissa's mortifying speech, was trying to correct a partiality for the sylphs. Had he been drawn to the old sanguine ideal of the gothick world? Beyond question he gave the aerial spirits by far the best press. They displace the others to such an extent that many write 'sylphs' when they mean 'spirits'.[29] If Pope's ironies take a 'melancholic' stance, his primary meanings are mostly sanguine.

Critics have taken over Dennis's perception of the sylphs as malignant; although they are not anxious to acknowledge *that* debt. Tillotson, Wasserman, Boire, Grove: all expose Ariel's dishonourable motive for being in Belinda's lap, and trace his evil influence on her character. On Dennis's assumptions, this should mean approval of Umbriel and the darker view. However, it is striking that no active opposition of sylphs and gnomes actually occurs. (Dennis in fact censures this.) For of course all four spirit categories are on the side of evil. Indeed, Pope's note to 1.145 half-encourages one to think of them in terms of fallen angels, subjects of 'the prince of the power of the air' of Ephesians 2.2. (Doubtless he had in view *Paradise Regained*, where Milton identifies the devils with 'Powers of Fire, Air, Water, and Earth beneath'.[30]) But this solemn viewpoint cannot be Pope's either: he has taken too much care to interiorise his spirits. As Thomas Parnell writes, 'The Sylphs and Gnomes are but a woman's heart.'[31] Besides, if it is true that 'unless the sylphs could gain an earthly lover they never achieved immortality',[32] was their aspiration so very evil?—or different from that of most earthly maidens? Coquetry is as reprehensible as Wasserman says. And Belinda's dream indeed resembles that of Milton's Eve. But to call Ariel's influence *demonic* seems a bit gnomelike, or superstitious.

And the moralists cannot claim that Belinda improves when Ariel abandons his guardianship and leaves her to other spirits, so that, after Umbriel's prayer, she falls into a melancholy, and much of the Fourth Canto is devoted to a hell of spleen. And these are not the only female disorders. Earlier, at the crisis of the ombre game (and the exact midpoint of 1714) 'Blood the Virgin's Cheek forsook' (3.89). Her 'livid Paleness' shows she has become as 'distemper'd' as the political state she is likened to. Already at 3.25, indeed, she burns with a Martian 'Thirst of Fame'.[33] Pope gives a crucial role to 'Rage, Resentment and Despair' (4.9): to the choleric promptings of the fierce termagant Thalestris. This Amazon is neither the (sanguine) 'resolute coquette' Wasserman would have her (p 434), nor the mere phase of melancholy detected by Boire. Anger might be thought of as 'preparing the body to melancholy, and madness itself'.[34] But to make Belinda's anger a feature of her melancholy is to give her too individualised a personality. There is no evidence that Pope knew Arabella Fermor.

Belinda doubtless suffers from love melancholy, in the general sense that most girls do. But she can also be choleric: after the 'rape' she 'burns with more than mortal Ire' (4.89), and is an 'incens'd Virago' (5.87). Tillotson (p 396) thinks she is virago-like merely in order to resemble a Homeric hero. But Dennis significantly thinks her 'a terrible Termagant' (p 335); thus connecting her with the salamander type. At a turning point of the tragic action— her triumph at ombre—she is guilty of the *hubris* of a bad winner: 'The

Nymph exulting fills with Shouts the Sky/The Walls, the Woods, and long Canals reply' (3.99–100). To Dennis, Belinda appears 'an arrant Ramp and a Tomrigg . . . Must not this be the legitimate Offspring of Stentor, to make such a Noise as that? The Nymph was within Doors, and she must set up her Throat at a hellish Rate, to make the Woods (where, by the by, there are none) and the Canals reply to it' (p 334).

Critics, ever protective of their author, have proved there *were* woods at Hampton Court, without attending to Dennis's point. Belinda is not being a light coquette, but a bold hoyden. (A ramp was a bold, ill-behaved woman, a tom-rig a 'strumpet, romping girl, a tomboy'.[35]) Indeed, the entire ombre game arises from a dangerous boldness on her part: she 'Burns to encounter two adventrous Knights,/At Ombre singly to decide their Doom' (3.26–7). Again the salamandrian 'burns'. This is not sylphlike.

From one point of view, Belinda is going too far. In playing men at their own game (*ombre* = man), and 'singly' at that, she ignores gender differences, and endangers her reputation. (Although the game is probably played in company, it symbolises another that need not be.) Her behaviour has something of the dangerous 'innocence' described in *Spectator* 198 (17 October 1711), in a passage that has oddly remained unconnected with *The Rape of the Lock*. Although not itself Rosicrucian, Addison's essay may well have suggested to Pope his interiorisation of the spirits:

> There is a Species of Women, whom I shall distinguish by the Name of Salamanders . . . a kind of Heroine in Chastity, that treads upon Fire, and lives in the Midst of Flames without being hurt. A Salamander *knows no Distinction of Sex in those she converses with* . . . She admits a Male Visitant to her Bed-side, *plays with him a whole Afternoon at Pickette*, walks with him two or three Hours by Moon-light; and is extreamly Scandalized at . . . the severity of a Parent, that would debar the Sex from such innocent Liberties. Your Salamander is therefore a[n] . . . admirer of the French Good-breeding, and *a great Stickler for freedom in Conversation*. In short, the Salamander lives in an invincible State of Simplicity and Innocence: Her Constitution is preserv'd in a kind of natural Frost: She wonders what People mean by Temptations; and defies Mankind to do their worst. Her Chastity is engaged in a constant Ordeal, or fiery Tryal . . .[36]

Belinda does not altogether escape the dangers of such boldness. When she comes to ask 'What mov'd my Mind with youthful Lords to rome?' (4.159), the answer might be a salamander almost as much as a sylph.

Belinda's boldness also appears in her solar role. Like a Stuart monarch, 'Bright as the Sun, her Eyes the Gazers strike,/And, like the Sun, they shine on all alike'.[37] So firmly is the role established that 'Belinda smil'd, and all the World was gay' (2.52) seems to follow naturally from the 'Sun-beams trembling on the floating Tydes' a few lines earlier. However, to take the role for granted as no more than Belinda's due hardly does justice to Pope's subtlety. She makes a rather dubious *Sol iustitiae*—'declining from the Noon' of justice, in fact: 'The Sun obliquely shoots his burning Ray' (3.20) as hungry judges hurry their sentencing. This is not a matter of contrast with a 'larger, more disturbing world' outside, as Grove has it (p 72): Belinda herself participates in the disorder actively. In her cosmic sovereignty she is something of an overreacher, like Spenser's Dame Mutabilitie.

Pope suggests as much, by insinuating suggestions of a better alternative to solar aspiring. So he associates Belinda with silver: the 'silver Sound' of her watch (1.18); her 'silver Token' (1.32); her 'Silver Vase in mystic Order laid' (1.122); 'the Bosom of the Silver Thames' (2.3–4) reflecting the true sun. And her petticoat, cardinal emblem of her chastity, has a 'Silver Bound' (2.121); conspicuously avoiding the subtext's gold.[38] It was a commonplace of the older world picture that silver belonged to Diana, Luna or Venus, not to golden Sol.[39] Thus Belinda's solar role is made to conflict with her nature either as a Diana or a chaste Venus (Venus-virgo).

Perhaps the second of these mythological colorations better suited a fashionable sex-goddess like Arabella Fermor. Pope may not have known his patroness personally; but it seems he could count on her salamandrian 'innocence' in the face of some fairly gross sexual innuendos. True, he went a little warily at first: in 1712 the notorious speech wishing the youth had been 'content to seize/Hairs less in sight—or any Hairs but these!' was given to Thalestris. (Perhaps Pope felt surer of Mrs Morley.) But in 1714 it is spoken by Belinda herself, at an extremely prominent Canto end. It is hard to assess coarseness over a gap of centuries. Grove is not unpersuasive when he finds in Belinda's 'half innocent heroics' a passionately indignant appeal '*just* polite enough to lie within [her] range' (p 82). But we have contemporary testimony. The invaluable Dennis writes that Pope 'could not forbear putting Bawdy into the Mouth of his own Patroness' (p 130). He complains that Belinda 'talks like an errant Suburbian [whore]' (p 335): Pope gives her 'Breeding, Modesty and Virtue in Words, but has in Reality and in Fact made her an artificial dawbing Jilt; a Tomrig, a Virago, and a Lady of the Lake [kept woman]'. And Charles Gildon makes a similar point.[40]

Other passages present much the same problem. In Ariel's order for Belinda's petticoat, as Dennis again objects (p 342), the verse 'Oft have we known that sev'nfold Fence to fail' (2.199) can ludicrously be taken to mean that this particular petticoat has often failed to protect its wearer's chastity. Indeed, sexual *doubles entendres* (like that at 2.106, 'frail China Jar') abound throughout, making *The Rape of the Lock* one of the most erotic works in the canon. Even the stellification that gives the poem its exquisite closure makes another instance. Many will have felt Pope's subject here to be poetic idealisation itself—'The elevated lock is, in a sense, the poem' (Price p 242). 'Who made a lampe of Berenices hayre?' asks Jonson; and the answer is 'Poets, rapt with rage divine'.[41] The lock of hair sacred as a nuptial sacrifice or token of love is one of the great poetic subjects.[42] Yet in linking Belinda's lock with the 'dishevel'd Light' of 'Berenice's Locks', Pope also associated it with a constellation whose vulgar name was 'Bernice's Bush'.[43] Again and again the poem recurs to its sustained juxtaposition—an oxymoron not unknown elsewhere in Pope—of the low and the ideal in woman.

How could innuendo have been thought calculated to reconcile the families, to 'laugh them together'?[44] Part of Pope's strategy may have been to make Belinda's world so erotic that the Baron's action came to seem almost natural.

By tender ridicule of the way Belinda's heroics exaggerate the incident into a rape, he makes it seem a mere romp outwardly—while still sympathising with its subjective apprehension as an outrage. And by the lurking lover at 3.144 he hints that Belinda's heavy reaction may be due to her having formed a serious attachment. Wasserman (pp 428–9, 435, 442) rightly draws attention to the antique symbolism whereby clipping a lock was a ritual preparation for marriage: Catullus makes tears for the lock ambivalent. Indeed, a 'glittering Forfex' such as that used to cut Belinda's hair—'The scissors double shaft,/Useless apart, in social union joined'—is regarded by Richard Jago as an 'Emblem how beautiful/Of happy nuptial leagues'.[45] Pope's innuendos, then, were perhaps not so counterproductively unsuitable as they may now seem. But in any case the mock-heroic occasional poem was soon left behind (by 1713 Baron Petre was dead); as Pope consciously recognised, his subject became nothing less than 'female sex'.[46]

In his treatment of women, Pope departed radically from the hostility of his satiric models. Thus, his finely poised description of Belinda's toilet is only from one point of view censure of those who 'dress all day'. Belinda is obviously vain—idolatrous, even, in her self-love—as our modern Umbriels have explained in detail. But to dwell exclusively on this 'moral' is to prefer gnomic heaviness to the poetic effect of erotic warmth. For, throughout the description, the poetry's own 'busy Sylphs surround their darling Care', like *putti* round a Renaissance Venus. Erotic nuances of language are here particularly marked. 'The Fair each moment *rises* in her Charms' (140); 'Arabia *breathes*' (134); and when the maid ('Th' inferior Priestess') 'begins the sacred Rites of Pride' she is 'Trembling'.[47] Wasserman legitimately spells out the 'Rites of Pride', reminding us how bad is Ariel's advice to know 'thy own Importance'; and that 'The mirror in which Belinda sees herself as a goddess is, of course, the traditional emblem of Pride' (pp 431–2). Pride is certainly a strong moral card, and Pope's readers would expect it to be played against Belinda. But we have not responded to the passage unless we also see the cosmetic rites as beautiful. The mirror is also, we recall, a traditional emblem of Venus.[48] Pope's description of the *garniture de toilette* is less a conventional *Vanitas* still life than a *Vénus à sa toilette*.[49]

To Parkin, 'the whole point of the metaphor' of worship is 'the actual disparity between the realms of make-up and religion'.[50] Certainly the metaphors are disjunctive morally. But it would be simplistic to take the 'heav'nly Image in the Glass' merely as Belinda's own reflection.[51] As Cleanth Brooks already recognised, Belinda also serves, paradoxically, as priestess in a religion of beauty.[52] To grave moralists, Venus is, of course, an idol—perhaps like Addison's coquette, 'An Idol . . . wholly taken up in the Adoring of her Person'.[53] But Venus could be a little more. The magic of female beauty, which everywhere enchants in *The Rape of the Lock*, was a serious interest for Pope in a way it never was for Addison.[54] It is the poem's concern with this magic, indeed, that makes its Rosicrucian machinery exquisitely appropriate.

In a Rosicrucian poem, Belinda's toilet can be the rite of a magical 'Art' (3.143), a purification of the quintessence of Venus. In this art, alchemic apparatus and symbols are evident. What is Belinda's glass but a magic mirror of intellectual reflection? or 'Each Silver Vase in mystic Order laid' but an alchemic vessel?[55] Indeed, the line (like several in the poem) has an explicitly alchemic subtext.[56] To Wasserman (p 434), 'The Tortoise here and Elephant unite' alludes to 'the Hindu emblem of the world' because the proud Belinda pretends to govern the universe. But Grove (p 64) notices that 'the verse . . . catches Tortoise and Elephant coupled in love-play, before the prudent explanation ('combs') returns the stage to rights'. The point of the Hindu world image for Pope probably lay in Locke's prominent use of it to destroy the illusion that qualities are supported by substance. (What supports the tortoise?) And Pope, too, has used the image for a metaphysic of perception—perception of beauty. For the union of elephant and tortoise is an alchemic *coniunctio* of opposites—strength and weakness, superhuman intellectual power and Venerean emotion.[57] The beauty that results from the Art, then, could truly be called a 'heav'nly Image'. It is hardly surprising that the Baron follows Prometheus in stealing its illumination:

> Sure shee is Heaven it self, and I
> In fervent zeal
> This lock did steal,
> And each life-giving thread,
> Snatcht from her beamy head,
> As once Prometheus from the skie.[58]

Burton, writing of love-melancholics who 'prank up themselves to make young men enamoured', asks 'why do they make such glorious shows with . . . whatsoever Africa, Asia, America, sea, land, art and industry of man can afford?'[59] But his elephantine attitude (which rests on the porcupine of misognystic satire) is far from Pope's.

Similarly with Pope's famous asyndetic couplet—

> Here Files of Pins extend their shining Rows,
> Puffs, Powders, Patches, Bibles, Billet-doux.
> (1.137–8)

Morally, it betrays Belinda's notorious confusion of values. But its diminutive organisation also delights, by enhancing a scene of delicate activity, thronged with 'busy Sylphs'. Pope the satirist is bound to censure the spending of resources on mere beauty—as Clarissa would say, it is not a 'Thing of Use' (5.22). Yet Pope the artist knows that beauty may be higher than use; and so he makes Belinda's rituals the mysteries of a separate world, with its own *magnum opus*. Gnomes compare the couplet with one of Halifax's (which is perhaps the origin of one used by Richard Steele on Philauthia's closet): 'Prayer-book, patch-boxes, sermon-notes and paint,/ At once t'improve the sinner and the saint.'[60] But Pope's lines are as close to Cowley's 'The Chronicle':

> But should I now to you relate,
> The strength and riches of their state,
> The Powder, Patches, and the Pins,

> The Ribbans, Jewels, and the Rings,
> The Lace, the Paint, and warlike things
> That make up all their Magazins:
>
> If I should tell the politick Arts
>   To take and keep mens hearts,
>   The Letters, Embassies, and Spies,
> The Frowns, and Smiles, and Flatteries,
> The Quarrels, Tears, and Perjuries,
>   Numberless, Nameless Mysteries![61]

—a poem whose tone is not at all misogynistic.

Political machinery

The chief of the aerial spirits who preside over the human race, as Ariel's Thames speech explains, 'guard with Arms Divine the British Throne' (2.89–90). Is, then, *The Rape of the Lock* a political poem?

A loosely politicised interpretation of the poem has become fairly common—as in discussions of Belinda's toilet articles in terms of 'commodity fetishism'.[62] This is perfectly legitimate, whenever a specifically political perspective is appropriate. Everything in literature can be seen in political and economic terms: every mention of every object. When Lear says 'undo this button', his speech reflects technological developments whereby buttons replaced points. But the decision how far to trace such reflections must depend on the pragmatic context. Doubtless Belinda's world could be described so as to seem one 'in which objects have taken over all meaning', by exclusion of human values and of 'the actual production of the commodities'.[63] But would this help us to appreciate what is specific to Pope's poem? Is it true that 'of all the major works of its period, *The Rape of the Lock* does the most to match imperialism and commodity fetishism, and the most to place the commodification of English culture in the context of imperial violence' (Brown p 22)? Is it true, even, that the poem's highly charged objects reflect the structural economic facts of Pope's time in a new way? After all, poems full of things that constitute the main repositories of value were hardly new. One thinks of Elizabethan satires, or of medieval romances with their overdetermined objects.[64] Pope may have given prominence to charming objects—cosmetic articles, and to tea and coffee—because they bulked distinctively large in female life. (They were also important in Pope's own, in ways that have little to do with his anti-mercantilism: he used to relieve his frequent headaches 'by inhaling the steam of coffee'—a surprising light on Ariel's threat that the punished spirit 'In Fumes of burning Chocolate shall glow,/And tremble at the Sea that froaths below!'[65])

If *The Rape of the Lock* was a political poem, why are politics never mentioned in Dennis's *Remarks*? True, Pope himself pseudonymously proposed a political allegory (concerning the Barrier Treaty). But if its logic is

27 Where Dennis speaks of Boileau's superiority in giving 'broad Hints as to what was his real Meaning', Pope writes 'Clarissa's Speach': see Mack 1982, p 407.
28 See Klibansky *et al.*, *passim.*
29 See, e.g., Tillotson, p 123: 'Pope . . . makes some of his sylphs "bad"'.
30 2.124; cf. 4.201: 'Tetrarchs of fire, air, flood, and on the earth.'
31 'To Mr Pope', cit. Wasserman, p 441.
32 Tillotson, p 143, n.32.
33 On her Martian boldness at this stage, see Plowden, p 83.
34 *The Anatomy of Melancholy*, 1.2.3.9.
35 See *OED* s.v. 'Ramp' sb.¹, 'Tom' sb., 7a.
36 Donald F Bond (ed), 5 vols (Oxford, 1965), 2.275–6 (my itals). Tillotson has compared *Spectator* 282, but unaccountably not this more relevant paper.
37 2.13–14. See Rebecca Parkin, 'Mythopoeic Activity in *The Rape of the Lock*', *ELH* 21 (1954), 30–8. In addition to her other instances, she might have mentioned the clipping of the sacred lock; since the sun's rays were often mythologised as hair, and his lessening power in winter as their cutting. Cf. Charles Cotton, 'Her Hair', st.5: 'Shee's now a Nazarite/Robb'd of her vigorous light,/For her resisting strength is gone.'
38 The Homeric and Vergilian 'stiff with gold' is replaced, as Tillotson notes, by 'stiff with Hoops'.
39 See e.g. John Maplet, *The Dial of Destiny* (1581), in *The Frame of Order*, James Winny (ed) (London, Allen and Unwin, 1957), p 187. There were a very few exceptions, as notably *Iliad* 20.91 in Pope's 1714 note. But in his own *Iliad* Pope actually mistranslates to keep the connection of silver with Diana.
40 *A New Rehearsal* (1714), p 43.
41 'To Elizabeth Countess of Rutland', 60–3.
42 Wasserman 428–9 cites many ancient examples. Callimachus's poem, on Berenice's lock lost from the temple, was itself lost so far as Pope was concerned; but Catullus's translation of it survived. The later tradition includes Drayton's *Ecl.* 9.216–22; Lovelace's 'On Sannazar'; Butler's *Hudibras* 2.3.844; and Cotton's 'Her Hair'.
43 R H Allen, *Star-Names and their Meanings* (New York, 1963), 170, citing Thomas Hill, *Schoole of Skil* (1599) etc.
44 Pope's own account of his brief: see Joseph Spence, *Anecdotes*, James M Osborn (ed), 2 vols (Oxford, Clarendon, 1966), no. 104.
45 *Edge-Hill* (1767), 3.545–8.
46 Marginalium to Dennis's *Remarks*, Mack 1982, p 407. Pope implies that this subject is comparable with the important ecclesiastical one of the *Lutrin*.
47 Cf. Robin Grove, 'Uniting Airy Substance: *The Rape of the Lock* 1712–1736', in *The Art of Alexander Pope*, Howard Erskine-Hill and Anne Smith (eds) (London, Vision, 1979), p 68.
48 See, e.g., Guy de Tervarent, *Attributs et symboles dans l'art profane 1450–1600* (Geneva, Droz, 1958), col 274.
49 Iconographically the sylph-putti are decisive against the harsher interpretation; cf., e.g., Oliver Millar, *Dutch Pictures from the Royal Collection* (London, The Queen's Gallery 1971), p 85, on the putto in a *toilette* by Steen.
50 Parkin 1955, p 103.
51 As Hugo M Reichard, 'The Love Affair in Pope's *The Rape of the Lock*', *PMLA* 69.1 (1954), 894; Parkin 1955, p 107; Grove, pp 64–5.
52 Cleanth Brooks, 'The Case of Miss Arabella Fermor: A Re-examination', reprinted in *The Well Wrought Urn* (London, Dobson, 1949), p 77.
53 *Spectator* 73, cit. Reichard 889.

54   It is seen also, for example, in the echo of The Song of Solomon, on beauty's power to draw with a single hair.

55   On the mirror, see Herbert Grabes, *The Mutable Glass*, trans Gordon Collier (Cambridge UP, 1982), pp 336–7; Jung, p 111; on the vessel, which was of central importance in alchemic thought, see ibid, s.v. *Vas*. Paracelsus (e.g. 1.14) has much to say about the 'silver pixis' or receptacle; see also ibid, 1.298, on the 'vase of the philosophers', quicksilver, or Mercury.

56   *Gondibert* 2.7.17. Cf. the notorious line 'Nor bound thy narrow Views to Things below', which echoes a central alchemic symbolon, 'As above, so below': see Stanislas Klossowski de Rola *Alchemy: The Secret Art* (London, Thames and Hudson, 1973), p 15.

57   As it happens, Pope's knowledge of the Renaissance elephant and tortoise can partly be documented, since he annotated Montaigne's account of the elephant's powers extensively: see Mack 1982, p 427.

58   Charles Cotton, 'Her Hair', st.3.

59   *The Anatomy of Melancholy* 3.2.5.5; 3.2.2.3, cit. Tillotson, Boire.

60   Tillotson, n. to 1.138; cf. Reichard 894, referring to *Spectator* 79.

61   *Poems*, A R Waller (ed) (Cambridge 1905), p 41.

62   Brown, pp 12–24; C E Nicholson, 'A World of Artefacts: *The Rape of the Lock* as Social History', *Literature and History* 5 (1979), 183–93; Robert Casillo, 'Dirty Gondola: The Image of Italy in American Advertisements', *Word and Image* 1.4 (1985), 344.

63   Brown, pp 13–14.

64   See, e.g., Sir John Davies, 'In Claium', or his Gulling Sonnet 6: *The Poems*, Robert Krueger (ed) (Oxford, Clarendon, 1975), pp 158–9, 166.

65   2.133–6. See *Gent. Mag.* (1775) 435, cit. Johnson, p 197.

66   Howard Erskine-Hill, 'The Satirical Game at Cards in Pope and Wordsworth', in *English Satire and the Satiric Tradition*, Claude Rawson (ed) (Oxford, Blackwell, 1984), p 190.

67   See ibid, p 186.

68   The 'bawdy intimations' of the game are well described in Grove, p 75.

69   Yates 1972, p 63.

70   Cf. 2.73–100: Ariel distinguishes aetherial spirits with translunary offices, and others 'less refin'd' with sublunary macrocosmic or national affairs. A third, yet lower, grade ('Our humble province') is Ariel's own sort. Pope's marginalium in Dennis underlines this subdivision: see Mack 1982, pp 408–9.

71   *A Key to the Lock*, p 189 might be taken to hint that characters can have dual roles.

72   See Douglas Brooks-Davies, *The Mercurian Monarch* (Manchester UP, 1983), p 193.

73   See Howard Erskine-Hill, 'Literature and the Jacobite Cause: Was There a Rhetoric of Jacobitism?', in *Ideology and Conspiracy: Aspects of Jacobitism, 1689–1759*, Eveline Cruickshanks (ed) (Edinburgh, Edinburgh UP, 1982); Douglas Brooks-Davies, *Pope's Dunciad and the Queen of Night: A Study in Emotional Jacobitism* (Manchester UP, 1985).

74   Alastair Fowler, *Triumphal Forms* (Cambridge UP, 1970), p 120.

75   W K Wimsatt, 'Belinda Ludens: Strife and Play in *The Rape of the Lock*', *NLH* 4.2 (1973), 357–74.

76   Cf. Plowden, p 87.

77   On the compromising significance of the lock in contemporary convention, see Reichard, pp 891, 900, 902.

78   2.80. On the confusion of 'aerial', see Tillotson, pp 118, 397.

79   Cf. Wasserman, p 435 *ad fin.*, on 1.12.

References

Agrippa, Henry C *Opera Omnia* (Cologne, 1533)

Boire, Gary A 'An Arrant Ramp and a Tomrigg: Pope's Belinda', *English Studies in Canada* 8.1 (1982), 9–22

Brooks-Davies, Douglas *The Mercurian Monarch: Magical Politics from Spenser to Pope* (Manchester: Manchester UP, 1983)

Brooks-Davies, Douglas *Pope's* Dunciad *and the Queen of Night: A Study in Emotional Jacobitism* (Manchester: Manchester UP, 1985)

Brown, Laura *Alexander Pope* (Oxford and New York: Blackwell, 1985)

Butler, Samuel *Hudibras*, John Wilders (ed) (Oxford: Clarendon, 1967)

Dennis, John (1728) *Remarks on* The Rape of the Lock, in *The Critical Works of John Dennis*, Edward Niles Hooker (ed), vol 2: 1711–1729 (Baltimore: Johns Hopkins, 1943)

Erskine-Hill, Howard (1982) 'Literature and the Jacobite Cause: Was There a Rhetoric of Jacobitism?', in *Ideology and Conspiracy: Aspects of Jacobitism, 1689–1759*, Eveline Cruickshanks (ed) (Edinburgh: Edinburgh UP, 1982)

Erskine-Hill, Howard 'The Satirical Game at Cards in Pope and Wordsworth', in *English Satire and the Satirical Tradition*, Claude Rawson (ed) (Oxford: Blackwell, 1984)

Grove, Robin 'Uniting Airy Substance: *The Rape of the Lock* 1712–36', in *The Art of Alexander Pope*, Howard Erskine-Hill and Anne Smith (eds) (London: Vision, 1979)

Johnson, Samuel *Lives of the English Poets*, George Birkbeck Hill (ed), vol 3 (Oxford: Clarendon, 1905)

Jung, C G *Psychology and Alchemy*, trans R F C Hull (London: Routledge and Kegan Paul, 1953)

Klibansky, Raymond, Saxl, Fritz and Panofsky, Erwin *Saturn and Melancholy* (London: Nelson, 1964)

Mack, Maynard *Collected in Himself* (Newark: Univ of Delaware, 1982)

Mack, Maynard *Alexander Pope: A Life* (New Haven and London: Yale UP, 1985)

Parkin, Rebecca P 'Mythopoeic Activity in *The Rape of the Lock*', *ELH* 21.1 (1954), 30–8

Parkin, Rebecca P *The Poetic Workmanship of Alexander Pope* (Minneapolis: Univ of Minnesota, 1955)

Plowden, G F C *Pope on Classic Ground* (Athens, Ohio: Ohio UP, 1983)

Paracelsus *The Hermetic and Alchemical Writings*, A E Waite (ed), 2 vols (London 1894)

Reichard, Hugo M 'The Love Affair in Pope's *The Rape of the Lock*', *PMLA* 69.1 (1954), 887–902.

Ripa, Cesare *Iconologia* (Padua, 1611)

The Spectator Donald F Bond (ed), 5 vols (Oxford: Clarendon, 1965)

Spence, Joseph *Polymetis* (London, 1747)

Tillotson, Geoffrey (ed) *'The Rape of the Lock' and Other Poems*, 3rd edn (London and New Haven: Methuen and Yale UP, 1962)

Villars, Abbé de *The Count of Gabalis*, trans P Ayres (London, 1680)

Wasserman, Earl R 'The Limits of Allusion in *The Rape of the Lock'*, *JEGP* 65 (1966), 425–44

Wind, Edgar *Pagan Mysteries in the Renaissance*, 2nd edn (London: Faber and Faber, 1967)

Yates, Frances A *Giordano Bruno and the Hermetic Tradition* (London: Routledge and Kegan Paul, 1964)

Yates, Frances *The Rosicrucian Enlightenment* (London: Routledge and Kegan Paul, 1972)

thus creating the following two lines:

> Tis my Reward that no Reward attends
> Friend alone to Virtue and her Friends

Pope went on to fill the space, and the lower left and adjacent right margins, with composition and revision elaborating upon these two lines, with particular reference to Twickenham and the friends to be found there.

Pope then transferred his text to the small quarto sheet, folio 3^r, reworking his lines in the process and, where he is evidently satisfied with a line, just indicating it with the first words. Here are the first of these lines down to and including the peroration of his imitation which has undergone yet further revision:

> What? armd for Virtue when I point ye pen
> & spout it in ye face
> Can there be wanting, to defend her Cause,
> Lights   or
> Friends, Patrons, Champions—nor here
> 2   Could Laureat Dryden
>   & neither Charles
> 1   Could pensiond Boileau lash in
> Flatt'rers
>   nor strip the gilding off a Knave
>   *unpla*
> And I, *unplacd, unpens unpayd no Mortals slave*
> Unplacd, unpensiond, no man's Heir, or Slave?
> *Friends, Patrons, Champions* (*doubt not*) *will be seen,*
> *Nor*
> & here a Statesman blush to be a Screen.
> I will, or perish in ye Glorious Cause:
> Hear this & tremble, you who scape ye Laws!
> To Virtue only & her friends a friend
> *I leave ye rest to* murmer or commend
> The world beside may   or

Though this sheet largely serves to record what Pope wishes to preserve from folio 2^v, original composition is also present, not least in the assertion:

> I will, or perish in ye Glorious Cause:
> Hear this & tremble, you who scape ye Laws!

Pope's shift from Horace's third person past tense to the first person present signals the difference here between translation and imitation and also alerts the 'skilful Reader' to the felt difference between the two men.

Pope took up a clean foolscap sheet, folio 4^r, and incorporating further adjustments, made fair copy including these lines:

> Is this my Care when Virtue arms my pen
> & spouts it in ye face of shameless Men

> *Fy* Fry'r
> Could Laureate Dryden Pimp & *Priest* ∧ engage
> & neither Charles nor James be in a rage
> Could pensiond Boileau lash in graver vein
> Flattrers & Bigots evn in Louis Reign?
> And can I want, to aid this bribeless cause
> Lights of ye Church, or Guardians of ye Laws?
> Another Colbert (FXX) shall be seen
> & here, with pride, a King may be Screen
> I leave ye World to murmer or commend
> To Virtue only & her friends a friend
> In Twitnams Grottoes, all ye noise ye keep
> Like distant Thunders but promotes my sleep
> There, my Retreat
> The best Companions my Retreat shall grace
> Chiefs, out of War, & Statesmen, out of place:

Before the text was issued from Gilliver's press, further refinements and adjustments of lines took place, with Pope often reverting to readings at folio 3^r.

Upon publication Pope's enemies did not fail to note a marked change in tone and a distinctive assertion of the personal in relation to Horace:

> In two large Columns, on thy motly Page,
> Where *Roman* Whit is stripe'd with *English* Rage;
> Where Ribaldry to Satire makes pretence,
> And modern Scandal rolls with ancient Sence:
> Whilst on one side we see how *Horace* thought;
> And on the other how he never wrote.
>
> *Verses Address'd to the Imitator of the*
> *First Satire of the Second Book of Horace,*
> 1733 (Foxon, V39)

What emerges clearly from the manuscript is how Bolingbroke's suggestion of how well the *First Satire* 'hit' Pope's case served as a stimulus, not least as he responded to those aspects he found to be inapt and was challenged to vary and even wholly depart from his original. Here the art of formal imitation became for Pope a process of self-definition and moral discrimination, in clarifying his role as opposition satirist and in affirming where he stood and what he stood for. Apart from his closest friends, it is perhaps for us today to be amongst the first to apprehend the extent of trial and error, energy and emotion that was engaged in its creation.

NOTE

1   This paper was originally presented at the Fifth David Nichol Smith Memorial Seminar in Eighteenth-Century Studies, the Australian National University,

Canberra, 26 August 1980. Presentation of the paper was made possible by a Visiting Research Fellowship at the Humanities Research Centre, the Australian National University, for which I am especially grateful to the Director, Ian Donaldson. An award from the British Academy made possible study of Pope's manuscript and his copy of Rochester's *Poems* (1696) in the Albert A and Henry W Berg Collection of English and American Literature, the New York Public Library, whom I wish to thank for permission to reproduce the plates illustrating this paper and my transcriptions from the documents. Quotation from Pope's annotations in his copy of Oldham's *Works* (1694) is with permission of the British Library. Previous reference to the manuscript will be found in *The Works of Alexander Pope*, J W Croker, W Elwin and W J Courthope (eds) (1871–89), III, 289–300, referred to as the Chauncy MS; in Maynard Mack, Introduction to his edition in facsimile of the manuscripts of *An Essay on Man* (Oxford, 1962), p xi; and *The Garden and the City* (Oxford and Toronto, 1969), pp 172 n 2, 181 n 5, 185 n 6. I am also indebted to the earlier study of Pope's methods of composition by George Sherburn, 'Pope at Work', *Essays on the Eighteenth Century Presented to David Nichol Smith* (Oxford, 1945), pp 49–64; by John Butt, 'Pope's Poetical Manuscripts', *Proceedings of the British Academy*, vol 40, pp 23–39; and by Maynard Mack (cited). For advice and comment I am specially grateful to S L Goldberg, Howard Erskine-Hill, MacDonald Emslie, and to Maynard Mack, who subsequently has made available a facsimile and transcription of the entire manuscript, together with discussion of the Mapledurham House fragment, in *The Last and Greatest Art* (1984), pp 168–89; corresponding references to this facsimile are incorporated in the text of this paper. For important recent discussion of Pope's imitation see Howard D Weinbrot, *Alexander Pope and the Tradition of Formal Verse Satire* (Princeton, 1982), pp 201–39; Howard Erskine-Hill, *The Augustan Idea in English Literature* (1983), pp 293–300; and Frank Stack, *Pope and Horace: Studies in Imitation* (Cambridge, 1985), pp 29–59.

References

Bloom, Lillian D 'Pope as Textual Critic', *JEGP*, xlvii (1948), pp 150–5

Brower, Reuben *Alexander Pope: The Poetry of Allusion* (Oxford, 1959)

Butt, John *et al.* (eds) *The Twickenham Edition of the Poems of Alexander Pope*, 11 vols (1938–68)

Foxon, D F *English Verse 1701–1750: A Catalogue of Separately Printed Poems With Notes on Contemporary Collected Editions*, 2 vols (Cambridge, 1975)

Griffith, R H *Alexander Pope: A Bibliography*, 2 vols (Austin, Texas, 1922–7)

Johnson, Samuel *Lives of the English Poets*, George Birkbeck Hill (ed), 3 vols (Oxford, 1905)

Mack, Maynard *The Garden and the City: Retirement and Politics in the Later Poetry of Pope* (Oxford and Toronto, 1969)

——'*The Last and Greatest Art*': *Some Unpublished Poetical Manuscripts of Alexander Pope* (1984)

——'Pope's Books: A Biographical Survey with a Finding List', *English Literature in the Age of Disguise*, Maximillian Novak (ed) (Berkley, Los Angeles, 1977), pp 209–305; revised 'A Finding List of Books Surviving from Pope's Library with a Few That May Not Have Survived', Maynard Mack, *"Collected in Himself"*: *Essays Critical, Biographical, and Bibliographical on Pope and Some of His Contemporaries* (1982), pp 394–460

'Pope's Copy of Chaucer', *Evidence in Literary Scholarship: Essays in Memory of James Marshall Osborn*, R Wellek and A Ribeiro (eds) (Oxford, 1977)

Sherburn, George (ed) *The Correspondence of Alexander Pope*, 5 vols (Oxford, 1956)

Spence, Joseph *Observations, Anecdotes, and Characters of Books and Men*, James M Osborn (ed), 2 vols (Oxford, 1966)

Wharton, Joseph *An Essay on the Genius and Writings of Pope*, Volume the Second (1782).

12

Text And Context:
Pope's 'Coronation Epistle'

W W ROBSON

Pope is a problem to anthologists. He is rarely at his best in short poems. Of course there are many passages in his longer poems—*The Rape of the Lock*, *The Dunciad*, *An Epistle to Dr. Arbuthnot*—that appear again and again in anthologies. But the understanding and appreciation of Pope's poetry has often been harmed by the habit of excerpting from his work. Pope explained one of the principles on which he wrote when he told Tonson the reason why he was not willing to show him the 'character' of the Man of Ross until he had completed the whole poem in which it was to appear. 'To send you any of the particular verses will be much to the prejudice of the whole; which if it has any beauty, derives it from the manner in which it is *placed*, and the painterly *contrast* (as the painters call it) in which it stands, with the pompous figures of famous, or rich, or high-born men' (Sherburn 1956 iii, p 390). The best choice for selection in an anthology would be a poem in which this consciously 'painterly' quality of Pope's poetry (if not himself a first-rate painter, he had a keen and devoted interest in the practice of that art) can be shown as operative in the work as a whole.

An early poem from the sunniest period of Pope's poetic career—the period of *The Rape of the Lock*—the poem called for short the 'Coronation Epistle', displays this quality admirably, and should long ago have been added to the 'canon within the canon', the short poems or passages which until quite recently were 'household words', familiar to all lovers of English poetry. Victorian taste, however, was evidently unable to recognise it as a serious poem. It does not appear in either *The Golden Treasury* (1861) or Quiller-Couch's *Oxford Book of English Verse* (1900). But with the great revival in Pope's popularity in this century the 'Coronation Epistle' is now widely recognised as one of the most beautiful of his poems. Even the most hostile twentieth-century critic of Pope, James Reeves (1976), has words of praise for it. This is remarkable; for on the whole it is the dark side of Pope, the surrealistic imagination of *The Dunciad*, the night world of dream-like complexities and metaphysical horror, that has captured the moderns: so much so that the sunlit world of Popean humanism, from *The Rape of the Lock* to the *Essay on Man*, while by no means neglected by scholars, does not seem to bulk large in the image of Pope as the poets of today receive it. (Once again the aesthetic significance of *contrast* has been neglected.) If so, the 'Coronation Epistle', in the form in which it appears in modern anthologies, e.g. Helen Gardner's *New Oxford Book of English Verse* (1972), or Roger Lonsdale's *New Oxford Book of Eighteenth Century Verse* (1984), is a timely reminder that it is possible to combine with the touch of realism favoured by modern taste the grace of art belonging to an age which still recognised the existence of artistic and moral ideals.

Here now is the poem as it appears in the one-volume edition of the Twickenham text, edited by John Butt (1965). I have made only one emendation ('delight' in line 23, for Butt's 'a delight'.)

Epistle to Miss Blount, on her leaving the Town, after the Coronation

As some fond virgin, whom her mother's care
Drags from the town to wholesome country air,
Just when she learns to roll a melting eye,
And hear a spark, yet think no danger nigh;
From the dear man unwilling she must sever, 5
Yet take one kiss before she parts for ever:
Thus from the world fair *Zephalinda* flew,
Saw others happy, and with sighs withdrew;
Not that their pleasures caus'd her discontent,
She sigh'd not that They stay'd, but that She went. 10
    She went, to plain-work, and to purling brooks,
Old-fashion'd halls, dull aunts, and croaking rooks,
She went from Op'ra, park, assembly, play,
To morning walks, and pray'rs three hours a day;
To pass her time 'twixt reading and Bohea, 15
To muse, and spill her solitary Tea,
Or o'er cold coffee trifle with the spoon,
Count the slow clock, and dine exact at noon;
Divert her eyes with pictures in the fire,
Hum half a tune, tell stories to the squire; 20
Up to her godly garret after sev'n,
There starve and pray, for that's the way to heav'n.
    Some Squire, perhaps, you take delight to rack;
Whose game is Whisk, whose treat a toast in sack,
Who visits with a gun, presents you birds, 25
Then gives a smacking buss, and cries—No words!
Or with his hound comes hollowing from the stable,
Makes love with nods, and knees beneath a table;
Whose laughs are hearty, tho' his jests are coarse,
And loves you best of all things—but his horse. 30

> In some fair evening, on your elbow laid,
> You dream of triumphs in the rural shade;
> In pensive thought recall the fancy'd scene,
> See Coronations rise on ev'ry green;
> Before you pass th'imaginary sights   35
> Of Lords, and Earls, and Dukes, and garter'd Knights;
> While the spread Fan o'ershades your closing eyes;
> Then give one flirt, and all the vision flies.
> Thus vanish sceptres, coronets, and balls,
> And leave you in lone woods, or empty walls.   40
>   So when your slave, at some dear, idle time,
> (Not plagu'd with headachs, or the want of rhime)
> Stands in the streets, abstracted from the crew,
> And while he seems to study, thinks of you:
> Just when his fancy points your sprightly eyes,   45
> Or sees the blush of soft *Parthenia* rise,
> *Gay* pats my shoulder, and you vanish quite;
> Streets, chairs, and coxcombs rush upon my sight;
> Vext to be still in town, I knit my brow,
> Look sow'r, and hum a tune—as you may now.   50

It takes no very profound analysis to perceive that the distinctive pleasure given by this lively poem derives from a series of contrasts. The poem consists of five sections of paragraphs, of approximately equal length (1–10, 11–22, 23–30, 31–40, 41–50), and it proceeds by showing a different picture in each: each piquantly different from its predecessor. A glimpse of 'fair *Zephalinda*', in flight from 'the world', is followed by the detailed evocation of quite another world, that of

> Old-fashion'd halls, dull aunts, and croaking rooks.

with fast and prayers in her 'godly garret' after seven o'clock in the evening. Then broad comedy supervenes, with the innocent flirtation with the 'coarse' and 'hearty' Squire. The tone changes completely as we identify with the romantic girl dreaming of 'triumphs' and 'imaginary sights' picking up the reference in the title to the recent Coronation. The last turn in the emotional sequence introduces the poet himself. The implied sympathy with the girl which has pervaded the poem now emerges from the amused detachment of the narrative and is revealed as tender love and longing. The delicate playing to and fro between the real and the imaginary which characterises this poem is illustrated in the simultaneous parallel and contrast between the girl and the poet. The parallel is drawn clearly. *She* indulges in day-dreams

> Of Lords, and Earls, and Dukes, and garter'd Knights

but she gives her fan a 'flirt', and reality breaks in. *He* 'stands in the streets', seeming to 'study', but really thinking of her, when corresponding to her 'flirt' of the fan,

> *Gay* pats my shoulder . . .

and she disappears. But the contrast is equally firm. They are both dreamers, but while *he* is dreaming of *her*, *she* is not dreaming of *him*. *She* is in the country, longing to be back in Town—but not because she wants to be with him; *he* is in Town, but 'vext' to be there, because he wants to be with *her*.

The aesthetic effect of simultaneous similarity and difference can be illustrated in the verse movement. Everything, of course, is under the control of the regular Popean five-beat couplet; yet the changes of tempo dramatically mark out the changing of moods in this opalescent miniature. Opening with an *allegro con brio*, the epistle sweeps along, with one line that seems to contain no pause at all:

> Thus from the world fair *Zephalinda* flew

but in line 10 slows down drastically:

> She sigh'd not that they stay'd, but that She went.

The pause at 'She went' is enhanced by the repetition of the words at the opening of the next section (the comma here seems more appropriate that Lonsdale's omission of it in the text in his *Oxford Book*). The adagio of the second edition is epitomised in that line of nine words which seems interminable:

> Count the slow clock, and dine exact at noon

(and the slow clock seems to go on clacking in the second part of the hemistich). 'That's the way to heav'n' could have come appropriately as the resonant end of a pious adjuration. But everything changes at once with the immediately following scherzo of the Squire, with his gun and birds, his 'smacking buss', 'hollowing' from the stable like his hound: blunt monosyllables, emphatically masculine vocabulary; all is 'coarse' (but amiable), down to the final joke (in line 30).

If the epistle had ended here, its probable effect on the modern reader who finds it appealing might be similar to the effect of the passage in Sheridan's *School for Scandal* (1777), which it perhaps suggested.

> *Sir Peter Teazle* Yes, yes, madam, you were then in a somewhat humbler style—the daughter of a plain country squire. Recollect, Lady Teazle, when I first saw you sitting at your tambour, in pretty figured linen gown, with a bunch of keys at your side, your hair combed smooth over a roll, and your apartment hung round with fruits in worsted, of your own working.
> *Lady Teazle* Oh yes! I remember it very well, and a curious life I led. My daily occupation to inspect the dairy, superintend the poultry, make extacts from the family receipt book, and comb my aunt Deborah's lap-dog.
> . . . . .
> And then, you know, my evening amusements! To draw patterns for ruffles, which I had not material to make: to play Pope Joan with the curate; to read a

sermon to my aunt; or to be stuck down to an old spinet to strum my father to
sleep after a fox-chase.

[From Act II, Scene 1]

The charm of this for moderns may be greater than it was for Sheridan's
contemporaries: what for them may have sounded symbolic of dullness and
dreariness may to us seem pretty, picturesque, and nostalgic. Similarly with
Pope's evocation of a milieu which alternates pietism and bucolic vulgarity:
his verse makes it seem attractive to us who live in Philip Larkin's world,
disjointed, unserious, yet not cheerful either. But surely the last two sections
of the epistle add something which goes deeper than the first three, and shows
the whole piece as the work of a major poet, quite un-portentous, but deeply
engaged? The bringing in of the poet himself and his love for the girl internalise
the narrative, and create a total effect which is not easy to sum up.

Why, after all, have twentieth-century readers been taken with this poem,
and (implicitly) discriminated in its favour against other early poems that
obviously are related to it, such as 'To Miss Blount, with the works of
Voiture', or the Epistle to Jervas? It is notoriously difficult to say what
makes a poem good, or outstanding (fault-finding is much easier). But in all
probability what has made *this* poem stand out is the vivid evocation of the
Young Lady (as the recipient of the Epistle was called when it was first
published in Pope's *Works* of 1717). Now since she is so fully 'there' the poem
is self-sufficient (it might be said). There is no need to go beyond the fictional
mode. If we need points of reference outside the poem, we need only think
about some young 'Sloane' of our acquaintance, and imagine (or remember)
what it is like to be her 'slave'.

If the reading of poetry is just a private pleasure, that is clearly all that
needs to be said. There is a great deal in favour of the commonly expressed
view that the reader of poetry is better off without academic rigmarole and
scholarly commentary. The difficulty in the view that one should just enjoy
poetry and not think about it comes when we realise that people who enjoy
poetry sometimes want to *talk* about it. But in that case thinking about poetry
(i.e. criticism, scholarship, &c.) comes back again, for surely it will not be
held that it is possible to talk about poetry without thinking?

This is a general reflection which, if correct, holds good for all poems and
works of art without exception. In the case of the 'Coronation Epistle',
moreover, there are grounds for thinking that this is a poem which is not
quite so self-sufficient as it seems. Apart from the bio-literary problem about
the Young Lady (not identified as 'Miss Blount' until the 1735 edition of the
Works) the very first word of the Epistle is an invitation to deconstructive
unravelling, for here we have a simile that doesn't compare: As some fond
virgin . . . &c. down to Thus . . . (line 7). Of course for most readers the 'As'
(i.e., the analogical status of what follows) is rapidly elided, and may well
have been so for Pope himself. At any rate scholars who insist that the so-
called 'suppressed lines' of this poem (included by Butt under the title 'Epistle
to a Lady' at his page 308) could not have ever been an alternative ending or
coda are apt to point out the impossible indecorum of their being addressed

to the 'fond virgin' of the opening lines. But if the sustained comparison in the opening is to be taken seriously then the Young Lady is *not* a 'fond virgin'. In his discussion of Dryden's *Eleonora* Samuel Johnson says of the opening lines

As, when some great and gracious monarch dies, &c.

that 'there is so much likeness in the initial comparison that there is no illustration. As a king would be lamented, Eleonora was lamented.' But here there is a question not merely of likeness, but of identity!

The problem about the tone of the poem which this raises, and its relation or lack of relation to the so-called 'suppressed lines', may now be approached from another side. Instead of taking the poem by itself and as it stands we may attempt to reconstruct something of its original 'setting in life' (*Sitz im Leben*). First there is the question of form. Although the 'Coronation Epistle' seems to have no analogue in Horace's poetry it cannot be doubted that, as in the other epistles to 'Miss Blount', and in the late 'Epistle to a Lady', Pope is writing in his own personal variation of Horace's satiric-epistolary mode (cf. Brower, 1959, ch. VI). In this mode his view of women has always been the subject of controversy from his own time to ours, and hostile things have been said about it, for instance by James Reeves (1969): 'Pope's attitude to women is cynical, and breathes the all-male atmosphere of the clubs and coffee-houses' (p 89). But it may be that this does not take sufficient allowance of the realities of the society and culture in which Pope was writing his compliments, and his sermons, to women. As Pat Rogers puts it (1974), he is telling them 'how to succeed in a man's world' (p 91), a world in which they were admired, respected, teased, patronised and cajoled by men, but not treated with intellectual respect. Pope can be seen not as reinforcing the constrictions of the polite code but showing, from the inside, how to defeat them.

However that may be, there appears to be a continuity in the 'Blount' poems which makes them immediately relevant to the interpretation of the 'Coronation Epistle'. They begin with the poem that was first entitled 'To a Young LADY, with the Works of Voiture', included by Pope in his first miscellany of 1712. This poem appeared in the first collected edition of Pope's *Works* (1717), and was there directly associated with another epistle immediately following it: 'To the same, On her leaving the Town after the Coronation', i.e., the 'coronation Epistle'. On the face of it, then, the Young Lady who was given the Works of Voiture is the same person who left the Town after the Coronation. She remained anonymous till the 1735 edition of the *Works*, when the title of the first epistle was changed to 'To Miss Blount, with the Works of Voiture'. The title of the second epistle was unaltered. All the biographers of Pope record that he early made the acquaintance of two sisters, Teresa and Martha Blount, grand-daughters of an elderly neighbour, Anthony Eaglefield. The younger, Martha, was to become Pope's dearest and lifelong friend. He quarrelled with Teresa, and by 1735 there can be no doubt that in Pope's circle 'Miss Blount' would have been taken to mean Martha.

Certainly Martha Blount is the addressee of the late 'Epistle to a Lady', which, as Maynard Mack (1985) puts it 'shows what happens to the Belindas . . . when the rose is blowing or has blown'. Mack calls it 'a guided tour of a gallery of female portraits, made in company with Martha Blount' (p 627). After the famous and terrible passage that begins

> See how the world its Veterans rewards

the two words that follow, says Mack, 'come like an awakening from nightmare':

> Ah Friend! to dazzle let the Vain design,
> To raise the heart and thought and touch the Heart be thine!
> That Charm shall grow, while what fatigues the Ring
> Flaunts and goes down, an unregarded thing.
> So when the Sun's broad beam has tir'd the sight,
> All mild ascends the Moon's more sober light.
> Serene in Virgin Modesty she shines,
> And unobserv'd the glaring Orb declines.
>
> (249–56)

This admonitory tone had already been heard in the portrait of 'Pamela' in the epistle 'with the Works of Voiture', where, in accordance with Pope's usual method of contrast, it is the foil to Voiture's trifling with life:

> The Gods, to curse *Pamela* with her Pray'rs
> Gave the gilt Coach and dappled *Flanders* mares.
> The shining Robes, rich Jewels, Beds of State,
> And to compleat her Bliss, a Fool for Mate.
> She glares in *Balls*, *Front-boxes*, and the *Ring*,
> A vain, unquiet, glitt'ring, wretched Thing!
> Pride, Pomp, and State but reach her outward Part,
> She sighs, and is no *Dutchess* at her Heart.
>
> (49–56)

We do not have a clear sense in the 'Voiture' epistle of the supposed auditress; she might be an ideal figure, or she might be the Martha Blount of the late poem. But no one supposes that Martha Blount is the Young Lady of the 'Coronation Epistle'. The general agreement of biographers today is that she is Teresa Blount—or else a purely fictitious person.

The evidence that she is Teresa Blount is not conclusive, but reasonably convincing. There is evidence that in the early manuscript the seventh line of the Epistle originally was:

> So fair *Teresa* gave the town a view

or perhaps

> Thus from the world the fair *Teresa* flew.

Scholars have also traced the names 'Zephalinda' and 'Parthenia' to a correspondence between the Blount sisters and a man called Moor (or Moore), abut 1713, in which Teresa is 'Zephalinda' and Martha 'Parthenissa' (*sic*). Pope knew this correspondence, and there is evidence that in the original manuscript in line 46 Martha was alluded to:

> Or see the blush of *Parthenissa* rise.

Martha was notorious for her shyness and blushing (see Mack, pp 242–3). Later Pope changed the name, in subsequent editions, to 'fair Parthenia', so sparing her blushes.

But why bother who the Young Lady of the Coronation Epistle 'really' was? Isn't it just a matter for gossip, or antiquarianism? Certainly a reader of literary interests must feel some qualms about venturing near the quagmire of Pope's relationship with the Blount sisters. Mack says that 'so many of Pope's letters to them are undated and undatable that to go about mapping the ups and downs of their relationship is like walking through a minefield' (p 340). The only way, it seems, to preserve some kind of coherence in this series of poems is to treat 'Miss Blount' as a composite figure, 'Martha Teresa Blount', as in Jervas's portrait of 1716, where the two young women are side by side, one the virginal Parthenissa, holding the laurel associated with Apollo, the other holding a wreath of myrtle sacred to Venus.

No wonder Norman Ault (1949) complains of Pope's 'wilful mystification' (p 49) about the Young Lady. Undoubtedlty this was a trait in Pope's character. But the explanation for it may not be wholly psychological. It may have derived from the habitual necessities for various kinds of subterfuge, given the numerous legal, political and social restrictions on Catholics at this time, comparable to those imposed on Jews in Hitler's Germany. And as for the mystification about these poems, we may see in it Pope's way of vindicating the autonomy of poetry, the extraterritoriality of the imagination. He wanted to say something serious to, and about, women which the badinage of Voiture &c. would not have permitted him to do; to suggest the presence of the real, particular, personal world out of which he wrote; but without being tied down to it.

If we decide to accept the composite status of the Young Lady it is possible, finally, to see the 'suppressed lines' in a somewhat different light. This is the text as given by Butt.

Epistle to a Lady

In this strange Town a different Course we take,
Refine ourselves to Spirit, for your Sake.

For Want of you, we spend our random Wit on
The first we find with Needham, Brooks, or Briton.
Hackney'd in Sin, we beat about the Town,   5
And like sure Spaniels, at first Scent lie down,
Were Virtue's self in Silks,—faith keep away!
Or Virtue's Virtue scarce would last a Day.

Thus, Madam, most Men talk, and some Men do:
The rest is told you in a Line or two.   10
Some strangely wonder you're not fond to marry—
A double Jest still pleases sweet Sir Harry—
Small-Pox is rife, and *Gay* in dreadful fear—
The good Priests whisper—Where'S the Chevalier?
Much in your Absence B___'s Heart endures,   15
And if poor *Pope* is cl-pt, the Fault is yours.

The Twickenham editors were not sure whether to accept these lines as the
work of Pope, since few of his early editors had felt able to print them. But
it is difficult to believe that any other poet of the time could have been capable
of these incisive, balanced and compact comic lines. The last line is almost a
signature! Yet as a conclusion to the 'Coronation Epistle' they seem quite
incongruous. Ralph N Maud (1958) admits that the lines are probably by
Pope, but holds that they were never part of that poem but were part of some
other poem. 'Zephalinda' of the Epistle and 'Madam' of the additional lines
seem to him different people. Zephalinda has only begun to recognise her
natural charms; her flirtation with the Squire is totally innocent. 'Madam' is
a sophisticate, who is expected to enjoy *double-entendres*, and to take it as a
compliment that her frustrated friends have to seek solace from such as
'Needham' (a brothel-keeper). Maud suggests that the world of the additional
lines is the same as that of such manuscript poems as 'A Farewell to London'
(*c*.May 1715) and 'The Court Ballad' (December 1716). The lines could be
the end of a verse-letter to one of the ladies-in-waiting. Pope knew Mary
Bellenden and Mary (or Molly) Lepell intimately. The 'Coronation Epistle'
is virtually self-sufficient in its fictional mode; whereas the additional lines
are full of specific references and topical allusions. The *persona* of the poet is
now that of the man-about-town, writing in a knowing jocular manner, quite
unlike the 'slave' he has just portrayed.

These arguments have some force. And no one, if only on aesthetic grounds,
is going to suggest that these lines should be printed in future as the authentic
close of the 'Coronation Epistle'. But in taking that view it has to be recognised that it rests ultimately on an aesthetic, a critical, decision by *us*, i.e.
modern readers or editors. If we take a non-biographical view of the 'Blount'
poems they can be seen as illustrating the shifting moods and inconsistencies
in the relations between men and women. Pope likes to dwell on the traditional
theme of female mutability: taking his metaphors from painting, he exhorts
himself to

Come then, the colours and the ground prepare!
Dip in the Rainbow, trick her off in Air,

> Chuse a firm Cloud, before it fall, and in it
> Catch, ere she change, the Cynthia of this minute.
> (Epistle II, To a Lady. Of the Characters of Women, 16–19)

But he also likes to expatiate on the inconsistencies of men, and himself in particular. 'What is Man altogether, but one mighty inconsistency,' he wrote to Caryll. In the 'Farewell to London. In the Year 1715' he paradoxically depicts himself as

> Still idle, with a busy Air,
> Deep Whimsies to contrive;
> The gayest Valetudinaire,
> Most thinking Rake alive.

It seems impossible to rule out the suggestion that the 'suppressed lines' continue the sequence of contrasts which the canonical version of the Coronation Epistle' consists. Wise as Pope may have been to finally exclude them, they serve a purpose in reminding us that cynicism as well as idealisation, matters of fact and artifices, *all* belong to 'reality'. Protesting against the analytical tradition in Anglo-American philosophy, Jacques Derrida exclaims: 'As though literature, theater, deceit, infidelity, hypocrisy, infelicity, parasitism, and the simulation of real life were not part of real life!'. We might think of these words when, now and then, we read through the 'Coronation Epistle'—and add its 'coda'.

References

Ault, N *New Light on Pope* (London: Methuen, 1949)

Brower, R A *Alexander Pope the Poetry of Allusion* (Oxford: Oxford UP, 1959)

Derrida, Jacques *Limited Inc.*

Mack, Maynard *Life of Pope* (Yale: Yale UP, 1985)

Maud, R N *Review of English Studies*, IX (1958), 146–51

Reeves, James *Commitment to Poetry* (London: Heinemann, 1969)

——*Reputation and Writings of Alexander Pope* (London: Heinemann, 1976)

Rogers, Pat *The Augustan Vision* (London: Methuen, 1978)

Sherburn, George (ed) *The Correspondence of Alexander Pope* (Oxford: Oxford UP, 1956).

13

Pope's Mediaeval Heroine:
Eloisa to Abelard

RDSJACK

Pope's *Eloisa to Abelard* has met with a mixed critical reception. Particularly, there is disagreement over its literary quality and over what, precisely, are the nature and the outcome of the heroine's dilemma. This confusion in part stems from the complexity of the poem's origins. It is after all based on a classical literary form and celebrates a mediaeval heroine whose history Pope derived from a very free eighteenth-century version of the original Latin letters. Establishing the nature and relative importance of these varied influences helps to clarify some of the issues involved.

In terms of genre *Eloisa* unquestionably stems from the Heroic Epistle. In the Preface to the 1717 *Collected Works* in which it first appeared Pope writes:

> All that is left us is to recommend our productions by the imitation of the Ancients: and it will be found true, that in every age, the highest character for sense and learning has been obtain'd by those who have been most indebted to them.

(I, 7)

The Heroic Epistle was a form with a clear classical pedigree both admired and practised in his own day. As such it was an obvious choice for the young Pope. Its conventions lie behind *Eloisa* and readers who lament the poem's forced 'rhetoric' should remember that Ovid's *Heroides* are also full of extravagant rhetorical flourishes.

Two features of the Heroic Epistle, one obvious the other less so, are of prime importance in establishing the criteria governing Eloisa's conflict. The traditions of the Heroic Epistle provide for an emotional, often erotic argument. The context however is almost always both practical and persuasive. So, when Pettit claims that the 'conflict in the *Eloisa* is entirely within the heroine' (Pettit 1964, p 302) his opinion is at odds with the usual practice of Pope's chosen genre. As Jacobson argues, that form 'has the advantages of both monologue and dialogue' (Jacobson 1974, p 337). It therefore draws in the situation and the character of the addressee as well. Pope may, of course, have chosen to ignore this convention but the comparative evidence strongly suggests that he did not. A study of his major source, Hughes' 1713 version of the *Letters*, reveals that many arguments used by Eloisa are in fact based on letters there attributed to Abelard. The conflict, although largely with herself, is usually determined to some degree by the way she believes her correspondent views it.

In all versions of the *Letters* Eloisa does present her amorous torment in a manner designed to encourage her lover to return or, at worst, to reply. Equally the elegiac and erotic appeals of the Classical heroines of the Heroic Epistle—even their most extreme protestations such as Penelope's threat that soon she will die—are usually not stratagems of despair but designed to effect in the lover a change of heart. This intensely practical line of argument is emphasised in Pope's poem.

Pope chose, however, to set within this classical form a heroine who 'flourish'd in the twelfth Century' (II, 298). Having earlier translated lines from Boethius and imitated three Chaucerian works he was well aware of mediaeval literary conventions and the distinctive Christian world view fostered in that period. Part of his 'Invention' in *Eloisa* lies in translating a dilemma, shared in its essentials with mythic classical heroines, into terms consistent for a mediaeval prioress. The degree to which this alteration was effected should not be gauged through a comparison with the original Latin letters for Pope did not possess these. Measured against Hughes' version, *Eloisa* emerges as a thorough attempt to return both hero and heroine to the mediaeval world. It is not simply that Pope ignores entirely Hughes' vision of Abelard as a late-seventeenth or early-eighteenth-century gentleman, restores to Eloisa her intellect and dismisses the lecherous maids and avaricious music masters created by Hughes' fertile imagination. He returns to the mediaeval categories of self-examination ('grace and nature, virtue and passion') (II, 298) and to the hierarchy of that categorisation (see Kalmey 1968, p 169). Eloisa knows that according to the Christian creed her situation must not only be measured against spiritual as well as practical and emotional criteria but that these spiritual values ought to have priority.

If the three major—and often conflicting—criteria are thus established, a fourth consideration of more than peripheral importance is suggested both by source study and considerations of genre. When Pope decided to imitate Ovid's *Heroides* he characteristically chose *Sappho Phaonis*, the one in which the heroine's amorous problems were linked 'in a lower key' to a 'concern with her role as artist' (Jacobson 1974, p 289). Eloisa is not a creative writer in this sense but as the wife and mistress of an outstanding man of letters she needs to prove her value as a worthwhile literary correspondent. In Pope's poem she draws our attention to the epistolary form much more often than she does in Hughes. She discusses in some detail the differences between literary and divine creation as understood in the Middle Ages. She attributes to herself the sensitivity of the artist and discusses those very qualities of Memory and Fancy which in heightened form mark out the artistic personality. Most significantly of all, her argument begins and ends with the problem of how her fate may most effectively be communicated. Brendan O'Hehir may well be right in labelling Eloisa the 'only major poem written in the first person in which the speaker is not to be labeled as, in some way, Alexander Pope the Poet' (O'Hehir 1964, ρ 313) but the chosen dramatic voice does introduce a literary dimension to her complex testimony.

Indeed, I think even more can be claimed. D W Robertson Jr in his analysis of the original letters rightly notes that they are a 'fabulous narrative' in the sense that 'the characters are usually exemplifications of ideas and are never 'personalities', and their actions are for the most part disguised developments of an underlying theme' (Robertson 1974, p 101). While, clearly, Pope's Eloisa does emerge as a powerful personality, the poem, particularly at the end, seeks to broaden the significance of her struggle in a recognisably 'exemplary' fashion. Given that the mythic status of the classical heroines of the Heroic Epistle gives their fates a degree of universality, it is at least plausible to argue that Pope has ingeniously used mediaeval literary conventions to supply what, in his classical models, was inherent in character definition. In so doing he also, unknowingly, brought his epistle closer to its original Latin source.

The analysis which follows seeks to discuss the poem against this background and in particular to discover how literary considerations are worked into an argument where practical, emotional and spiritual criteria at once define and compound Eloisa's dilemma. Such an approach may help to answer the vexed questions of whether she is properly to be regarded as a mediaeval heroine and whether she resolves her problem on any or all of these levels.

Abelard's letter (lines 1–58)

Eloisa's chance discovery of Abelard's letter initiates the correspondence in all versions. For Hughes it works simply as explication and provides a dramatic opening. For Pope its function is more complex. The letter not only introduces considerations of literature in relation to creativity but is at once related to the practical, erotic and spiritual problems faced by Eloisa.

On the simplest level, Eloisa values letters as practical aids:

> Heav'n first taught letters for some wretch's aid,
> Some banish'd lover, or some captive maid.
>
> (51–2)

As such she intends to use hers. Letters may enable her to win back Abelard. This hope, however, throughout the section is associated with the physical union of which Abelard's castration has for ever deprived her. As she warms to this topic the idea of letters as a substitute for such a union is suggested by vocabulary and imagery with erotic overtones.

> Yet write, oh write me all, that I may join
> Griefs to thy griefs, and eccho sighs to thine.
>
> (41–2)

Ah more than share it! Give me all thy grief.
(50)

Speed the soft intercourse from soul to soul
And waft a sigh from Indus to the Pole.
(57–8)

But the opening section also introduces a plea for letters as a means of creation and explores it on the highest, spiritual level. It was a commonly held mediaeval belief that literary endeavour was a shadow of God's act of creation. The text which formed the basis for this understanding (John 1.1: In Principio erat Verbum) also laid stress on the word as name (John 1.1: Et Deus erat Verbum). In Hughes no such connection is made. Eloisa's first letter mentions names briefly. Emotional upset at the sight of them is one of her reasons for replying but that is all. Pope not only pays much more attention to Abelard's name in particular, he introduces a more complex reaction from Eloisa. Abelard's name becomes the word which recreates her out of coldness into 'long-forgotten heat'. His 'fatal name' brings her from silence to the creativity of writing. But it is also 'that well-known name' which re-creates all her miseries by bringing back memories of him through his writings.

If the opening paragraphs establish the heroine as writer and relate the letters to the three levels on which her unique problem must be posed and answered, they also establish that whatever hope may be gained from them, they are in each realm substitutes. Practically the letter is not written to her but to console a male friend; erotically the idea of union is a mere metaphor, and spiritually all human writing stands at one remove from God's act of creation.

This is only the start of the problem. Given the mediaeval, religious context, it is the spiritual judgement which is the highest and, while Eloisa's worldly hopes are encouraged by the letter, all the mediaeval categories of self-examination re-introduced by Pope suggest that she is wilfully choosing lower, worldly values. For, set against the pathetic picture of the forlorn prioress tenderly remembering her love, is a structure of conflict in which the tears and prayers associated with penance either become worldly in their focus or are opposed to the powers of passion:

In vain lost *Eloisa* weeps and prays,
Her heart still dictates, and her hand obeys.
(15–16)

Still rebel nature holds out half my heart;
Nor pray'rs nor fasts its stubborn pulse restrain,
Nor tears, for ages, taught to flow in vain.
(26–8)

As expressions of affection for Abelard, they may assist the act of writing but as the mystic language of spiritual communication they are set—here and throughout the poem—in opposition to the primary creative process. Thus, despite the many positive associations connected with Eloisa's newfound life and fire, judged against the severer theological ideals embraced by Abelard each worldly advance implies spiritual regression. Love and fame may be the 'best' but only of 'passions'. Religion's teaching may be 'stern' but it still presents truths however unpalatable.

It is no coincidence, therefore, that her ecstatic decision to write (49–58) is couched in language which consistently uses religious terms to define worldly aims—

Heaven	— to aid some banish'd lover
Inspires	— (earthly) love
Faithful	— to (love's) fires
Soul	— speed the soft intercourse

Indeed Eloisa only finds joy in the substitute device of letters because her continued love for Abelard prevents mystic communion with God through prayers and penitential tears. The spiritually reconciled Abelard is thus dramatically made aware of how far Eloisa is from sharing his state and of who is ultimately responsible for her misery.

Eclectic biography (lines 59–176)

Eloisa now moves on to an account of their relationship, highlighting in successive paragraphs the seduction, the joys of love, Abelard's castration, her initiation into the Church, life at the Paraclete and finally the Death which will end all. Neither the Latin letters nor Hughes' version of them orders this material so economically. Equally, neither uses the material to present so subtle a condemnation of Abelard. In the Latin letters Eloisa is concerned with boosting a lover whom they both consistently view as her superior. In Hughes, the element of accusation is present but not so persistent. The biographical section of *Eloisa*, which uses material from the 1713 letters attributed to Abelard as well as those of Eloisa, is carefully designed to awaken both pity and guilt.

Eloisa begins with the vision of Abelard as false teacher, a role he often attributes to himself in Hughes' letters:

'I was earnest to teach you vain sciences.'

'I have thought myself hitherto an abler master to instil vice than to teach virtue.'
(Hughes 1901, pp 44, 50)

He becomes the experienced seducer of a young innocent who was ready to see in him a type of God. It was Abelard the scholar and artist who reversed this process through his skills in dialectic and song. The subtlety of his method is cleverly suggested by words capable of both positive and negative meanings:

And truths divine came *mended* from that tongue.
(66)

But the retreat with which the paragraph ends is unambiguously described. As she runs 'back thro' the paths of pleasing sense', the saintly joys become 'dim and remote' while Abelard sets himself up as the idol to be adored in God's place. The argument is presented by inverting the Ficinian progression of the 'strada al Dio'. Spiritual joys are rejected for the pleasures of physical love. Spiritual and erotic values again clash but in such a way that Abelard's guilt is throughout confirmed.

From this Pope moves in the next paragraph to a description of the genuine love they experienced:

> When love is liberty, and nature, law:
> All then is full, possessing, and possest.
>
> (93–4)

There is no obvious attempt to diminish the perfection of this moment. Eloisa accepts that they have shared the highest of earthly joys. But in fact only lines 91–6 describe this perfection and do so by using a vision of Nature as uncontrolled freedom, opposed vigorously by the Fathers and dramatically rejected in Milton's *Comus*. The first eighteen lines re-state (without the theological precision of the Latin letters) Eloisa's arguments against marriage and her hypothetical sacrifice of Caesar's love in favour of Abelard's. But while, in the Latin letters, these views were advanced as part of a theological debate and in Hughes as proof of Eloisa's determination, in Pope's poem they complement the negative picture of Abelard as seducer and false teacher with the positive one of Eloisa as selfless martyr to temporal love. The glorifying of that love becomes another means of awakening Abelard to a sense of duty. And in the last two lines even that glory is modified by a parenthesis comparing it unfavourably to spiritual love and a change of perspective which—in essence—obliterates it:

> This sure is bliss (if bliss on earth there be)
> And once the lot of *Abelard* and me.
>
> (97–8)

The horror of the castration, which follows, is marked out by a more urgent tone and a staccato style characterised by exclamations and rhetorical questions. It ends with a clever variation on the traditional mediaeval use of 'Occupatio'. Eloisa is unable to continue the description not because she lacks adequate literary powers but because of the fierce emotions aroused by memory of the event. The role she adopts is still that of selfless lover but she moves, at least in hypothesis, from passive martyrdom to active martial defence of the helpless Abelard:

> Where, where was *Eloise*? her voice, her hand,
> Her ponyard, had oppos'd the dire command.
>
> (101–2)

What this carefully selected biographical sequence has achieved so far is to set positive visions of Eloisa as martyr and defender against negative visions of Abelard as seducer of body and mind. But these opposed visions are all used to underline a single message—the unreasoning, irrevocable nature of her love. The castration episode makes any physical solution to this impossible and renders her plight at once more desperate and less natural. By moving immediately from it to the memory of her vows, Pope introduces a subtle psychological argument suited to the new situation.

This incident is the one which Hughes' Abelard regrets most unreservedly. He confesses at some length that his decision to commit Eloisa to God before doing so himself revealed jealousy and false faith. Pope's Eloisa focuses on this guilt by stressing the poignant irony of their situation. The man who hypocritically drew her away from God and then forced her into a marriage to which she was firmly opposed now hypocritically marries her to that God against her will and in a state of self-confessed spiritual blindness for which he is largely responsible.

But the argument from guilt is complemented by an argument from love, which is equally ironic. At the moment when he ceases to be a full lover, Eloisa appeals to him as just that. The word 'come', with its sexual undertones, leads into a sensual description cut short because he can no longer complete the act of love. To counter this, she is willing to retreat into the world of imagination, using the qualities of the artist as a substitute for reality—

> Give all thou canst—and let me dream the rest.
> (124)

And if he proves obdurate to either the claims of guilt or pity, there is a third ironic appeal—to duty. Having depicted the depths of her spiritual confusion as she drinks the 'poison' of sensual pleasure now incapable of gratification, she suggests that here is his opportunity to take on the role of true teacher. The horrific uniqueness of her situation, thus affords the once false tutor an opportunity to become her true, spiritual guide.

It is important to notice that while all these arguments again combine practical, erotic and spiritual considerations, it is the last—the clearest appeal to Abelard as man of God—which leads into the longest of all the biographical sections. This deals with Eloisa's life among the nuns at the Paraclete. In it spiritual considerations become paramount and the frame of reference broadens from Eloisa herself to the convent as a whole. But, precisely because this appeal is, at least on the surface, the least worldly it is the most likely to bring some practical success. The severely ascetic Abelard did respond to this call, first through letters and later through visits. And D W Robertson Jr perceptively notes that one of the reasons for this was that it offered him a means to fame now that his scholastic career was effectively finished:

> The new nunnery gave him, at last, something useful to do. He could make little

progress with his monks at St. Gildas, but he could help Héloise in a great many ways.

(Robertson 1974, p 85)

Certainly, it is in this section that Eloisa makes her most direct appeal for Abelard's return, setting it in the context of serving others rather than herself:

Ah think at least thy flock deserves thy care.
(129)

But any optimism that may seem to be implied by this request is severely modified by the fact that the gulf between Abelard's spirituality and Eloisa's worldliness (accentuated by the castration) is still widening. The Paraclete section shows Eloisa accepting the superiority of spiritual values. She also accepts that Abelard is reconciled with God and so shares these values. On this level her argument is a confident one. She returns to the vision of him as a teacher, which had opened the biographical section. The man who had guided her away from God may now lead the Nuns to God. But the counter-pointing of the two situations is carried further. Abelard has introduced her innocence to worldly ways and then deserted her. Now he has taken the nuns 'in early youth' away from the world, only to desert them as well. The single consistent factor is his retreat from responsibility; the only solution, the very return which Eloisa craves.

If he does so out of duty for the nuns, the picture of Eloisa suggests that the challenge of recovering her may test even his great talents. Through subtle contrasts between her state and that of the sisters, she emphasises that her real reasons for wishing his return are still almost exclusively worldly; that when she looks at Nature it becomes infused with her repressed sexual desires and that she has passed beyond communion into a silence presaging death. Most importantly, her sense of desertion is more acute than that felt by the others and imaginatively his place has already been taken by Black Melancholy.

So the 'Biography' ends on a predominantly bleak note, highlighting the distance which separates the lovers geographically and spiritually. But the situation is not hopeless and Eloisa has not given up her attempts at persuasion. In the Paraclete section she has recognised the superiority of spiritual values; she has included the first direct plea for a return and used the very extremity of her own state as a challenge well suited to appeal to Abelard's known intellectual arrogance. In fact, any expression of despair is reserved for the discussion on Death which follows. The mixing of her 'cold dust' with his is a solution presaging defeat on all levels. It implies her failure practically to re-establish re-union in other ways. The imagery of coldness and the extinction of flames signals the end of that erotic love which has been the reason for her continued endurance. Finally, without any vision of joys beyond the grave it is the negation of Christian hope.

Memory, Fancy and Ideas (lines 177–302)

The account of the battle for her soul which follows is still part of the persuasive process. It is Abelard's continued absence which drives her from fact to fancy as she seeks to find some comfort after the failure of the biography. Relying increasingly on the power of imagination she first continues the device of contrast opposing her state unfavourably with the Nuns and Abelard.

The contrast with the Nuns centres first on the power of Memory. Abelard in Hughes' version was the one who most often discussed this problem, so Pope is once again allowing Eloisa to voice concerns drawn from the evidence of her lover. On the simplest level, her contention is that the biography just recounted makes it impossible for her to break free into a new purity:

> Of all affliction taught a lover yet,
> 'Tis sure the hardest science to forget!
> (189–90)

The Nuns, by contrast, have nothing to remember. Their state is also summed up by the word 'forget'.

> The world forgetting, by the world forgot.
> (208)

But in neither instance does that word have its usual modern sense. 'Forgetting' means a positive choice and so comes close to 'rejecting'; 'forgot' implies the innocence of withdrawal from all worldly temptation.

For both mediaeval and neoclassical philosophers, Memory's positive function was the ordering of experience. In the earlier period it was viewed as ordering the universe, in the later merely the individual. Misused in either case it brought chaos. As a writer, Eloisa not only employs Memory to order her material, she uses antithetical constructions in the first two paragraphs to underline that literary control. The same rhetorical technique highlights contrasting states. Applied to her own psychological state it is used to present irreconcilable oppositions. For the Vestals, on the other hand, the oppositions become part of a complementary harmony. In each case too there is an attempt to define precisely in order to arrive at the most accurate picture possible. But while each detail recalled for the Nuns contributes to an orderly pattern, the much greater energy devoted to pinning down the nuances of her own state results in a chaos of unconnected or self-defeating passions, only just contained by the listing techniques adopted to express them.

Her misuse of Memory means that its obverse side, future hope, can only express itself in images of warfare (Abelard against God; Heaven against fire) and incompletion (the failed consummation of marriage with either Abelard or God). This is again clearly contrasted with the heavenly thought and angelic visions of the Nuns singing their 'Hymeneals' to 'sounds of heavenly harps'.

The use of Memory provides a focus for the opposition between correct literary and incorrect spiritual usage earlier noted. The concept, however, is also related to all three levels of reference. Its spiritual potential is set against its particular erotic power for Eloisa. But again there is a practical dimension, Eloisa in lamenting her misuse of the power seeks to re-awaken Abelard's own miseries. Pope this time even employs specific arguments taken from Abelard's letters in the Hughes edition:

> It is difficult in our sorrow to distinguish penitence from love. The memory of the crime and the memory of the object which has charmed us are too nearly related to be immediately separated.
>
> (Hughes 1901, p 47)

Such use of his major source again suggests that he conceived of the work as an appeal directed towards the correspondent's 'known' vulnerabilities.

Continuing to order her material carefully, Eloisa contrasts her inner life with Abelard's. But, in her most daring confession so far, she moves from conscious thought and Memory to unconscious thought and Fancy. It is no coincidence that Fancy refers to the literary imagination specifically, nor that—in dissociating it from judgement—she suggests that it is being misused on both levels. The depths to which she has been brought are now self-indulgently described and their horror ironically referred to the very vision of freedom in love and nature which she had held up as a model when enjoying the fruits of a mistress's love. Spiritually, her dreams not only welcome Daemons but find that 'guilt exalts delight'. Practically, they bring home to her how far she is from meeting her lover. Fancy alone can bring them together and even in Fancy he flees from her. Erotically, the vision is one of horror and abnormality. The natural setting in aggressive guise comes between them and prevents a rape from which she awakens shrieking.

But the full enormity of her situation lies in the fact that these nightmarish images are still preferred to reality. They remain 'soft illusions' and 'dear deceits'. That is, even knowing the viciousness and the impossibility of her yearnings, her soul is still Abelard's. Seen from this point of view the brief account of his state as she imagines it marks the emotional and spiritual nadir of the poem. To the picture of a woman ready to damn herself for the shadow of a shadow, it adds the vision of a lover who is removed from any other level of communication. Physical love is made impossible by the castration. She is dominated by emotions; he removed from them. He seems already to sit among saints in a state beyond time and sin; she is beset by devils and overcome by the world.

At each crucial moment in the argument Pope draws in a discussion on death. This device of charting spiritual progression or regression by re-introducing at successive stages the same topic is often used in mediaeval literature. It allows a character's spiritual state to be gauged by noting any changes in reaction. Eloisa's second assessment, though still persuasive in form ('Come Abelard!'), is every bit as pessimistic as the 'mixed ashes' conclusion to the biographical section. Abelard is in a sexual sense already dead through castration but he is also dead to her through having transcended the worldly problems in which she is still immersed. Memory and Fancy have not, any more than history, succeeded in bridging the vast gulf of experience which separates them.

The next major movement (lines 263–302) differs from this earlier argument in two ways. The method of vision and dream continues but there is a much more determined attempt to find a spiritual solution. Equally, Eloisa tries, however hopelessly, to find some means of reconciling the different claims made on her by Abelard and God. Although the three solutions proposed are all inadeqate for their case and seem to intensify her tragedy, she is now looking in the true direction and dealing with ultimate questions. The vision of death at the end is therefore not so bleak as the earlier ones. It promises rest and is defined in terms of the theological virtues. Hope and Faith are present. Only Love, the crucially unresolved question, is weakly represented by the adjective 'amicable'. Despite the dramatic failure of each proposed solution, Eloisa is now readier for divine aid than at any other point in the poem.

The three failed attempts at finding harmony are all drawn from Hughes' version of Abelard's first letter, where they are related to *his* confusion (Hughes 1901, p 49). Pope transfers the arguments to Eloisa and focuses them round the central concept of the 'Idea'. In *Eloisa* this can have either or both the Platonic sense of 'higher form' and Locke's sense of 'retained sensual image'. It can, therefore, work on both spiritual and temporal planes of reference. First the sensual Idea of Abelard pursues Eloisa BLOCKING her perception of God. Here he acts again as the false, seductive intermediary of the opening. Unable to find peace in this way Eloisa goes a stage further and urges Abelard to align himself with the fiends and effectively BLOT OUT the spiritual Ideas completely. These are two paths back to worldliness in which Abelard's intermediacy is destructive and would assist Eloisa towards hell. Finally she urges him to 'QUIT' her and bid adieu to the 'Long lov'd, ador'd ideas'. (As 'idea' is not capitalised, it seems likely that the reference here is solely to Locke's sensual memories.) But to leave Abelard out of count is as unreal an alternative as making him her idol. If Eloisa is to achieve salvation by meeting death in the correct spirit, she must neither wholly accept nor wholly deny the unique passion which is at the root of her dilemma.

Resolution (lines 303–366)

I have no doubt that in the conclusion Eloisa presents to Abelard a vision in which she sees herself reconciled to death in a suitably holy manner. Arguing increasingly in theological terms she answers her various problems in a recognisably mediaeval manner—by transcending them. The change of focus:

> See in her Cell sad *Eloisa* spread
> (303)

prepares us for this higher solution. Distanced, she now looks upon herself as a character within a drama she does not fully understand. Mystic aid is provided by the 'sainted maid' who builds on her earlier vision of death (rest/sleep) and makes the all-important transition from self-reliance to trust in God. Once this alteration of perspective has been achieved, hitherto insoluble conflicts fall into place. Death is at last seen in an unequivocally Christian context as a gateway into spiritual joys and the leitmotiv word 'Come', until now associated with impassioned appeals or erotic imaginings, heralds her desire to pass into Paradise. After the last moment of worldliness—the orgastic vision of lines 323–4—she finds a world view which can comprehend both God and Abelard, yet bring her peace. In this new sacramental context her lover is neither opposed to God nor a false intermediary. Instead, as priest, he is the true intermediary leading her towards divine love. On the level of communication and communion she now sees Death, the worldly ally of silence, as mystically 'all-eloquent'. Even the language of sensual pleasure ('extatic'; 'embrace') can be used to describe the joys of ascension. Such a triumph is not and cannot be granted to the heroines of the classical Heroic Epistle. Its nature and the dialectical method used to reach it go back rather to mediaeval examples such as *Everyman*.

In this state, as one freed from worldliness, Eloisa does not think of her tomb as do the heroines of the *Heroides*. It is not used as an excuse for pathos or a dire warning to the wayward lover for now it can have the exemplary force of mediaeval mythic narrative.

Specifically she sees three groups who may learn from her tale. For youthful lovers it warns against excesses of worldly passion:

> Oh may we never love as these have lov'd!
>
> (352)

To those involved in spiritual devotion it may teach the virtues of pity and forgiveness. The value of the story, then, lies in the range of people who may profit from it and from the feelings of sympathy it will evoke.

The third and final example of the tomb—to future bards—is, therefore, a wholly fitting conclusion. The letter ends as it began with a discussion of writing. The return to this question provides the circular form advocated by mediaeval writers as particularly appropriate for poetry dealing with anagogical matters. It is fitting for a writer (Eloisa) who has emphasised the power of art as a 'type' of creation and union, and whose practical aim is to retrieve her lover through correspondence. It provides a category of people who may profit from the tale but who may (unlike the others) give their love a secondary type of immortality more eloquent than the silence of stone referred to in the opening section. Finally, in a poem which is at once Eloisa's consolation to and appeal for consolation from Abelard, the bard's songs will provide spiritual solace for her however successful or unsuccessful her own petitions for a reply have been.

The battle, then, has been the battle of a twelfth-century Christian concerned not only with practical persuasion and emotional conflicts but with spiritual values. The form of the poem and the nature of the argument points to resolution through the final transcension of passion by grace in an 'exemplary' narrative. Yet, there is a sense in which it remains open-ended. Eloisa has presented Abelard with the outcome he wanted to hear. But it is so narrowly won after such a torrid debate that there is no guarantee that the end of the letter represents the end of her torment. It may well be that she has, with divine assistance, found the true way. The journey, however, has accentuated the duties he owes to her and her proneness to alternate between joyful and despairing conclusions. The ecstasy of mystic insight may indeed signal the end of conflict. It might also be a prelude to continuing doubt. The last picture of a heroic, spiritually receptive but still vulnerable soul leaves him no excuse for ignoring her appeals. Is she truly saved or has she used her own art skilfully to develop the scenario most calculated to achieve her practical aim—his own reply and eventual return? The evidence of the poem provides no clear answer and in so doing prevents Abelard washing his hands of her either as unregenerate sinner or self-sufficient saint. In the Latin letters he does reply. Faced with Pope's Eloisa he would have had even more compelling grounds for so doing.

References

Hughes, J (1713) *The Love Letters of Abelard and Heloise* H Morten (ed) (London: Temple Classics, 1901)

Jacobson, H *Ovid's Heroides* (Princeton: Princeton UP, 1974)

Kalmey, R P 'Pope's *Eloisa to Abelard* and "Those Celebrated Letters"', PQ 47 (1968), 164–78

O'Hehir, B (1964) 'Virtue and Passion: The Dialectic of *Eloisa to Abelard*', in Maynard Mack (ed) *Essential Articles for the Study of Alexander Pope* (London: Frank Cass & Company, 1964)

Pettit, H 'Pope's *Eloisa to Abelard*: An Interpretation', in Mack, op. cit.

Robertson, D W (Jr) *Abelard and Heloise* (London: Millington, 1974).

Here in the rich, the honour'd, fam'd and great,
See the false scale of Happiness complete!—

ETHIC
EPISTLES.

BY

ALEXANDER POPE Esq;

LONDON:

Printed for J. and P. KNAPTON in *Ludgate-street*.

MDCCXLVII.

14

Pope's 1747 *Ethic Epistles* And The *Essay On Man* Frontispiece: An Abandoned 'Opus Magnum'?

DONALD W NICHOL

Now that R H Griffith's bibliography has passed mandatory retirement age, Pope scholars have clamoured for a replacement.[1] Twenty years ago Keith Maslen shed light on a 'bibliographical limbo' by uncovering two previously unrecorded editions of Pope's *Essay on Man*.[2] These he compared with four other small octavo editions of *An Essay on Man* (Griffith 607, 608, 620, 631) published by John and Paul Knapton between 1745 and 1748, one of which is 'presumably piratical'. Yet another edition, entitled *Ethic Epistles*, escaped Griffith's notice in this period between Pope's death in 1744 and his 1751 *Works*. Dated 1747, *Ethic Epistles* contains *An Essay on Man*, the four *Epistles to Several Persons* and 'The Universal Prayer'.[3] The accession date of the National Library of Scotland copy is 12 July 1927; this might account for its absence from the second part of Griffith's bibliography (from 1735 to 1751) which came out in the same year.[4] While this small octavo edition of *Ethic Epistles* will have little if any bearing on the textual apparatus of the Twickenham volumes of *An Essay on Man* (III, i) and *Epistles to Several Persons* (III, ii), it nevertheless occurs at an intriguing moment in Pope bibliographical history.

Like the six *Essay on Man* editions described in Maslen's appendix (184–8), the 1747 *Ethic Epistles* bears the Knapton imprint. John and Paul Knapton were the principal booksellers of the first five Warburton editions of Pope's *Works* (1751–4).[5] No price is indicated for *Ethic Epistles*, although it probably would have sold for eighteen pence; no listings appear in *Gentleman's Magazine* or *London Magazine* (although not every *Essay on Man* edition was

[*Overleaf*, pp 220–1]
10   Frontispiece and Title Page of Pope's *Ethic Epistles* (London: 1747). By permission of the National Library of Scotland.

advertised); no record of its printing appears in the Bowyer ledgers;[6] nor is there any indication that John Wright, Henry Woodfall or William Strahan, the other main printers of Pope's works in this period, had a hand in it.[7] There are no ornaments, press figures or water marks to indicate the origin of this edition. As in Maslen's *Essay on Man* 1745c, both the frontispiece and title-page vignette of *Ethic Epistles* have been re-engraved. No mention of *Ethic Epistles* is made in the correspondence between Warburton and Knapton.[8] Without sufficient evidence, the legitimacy or piracy of the 1747 *Ethic Epistles* is impossible to determine.

While neither Griffith nor the Twickenham editors notes its existence, at least two prominent Pope scholars have known about the 1747 *Ethic Epistles*. W K Wimsatt mentions it in a footnote to a series of medallions appearing in editions of *An Essay on Man* between 1745 and 1753:

> An inferior medallion of this type [43.3] but lacking the signature of A Pond appears on the title page of a volume I once saw in the collection of Professor George Sherburn: *Ethic Epistles by Alexander Pope Esq*; *London, Printed for J and P Knapton in Ludgate-street. MDCCXLVII* (not recorded in Griffith). This volume contained the *Essay on Man* and *Moral Essays*. It had a frontispiece from Pope's design.[9]

The title-page and medallion of the National Library of Scotland copy of the 1747 *Ethic Epistles* substantiate Wimsatt's description: this unsigned profile of Pope looking left is a rougher version of the medallion by Arthur Pond ('APond f.') on the title-page of the 1745 Warburton edition of *An Essay on Man*.[10] Pope looks worse for wear in the 1747 profile: heavier facial stippling makes the poet look hirsute, his eye has become puffier, and his once sharp nose has been rounded off. Side by side, the 1745 image radiates Roman manliness while the 1747 re-engraving suggests an aftermath of drinking deep from something other than a Pierian spring.[11] One slight anachronism in Wimsatt's description needs to be clarified: the *Moral Essays* title did not exist until 1751; in the 1747 *Ethic Epistles* the half-title for the second part reads 'Ethic Epistles, The Second Book. To Several Persons'.

The 1747 text of 'Epistle to a Lady' is the shorter version—196 lines as opposed to Twickenham's 292 lines. *Ethic Epistles* lacks the portraits of 'Philomedé' (69–86), 'Atossa' (115–50) and 'Cloe' (157–98) which had been included in the 1744 'death-bed' quarto. The 'Atossa' sketch was published in 1746 as 'Verses upon the late D——ss of M———' (Griffith 613–15) with Bolingbroke's vicious footnote concerning Pope's acceptance of £1000 from the Duchess of Marlborough in exchange for the suppression of 'Atossa'. *Ethic Epistles* may have been an inept attempt to correct the balance by perpetuating the 'safer' text; if so, *Epistles to Several Persons*, supposedly

[*Overleaf*, pp 224–5]
11   Frontispiece and Title Page of Pope's *An Essay on Man* (London: 1755). By permission of the National Library of Scotland.

Here in the rich, the honour'd, fam'd and great,
See the false scale of Happiness complete!—

Published by J. & P. Knapton Feb. 6.th 1744.

A N

E S S A Y

O N

M A N.

B Y

ALEXANDER POPE, Esq.

Enlarged and Improved by the AUTHOR.

Together with his MS. Additions and Variations,
as in the Laft Edition of his Works.

With the NOTES of
Mr. WARBURTON.

LONDON,
Printed for J. and P. KNAPTON in Ludgate-ftreet.
MDCCLV.
[Price Eighteen Pence.]

released in the following year, might be regarded as a counter-reaction. *Ethic Epistles* also omits the couplet on Samuel Clarke from the 'Epistle to Burlington' added in 1744 (Twick. III, ii: 140, lines 77–8). The text for the most part follows that of the octavo 1735 *Works* II (Griffith 389), although capitalisation has been modernised (not so in 1751) and italics—which fashionably adorned 'Epistle to a Lady' in 1735—have been removed.

There are various reasons why Warburton would not have welcomed *Ethic Epistles*. While Warburton's imprimatur is evident on the title-pages to all *Essay on Man* editions from 1745 to 1753, the name of Pope's editor is nowhere to be found in *Ethic Epistles*. The 1747 edition does not reprint the five congratulatory poems that accompany most of the *Essay on Man* editions of this period. Warburton's notes and commentaries—an overabundance of which characterised *An Essay on Man* and *Epistles to Several Persons*—have been eliminated. In *An Essay on Man* there are two of Pope's footnotes in Epistle I (to lines 182 and 213); none in Epistle II; two in Epistle III (to lines 68 and 177); and none in Epistle IV. The forty-eight footnotes in the second part of *Ethic Epistles* are again all Pope's own. But the most obvious objection Warburton would have had to the 1747 text appears in the 'Epistle to Bathurst' at line 107 where the name 'SUTTON' is given in full capitals. Sir Robert Sutton (1672–1746) had been Warburton's first patron. After Sutton became implicated in the Charitable Corporation scandal, Warburton wrote *An Apology for Sir Robert Sutton* in 1733. When Warburton was assured of his editorship of Pope's works, he defended his former patron to his new one.[12] Pope accepted Warburton's vindication of Sutton's character and authorised the textual change (*Corr.* 4: 495–6; 27 January [1743/4]). Having diplomatically released Sutton from the eternal ignominy of Pope's satire, Warburton would no doubt have been infuriated to witness Sutton's textual reinstatement.

If legitimate (that is, if Warburton was too pre-occupied with the critics of his 1747 Shakespeare edition to proofread this slim volume), *Ethic Epistles* would warrant attention in light of recent debates over Pope's plan to create an 'opus magnum' out of the *Essay on Man* and *Epistles to Several Persons*. From its inception the *Essay on Man* has had a curious history. At first, each epistle was issued anonymously, enthused readers were allowed to make wild guesses as to its origin. Pope eventually revealed his authorship after his would-be detractors lavished praise on this new, unexpected, philosophical poem, thereby securing its reputation. This stratagem worked remarkably well. One of the reasons for Pope's initial secrecy was the fact that he was in the midst of one of his fiercest pamphlet wars—against the combined forces of Lady Mary Wortley Montagu and Lord Hervey—and did not wish his harsher critics to know of his involvement in what he privately considered to be his most ambitious production. The publication of his *Imitation of Horace, Satire II, i,* had aroused considerable ill feeling; and yet, ironically, Pope's satiric prolificity provided just the kind of smoke-screen he needed to usher *An Essay on Man* into the world. These psychological polarities of satire and system-making need further exploration in light of the 1747 *Ethic Epistles*.

Pope's main stumbling block in pursuing his 'Opus Magnum' might have had something to do with the generic problems of his four epistles—to Cobham, a Lady, Bathurst and Burlington—referred to at different times as *Ethic Epistles, The Second Book. To Several Persons* (1735), *Epistles to Several Persons* (1744/48) or *Moral Essays* (1751). The publication history of Pope's *Ethic Epistles* has been clouded by a number of factors, not the least of them being the poet's own undecided mind about their basic position in his œuvre. One example of Pope's change of mind over the arrangement of his works may be seen in the 1743 small octavo *Works* II, part i. A note at the end of this volume informs the reader: 'Those Satires and Epistles of Horace, with the Satires of Dr. Donne, hitherto printed in this Volume, are in this new Edition placed at the beginning of the Second Part, in their proper Order with others of the same kind by the Author, which compleat his Poetical Works.'[13]

The other main problem with this important body of Pope's works lies with Warburton. Pope ordered a limited edition in quarto of *An Essay on Man* and *Epistles to Several Persons* shortly before his death to give to friends. The discovery of one of the copies of this edition in the British Museum led F W Bateson to parenthesise the *Moral Essays* title, adopted by Warburton for the 1751 *Works*, in his Twickenham volume of *Epistles to Several Persons*. Bateson viewed Warburton's innovation with some disdain and based his own editorial decision on the authority of Pope's 'death-bed' *Epistles to Several Persons* which was suppressed until 1748. Bateson defended his decision by referring to the poet's correspondence: 'All Pope's references to the four poems in his letters are to his "Epistles". The expanded alteration "Ethic Epistles", used by some modern scholars . . . would not have been acceptable to Pope himself, who only uses it as a general title for *E. on Man* [*sic*] and the four Epistles *considered as a single entity*.'[14] Apart from these intimations of authorial intention, Bateson offered a semantic explanation. The title, *Epistles to Several Persons*,

> describes more accurately the nature of the four poems. To a reader of the early eighteenth century the word 'essay' had a more formidable connotation than it has today. The combination of 'moral' and 'essays', instead of suggesting, as it might to us, Addison's Saturday numbers of *The Spectator*, would then have been more likely to suggest some such dismal treatise as James Lowde's *Moral Essays wherein some of Mr. Locks and Mons. Malbranch's opinions are briefly examin'd* (1699). The effect of Warburton's title therefore was to put all the emphasis on the didactic elements in the poems. Here, it proclaimed, is another *Essay on Man*! It called attention, in other words, to all that is weakest and most pretentious in the four Epistles and ignored altogether the social satire and worldly wisdom in which their real strength lies.
>
> (Twick. III, ii: xxxvii)

There is a more contemporary example of a 'moral essay' title than Lowde's; yet Hume's *Essays Moral and Political* (1741/48) attempted to reach a wider audience after the 'dead-born' reception of his *Treatise of Human Nature* by adapting the *Spectator* formula of urbane argument to mid-century issues.

When John Butt, the general editor, condensed the Twickenham series into the one-volume edition of 1963, he reversed Bateson's title thus: *Moral Essays* [*Epistles to Several Persons*] at the end of the four poems and restored *Moral Essays* to the contents page, the chronological table and the running head. Further complicating (or at least challenging) the issue, Herbert Davis completely banished the *Moral Essays* title from the 1966 Oxford Standard Authors edition of Pope's *Poetical Works*, retaining the 1744 *Epistles to Several Persons* title. Davis added a fifth epistle, 'To Mr *Addison*' which Pope wrote in 1715 and Warburton later added to this group of poems. 'It is my modest hope', concluded Davis in his preface, 'that it [his edition] may demonstrate that there are more ways than one of editing texts printed in the eighteenth century.'

In this context it is worthwhile noting similar problems of nomenclature occurring in American editions. In *Alexander Pope: Selected Poetry and Prose*, William K Wimsatt, Jr, following Warburton's example, adopted the *Moral Essays* title for a section which also included 'To Mr Addison' and repeated the 1751 oversight by maintaining the subheading 'In Four Epistles to Several Persons' to the group now consisting of five poems.[15] On the other hand, James E Wellington mirrored Bateson's compromise on the title-page of his edition of *Epistles to Several Persons (Moral Essays)* — 'this was, after all, Pope's personal and final choice for a title'.[16] In the Riverside edition, Aubrey Williams listed the four poems as *Epistles to Several Persons* in the table of contents, merged the 1744 and 1751 titles in the text heading — *Epistles to Several Persons* [*Moral Essays*] — but used *Moral Essays* in the running-head, thereby covering all bases.[17]

John Barnard brought up the matter of title designation in his commemorative article, 'F W Bateson, Pope, and Editing'. Looking at Bateson's Twickenham edition, he observed:

> Even the book's spine offers an immediate challenge. *Epistles to Several Persons* is a title embodying an editorial decision and implying a critical stance. . . . The more grandiose title reflects Pope's intentions, which actively occupied his mind from 1729 to 1735, and were never entirely given up, of creating an '*Opus Magnum*', of which the *Essay on Man* would have been the introductory part serving as a scale for '*a general Map* of MAN' with the four epistles to Cobham, to a Lady, to Bathurst and to Burlington, forming no more than the first two books of the whole.[18]

Barnard went on to say that 'the plan lost impetus' and suggested that the blueprint for the 'Opus Magnum' in the 1744 advertisement might have been drawn up by Warburton. One of the weaknesses in Bateson's argument concerning the title, as Barnard pointed out, lies in the fact that Pope referred to many of his epistolary poems as 'ethic epistles'. In the 1735 Works there are no fewer than seven poems grouped under the half-title, 'ETHIC EPISTLES, |THE| SECOND BOOK. |TO| SEVERAL PERSONS'. The last of these, '*To Dr Arbuthnot*', was to become an editorial oddity when Warburton turned it into a 'Prologue to the Satires' in the 1751 *Works*.

Underlying the ambiguity over titles is the larger, more complex problem of Pope's artistic direction in the 1730s. Was he content with the diversity of imitating and updating Horace or was he committed to a higher, more philosophically unifying ideal of the 'Opus Magnum'? Bateson's selection of the *Epistles to Several Persons* title suggests that he supported the formal proposal and that Pope, in the 'death-bed' quarto, was declaring his abandonment of the 'Opus Magnum' scheme in favour of the more socially urbane and chaotic atmosphere of the Horatian imitations. Yet Barnard leaned more towards the 'magisterial simplicity' of the *Moral Essays* title, although, following Bateson, he thought 'Pope's essential genius did not encompass the ability to build up large intellectual structures'. The split in critical opinion over Pope's intentions to build either a disparate collection of Horatian imitations or a unified *'general Map* of MAN' is exemplified in such works as Reuben Brower's *Alexander Pope: The Poetry of Allusion* which states that Pope's career became 'progressively an *Imitatio Horatii*' and Miriam Leranbaum's *Alexander Pope's 'Opus Magnum' 1729–1744* which emphasises the Lucretian influence on his well-structured moral system.[19]

Ethic Epistles does little to resolve the question of nomenclature, neither following Pope's 'death-bed' choice nor anticipating Warburton's 1751 alteration, but hearkening back to the 1735 half-title. Its main interest lies in the fact that it re-incorporates the *Essay on Man* with the *Epistles to Several Persons* in a single volume before the release of the suppressed quarto 'death-bed' edition of the *Epistles* in 1748. Might Bolingbroke, through Cooper and Webb, who published the 1746 'Verses upon the late D——ss of M——, have released *Ethic Epistles* without Warburton's notes in order to test copyright law and deprive the editor of some of the profits from his *Essay on Man* editions?[20] Yet the inclusion of Warburton's note on Pope's frontispiece might give the editor some legal foothold. Or perhaps Warburton followed Pope's example of allowing Curll to print an incorrect version of his *Letters* in order that he might release an 'authorised' edition; the publication of the 1747 *Ethic Epistles* may have expedited the release of the suppressed 'death-bed' quarto of *Epistles to Several Persons* in the following year. Griffith entered this as *Four Ethic Epistles* (no. 591), based on a description in an advertisement in the 1754 *Works* (4: 250–2), describing it as 'printed but not published' about 1 May 1744. In an undated letter to Marchmont, Bolingbroke mentions this

> edition of the four Epistles, that follow the Essay on Man. They were printed off, and are now ready for publication. . . . I have a copy of the book. Warburton has the propriety of it, as you know. Alter it he cannot, by the terms of the will. Is it worth while to suppress the edition?
>
> (Twick. III, ii: xiii)

It would seem most unlikely that John and Paul Knapton would publish an edition expected to arouse Warburton's antipathy; as the main publishers of Pope's works and of Warburton's religious tracts, they would certainly not have wanted to jeopardise their own best interests. They stood little to gain and much to lose by going against Warburton's wishes. However, Warburton was spending more and more time at Prior Park, away from the bustle of the London book-trade, and it is conceivable that crossed signals (perhaps between Warburton and Bolingbroke) could have resulted in the publication of an unsatisfactory edition. On the other hand, the 1747 edition might have been an enterprising publisher's way of cashing in before the quarto edition came on the market. As only three copies of *Ethic Epistles* appear to exist in British and American libraries, it is difficult to say in what sense the edition was 'published'. Was the edition sold by the usual means or was it withdrawn shortly after being printed?

Piracy would seem the simplest explanation, yet it is unlikely that any London printer would use the name of one of London's most established publishers. In 1747 Warburton also published *A Letter from an Author to a Member of Parliament Concerning Literary Property*. When John Sayer wanted to 'borrow' part of the *Essay on Man* for his Latin translation in 1754, Warburton replied, 'Soon after Mr Pope died I was necessitated to put half a dozen people, who pirated the Essay on Man, into Chancery since which I have been but little injured in my property of it' (Egerton 1954.f.78; 28 January 1754). Yet no evidence points directly to piracy or legitimacy in the case of the 1747 edition of *Ethic Epistles*.

The frontispiece likewise remains a mystery. As many critics have recently well established by various researches, verbal and visual arts often went hand in hand in Pope's imagination.[21] Sculpture, painting and book illustration concerned Pope from his earliest days as a fledgling writer to the 'Universal Darkness' of the *Dunciad*. Maynard Mack's recent biography reminds us that Pope trained as a painter under Jervas. On the basis of a copy of Kneller's portrait of Betterton ascribed to Pope, Mack surmises that the poet was 'no Michelangelo' (229; 91). True as this no doubt is, the illustrations to Mack's edition of *An Essay on Man* indicate Pope maintained an active interest in drawing until the end of his life. The *Essay on Man* frontispiece must be regarded as one of Pope's last artistic acts.[22]

This frontispiece is worth noting in detail as a post-*Dunciad* re-evaluation of *An Essay on Man*. Like 'Ozymandias' in its rendering of crumbled human greatness, Pope's *capriccio* reflects gloomily on the death of classical values— those very truths of order and precision upon which the poet had early sought to build his art and reputation. Pope's awareness of the sublime and absurd vicissitudes of human nature led him from the all-encompassing urbanity of *An Essay on Man* into the anti-classical morass of the revised *Dunciad*. The mock-apocalyptic vision of the latter, in part, derived from an artistic failure on his part to complete the impossible project of setting a comprehensive philosophical system down in rhyming couplets. The absence of Pope's *Essay on Man* frontispiece from the 1751 *Works* was detected by a correspondent to the *Gentleman's Magazine* in August of the same year.

QUERY. Whether the new edition of Mr *Pope*'s works can be called *a complete edition of his works*, as the editor has *omitted* the frontispiece to the Essay on Man, which he before had so highly praised, and which, as he had said before, in the advertisement to the small edition, *was designed and drawn up by Mr* Pope *himself.*

(A.L.[23])

In place of Pope's design, a new series of cuts designed by Blakey and engraved by Ravenet and Scotin was commissioned for the third volume of the 1751 edition. The 'small edition' referred to by the above reader could be any one of several small octavo editions of the *Essay on Man* published between 1745 and 1748. The writer's query may have had some effect on Warburton's evident decision to reinstate the frontispiece—in its original state of 1744—in the 1755 small octavo *Essay on Man.*[24]

The sepia drawing by Pope which is reproduced opposite the title-page of the Twickenham *Essay on Man* differs slightly from the frontispiece published by J and P Knapton. Two statuesque figures on the coliseum in the background have disappeared from Pope's design; and the frontispiece adds a candlestick holder (beside Pope's belaurelled skull) as well as four sunbeams. Pope's name appears above 'INV.' on a tablet in the lower left-hand corner in both states. Although the frontispiece is dated 6 February 1744—almost four months prior to Pope's death—it did not appear in an edition of *An Essay on Man* until the following year. Perhaps in the confusion surrounding Pope's final illness, the engraving was set aside. Pope's frontispiece was described in the press:

> On a kind of cornice is plac'd death's head crowned with laurel, on one side of which is a *candle* just going out, and on the other a faded rose, over which hangs a *cobweb curtain*, and beneath the whole on a scroll these words, *sic transit gloria mundi*, the sense of which seems further pointed out by a music book and broken flute below, as well as the ruinous pyramid and half decay'd tree over it.[25]

Like Hogarth's 'Tail Piece: The Bathos', Pope's design depicts a world that is falling apart. Hogarth's later Father Time exhales the word 'FINIS' in a puff of smoke while Pope's philosopher sits idly blowing bubbles. Pope's ironic Latin mottoes, 'VIRO IMMORT:', 'SIC TRANSIT GLORIA MUNDI', 'CAPITAL IMMOBILE SAXUM', and 'ROMA ÆTERNA' find loose translations in Hogarth's 'H Nature Bankrupt', 'The Worlds End', the bequest to 'Chaos', and the igniting 'TIMES'. Pope includes a fallen statue, a broken flute, a crumbling coliseum; Hogarth etches a dead Apollo, a broken scythe, a dilapidated tower. In the 1744 the tree still has leaves; by 1764 the tree is bare. Both designs have been executed by men acutely aware of impending death.

Pope's design seems entirely contrary to the spirit of the work it was intended to preface. One would expect some classical rendering, a Rome-in-all-its-glory scenario, to mirror the ordered rationale of *An Essay on Man*. This image of a world falling apart might better have suited the *Dunciad*, and yet Pope's intentions are clear enough. The sepia drawing bears the subscription: 'Author Ipse Inv[t.] & I M Delineavit . . ./Herein the Rich, the Honou'r, Fam'd, and Great,/See the false Scale of Happineſs Compleat . . .' The 1745 frontispiece carried both the instructions to the binder, 'Essay on

Man . . . to face the Title', and the above couplet (*Twick*. III, i: 155, lines 287–8). Thus Pope's directions were followed to the letter.

Why then depict such a scene of breakdown and decay? Does the frontispiece to the *Essay on Man* form an impressionistic confession of failure to fulfil the 'Opus Magnum' design? Perhaps Pope lost confidence in his 'Opus Magnum' after the constant barrage from his critics in the 1730s, especially after Crousaz published his *Examen* in 1735. Warburton ingratiated himself by publicly defending Pope, and yet it was Warburton who later urged him to revise *The Dunciad*. Pope ended his career by giving full vent to his satiric impulses, creating, as it were, an anti-Opus Magnum. In doing so he abandoned his 'general Map of MAN'. By prefacing his late (and ultimately posthumous) editions of *An Essay on Man* with his own ironic testament of the world's decline, Pope perhaps intended his philosophical masterpiece to be read as the beginning of an ideal scheme which failed to achieve fruition. To what extent Pope's grand design became thwarted by satire, cynicism or despair is still being pondered, but the 1744 frontispiece might be regarded as the ontological turning point between *An Essay on Man* and *The Dunciad*.

In the seven years between Pope's death and the publication of the first Warburton edition of his *Works*, the market for cheap editions of *An Essay on Man* was considerable: Maslen estimated that 'no fewer than 5000 copies' of *An Essay on Man* were printed by Bowyer between 1745 and 1748. *Ethic Epistles* suggests public demand was even higher. Griffith's bibliography remains the standard source up to 1751, although Maslen's findings demonstrate the need for a major overhaul in light of knowledge gleaned from Bowyer's printing ledgers. David Foxon, perhaps the last single-handed eighteenth-century bibliographer, prefaces his section on Pope with the note, 'Because of the complexity of the editions of Pope, the belief that a revision of Griffith's bibliography could not long be delayed, and the frequency with which copies of his poems occur, the account given here has been somewhat abbreviated.'[26] In his travels Foxon uncovered Pope editions not seen by Griffith and added considerably to the grey area of piracy through the identification of printers' ornaments; other editions unknown to Griffith have been discovered by individual scholars and the compilers of the *ESTC*.[27] As a collection of poems, *Ethic Epistles* would not have fallen under Foxon's purview, but its existence adds to the growing need for a revised Pope bibliography.

NOTES

1   R H Griffith, *Alexander Pope: A Bibliography*, 1 vol, 2 parts (Austin: Univ of Texas Press, 1922–7). See, for example, William B Todd, 'Concealed Pope Editions', *Book Collector*, 5 (1956), 48–52; David Foxon, 'Concealed Pope Editions', *Book Collector*, 5 (1956), 277–9; Maynard Mack, 'Two Variant Copies of Pope's *Works . . . Volume II*: Further Light on Some Problems of Authorship,

Bibliography, and Text', *The Library*, 5th series, 12 (1957), 48–53; rpt *Collected in Himself* (Newark: Univ of Delaware Press, 1982), 139–44 (see also Mack's desideratum which adds to the above, 113n); Phillipa Hardman, 'An Addition to Griffith's Bibliography of Pope', *The Library*, 5th series, 33 (1978), 326–8; and note 2 below. To revise Griffith is not to dishonour him, but to extend his work.

2 K I D Maslen, 'New Editions of Pope's *Essay on Man* 1745–48', *Papers of the Bibliographical Society of America*, 62 (1968), 177–88. See the bibliographical entry at end of this article which follows Maslen's format.

3 National Library of Scotland [cited as NLS], 10.1927.

4 Two other copies are listed in the *National Union Catalogue* at University of Illinois, Urbana, and Kansas State University, Manhattan [unseen].

5 See my article, 'So proper for that constant pocket use': Posthumous Editions of Pope's *Works* (1751–1754)', *Man and Nature*, 6 (Edmonton: Academic Printing and Publishing, 1987); 81–92.

6 I am indebted to Keith Maslen for supplying me with this and other information about the Bowyer press ledgers from his forthcoming edition.

7 M McLaverty's *Pope's Printer, John Wright: A Preliminary Study* (Oxford: Oxford Bibliographical Society, 1977) covers the period from 1728 to 1750 and lists thirty-nine Pope items, the last of these being the 1747 *Miscellanies*. Obviously *Ethic Epistles*, not bearing any ornaments, would not have been numbered in such a study, but Wright would surely have identified any Pope edition he printed. The ledgers of Henry Woodfall, Sr and Jr, cover this period: see the series of articles by P T P, *Notes and Queries*, 1st ser (1855), 'Pope and Woodfall', 9 May, 11: 377–8; 'Woodfall's Ledger, 1734–1747', 2 June, 11: 418–20; 'Pope and Henry Woodfall', 15 Sept., 12: 197; 'The Ledger of Henry Woodfall, Jun., 1737–1748', 22 Sept., 12: 217–18. Similarly, William Strahan, who shared with Bowyer the printing of Pope's *Works* in 1752 (by evidence of ornaments), had no hand in *Ethic Epistles*. See Patricia Hernlund's two articles, 'William Strahan's Ledgers: Standard Charges for Printing, 1738–1785', *Studies in Bibliography*, 20 (1967), 89–111, and 'William Strahan's Ledgers II: Charges for Papers', *Studies in Bibliography*, 22 (1969), 179–95.

8 British Library, Egerton 1954. The writer is currently preparing an edition of the correspondence between Warburton and Knapton for publication.

9 W K Wimsatt, *The Portraits of Alexander Pope* (New Haven: Yale UP, 1965), 192n3.

10 Compare the 1747 title-page medallion with Wimsatt no. 43.3. For a biography of the artist, see Louise Lippincott, *Selling Art in Georgian England: The Rise of Arthur Pond* (New Haven: Yale UP, 1983).

11 The 1747 medallion is fractionally smaller than the 1745 (1747 diameter = 41 mm; plate mark = 46 × 47 mm/1745 diameter = 42 mm; plate mark = 49 × 50 mm).

12 *The Correspondence of Alexander Pope*, George Sherburn (ed), 5 vols (Oxford: Clarendon Press, 1956), 4, 492–4 [1743/4]. This is the only extant letter from Warburton to Pope [cited as *Corr.*]

13 London: Printed for R Dodsley and Sold by T Cooper in Paternoster-Row, *181* (British Library: 239.h.39; Griffith 583).

14 Pope, *Epistles to Several Persons (Moral Essays)*, F W Bateson (ed) (London: Methuen, 1951; 2nd edn 1961), ixn3 [cited as Twick. III, ii].

15 (New York: Holt, Rinehart and Winston, 1951; rpt 1972), 171. This oversight remains uncorrected in subsequent Warburton editions—the 1752 large octavo (3: 169); 1753 small octavo (3: 175) and 1770 duodecimo (2: 107).

16 (Miami: Univ of Miami Press, 1963), 3.

17 *Poetry and Prose of Alexander Pope* (Boston: Houghton Mifflin, 1969), vii, 158, 160–96.

18 *Essays in Criticism*, 29, no. 2 (April 1979); 124–38; p 128.

19 Reuben Brower, *Alexander Pope: The Poetry of Allusion* (Oxford: Clarendon Press, 1959), 165; Miriam Leranbaum, *Alexander Pope's 'Opus Magnum' 1729–1744* (Oxford: Clarendon Press, 1977), ch 2.

20 W Webb's anti-Warburton 'Proclamation' (Foxon P1103) was reprinted in Mary Cooper's *Verses Occasioned by Mr. Warburton's Late Edition of Mr. Pope's Works*, 1751. Cooper's 1757 *Supplement to the Works of Alexander Pope* contained poems like 'Sober Advice from Horace' which Warburton had preferred to omit from the canon.

21 Robert Halsband, *The Rape of the Lock and its Illustrations 1714–1896* (Oxford: Oxford UP, 1980). W K Wimsatt's *Portraits of Alexander Pope* attests not only to the poet's desire to perpetuate his image in as many forms as possible, but also to the cottage industry which sprang up around this prodigious celebrity. The large folding frontispiece to 1717 *Works*, revealing Pope in pre-Byronic *déshabillé* might be regarded as an early 'pop' poster. Even his villa was targeted by Sunday painters long after his death until Lady Howe had it torn down in 1807. See the exhibition catalogue compiled by Morris R Brownell, *Alexander Pope's Villa: Views of Pope's Villa, Grotto and Garden: A Microcosm of English Landscape* (London: Greater London Council, 1980), 49–56. Maynard Mack writes in *Alexander Pope: A Life* (New York: Norton, 1985), 'Few poets, if any, have more self-consciously pursued an immortality in art than he, to say nothing of a settled livelihood' (111). Mack reminds us that Pope could, at times, be his own worst critic or best satirist: 'I have crucify'd *Christ* over-again in effigie' (228; 23 August 1713, *Corr.* 1: 188).

22 For a reproduction of Pope's sepia drawing, see the frontispiece facing the title-page of Twickenham III, i, *An Essay on Man*, Maynard Mack (ed) (London: Methuen, 1950; rpt 1958) and the 'Note on the Illustrations', xc. The frontispiece appears on the cover and title-page of an Open University booklet, *An Essay on Man, IV*, A204, unit 3 (Milton Keynes: Open UP, 1979). James Sambrook, 'Pope and the Visual Arts', *Alexander Pope: Writers and their Background*, Peter Dixon (ed) (London: G. Bell and Sons, 1972), 143–71, makes an unsubstantiated claim, 'Despite Warburton's assertion, it is doubtful whether Pope made the sepia drawing . . .' (144). Yet Benjamin Boyce, 'Baroque into Satire: Pope's Frontispiece for the "Essay on Man",' *Criticism*, IV (1961–2), 14–27 (whom Sambrook cites), exhaustively researches the *Varia Marci Ricci pictoris* which Pope knew and drew upon for his drawing. Had Warburton attempted to deceive his public by commissioning a fake 'Pope', his many detractors would have let the world know. Such dishonesty was not one of Warburton's shortcomings. He did not need to manufacture ways of promoting Pope's works; and his relationship with the Knaptons was based on mutual integrity. Neither Mack nor Maslen shares Sambrook's view.

23 *Gentleman's Magazine*, XXI (August, 1751), 344.

24 NLS: ABS.1.80.244 (1–3). The title-page medallion is signed A Walker.

25 *Gentleman's Magazine*, XV (February, 1745), 98.

26 David Foxon, *English Verse 1701–1750: A Catalogue of Separately Printed Poems with Notes on Contemporary Editions*, 2 vols (Cambridge: Cambridge UP, 1975), i, 613.

27 See note 1 above. The catalogue of the British Library Pope holdings contained in R C Alston and M J Jannetta, *Bibliography Machine Readable Cataloguing and the ESTC* (London: The British Library, 1978), includes several additions to

Griffith: *Works* II (London: R Dodsley, sold by T Cooper, 1739) [686.d.18]; *Four Ethic Epistles* (Glasgow: R Urie, for Daniel Haxter, 1750) [1607/4229]; *Letters* (Dublin: Richard James, 1751) [1083.f.6]; *The Dunciad* (Dublin: Philip Bowes, 1743/44) [Foxon P798; 1607/5245]; *An Essay on Man* (Dublin, George Faulkner, 1745) [Foxon P870; 1607/4236]; *An Essay on Man* (London: John and Paul Knapton, 1748) [Maslen 1748a (see note 2 above); Foxon P872; 11634.b.13; 1484.bbb.13]; *An Essay on Man* (London: J and P Knapton, 1743 [1749?]) [C.59.e.1(1)]; *An Essay on Man* (Glasgow: William Duncan, Jr, 1751) [1607/4228]; *Of the Knowledge of Men* (Dublin: George Faulkner, 1734) [Foxon P922; 11631.aa.47(6); C.136.aa.1(14)]; *Of the Use of Riches* (Dublin: George Faulkner, 1733) [Foxon P931; 11631.aa.47(4)]; *The Rape of the Lock* (Dublin: J Thompson, 1729) [Foxon P950; 11630.aaa.45(3)]; *Poems Occasioned by Reading the Travels of Captain Lemuel Gulliver* (Dublin?, 1727) [Foxon P359; 1872.a.1(11)]; and *Sober Advice from Horace* (Dublin: George Faulkner, 1735) [Foxon P971; T.902(10)].

15

The Self-portrait In The Letters

WENDY JONES

Traditionally the issue of Pope's publication of his own letters has been used as a stick to beat the poet for what critics have perceived as his duplicity and vanity. A more fruitful approach is suggested by Geoffrey Tillotson (1958), who observes that the first edition of Pope's letters, published in May 1735, appeared at a crucial time in Pope's career: 'His war with the dunces had left him sorer and shabbier than was comfortable.'

The implications of this observation have never been sufficiently assessed. While it is a commonplace that acquaintance with the pamphlet attacks on Pope's character and writings leads one to a greater appreciation of his mature poetry—and especially of the *Dunciad*, the *Moral Essays* and the *Imitations of Horace*—the fact that this applies with equal if not greater force to the letters Pope published has been largely ignored: a surprising omission in studies dealing with Pope's letters.

We know that, despite his cultivated pose of indifference, Pope was acutely affected by the hundreds of poems and essays published by Grub Street in an effort to destroy his personal and poetical reputation. Dr Johnson has left us, of course, the most famous anecdotal account:

> I have heard Mr. Richardson relate that he attended his father the painter on a visit, when one of Cibber's pamphlets came into the hands of Pope, who said, 'These things are my diversion'. They sat by him while he perused it, and saw his features writhen with anguish; and young Richardson said to his father, when they returned, that he hoped to be preserved from such diversion as had been that day the lot of Pope.

This expresses Pope's curiously ambivalent response to the pamphlet attacks: at once fascinated and tormented. The pamphlet warfare could not simply be ignored. Although 'paper wars' were an integral feature of the Augustan literary scene, Pope was the most maligned writer of his age. As Guerinot (1969) points out, 'It is, indeed, hard to think of any other figure in English literature who was so frequently attacked in his lifetime.'

Pope's preoccupation with the satire directed against him is most strikingly illustrated by the fact that he collected a great number of these pamphlet attacks, bound them in four volumes, and stored them in his library. On the one hand, Pope simply relished satirical literature and he was particularly intrigued by the public images of Alexander Pope as the age's foremost poet circulated by both his admirers and detractors. On the other, Pope's collection of the attacks was a somewhat masochistic act. He could not help but be deeply pained by the scurrilous nature of the generality of these pamphlets.

John Dennis's *Reflections Critical and Satyrical* on the *Essay on Criticism*, published in 1711, inaugurated the hostilities between Grub Street and Pope and may serve as an example. It is, indeed, possible to categorise the criticisms contained in Dennis's *Reflections* as representative because of a curious characteristic of the pamphlet attacks: an accusation against Pope, once printed, acquired the plausibility of truth and was repeated without question, let alone need for confirmation, in subsequent pamphlets.

Reflections is first typical of the many pamphlets for which it served as a model in its sense of injury out of all proportion to the offence it addressed. Dennis's thirty pages of bitter, implacable invective were ostensibly inspired by Pope's unwise but scarcely malicious description of the critic in his *Essay* as an irascible 'Appius'. Pope's epithet proved only too apt. Dennis was legendary for a sensitivity bordering on paranoia, which sensed injury where none was intended. This sensitivity unluckily did not extend to compassion for a twenty-three-year-old fledgling poet crippled physically by Pott's disease and socially by his allegiance to a despised religion.

Thus the disproportionate sense of grievance in Dennis's pamphlet is accompanied by numerous references to Pope's physical shortcomings which reduced his *Reflections* and most successive pamphlets to the level of crude personal libel. Dennis usually likened Pope to a monkey but here he attributed Pope's propensity for writing satire to his resemblance to another kind of being: 'As there is no Creature in Nature so venomous, there is nothing so stupid and impotent as a hunch-back'd Toad.' Dennis's fondness for describing Pope in terms of animal imagery led him to question whether the poet should even be considered human. He concluded that Pope's parents must have wished to abort such a 'monster' and that Pope

> has reason to thank the good Gods that he was born a Modern. For had he been born of *Graecian* Parents, and his Father by consequence had by Law had the absolute Disposal of him, his Life had been no longer than that of one of his Poems, the Life of half a day.

Another element of *Reflections* typical of subsequent pamphlets was its attack on Pope's religion. Pope's surname and Catholicism were unfortunate circumstances in an age with a morbid dread of a Jacobite invasion (and which witnessed one in Pope's lifetime). Dennis was only the first of many to accuse Pope of treason. Complaining that Pope's *Essay* had obliquely libelled William of Orange and Charles II in particular and the Dutch in general, he asserted that

he who Libels our Confederates, must be by Politicks a *Jacobite*; and he who
Libels all the Protestant Kings that we have had in this Island these threescore
Years . . . is, I suppose, politickly setting up for Poet-Laureat against the coming
over of the Pretender, which by his Insolence he seems to believe approaching.

Dennis's *Reflections* again anticipated many subsequent pamphlet attacks
on Pope in its accusation that Pope's friendships were largely compounded,
on the poet's part, of opportunism and ingratitude. Describing, for example,
Pope's intimacy with William Wycherley as a form of parasitism, Dennis
commented:

It has been observ'd that of late Years a certain Spectre exactly in the shape of
that little Gentleman, has haunted a certain ancient Wit, and has been by the
People of *Covent-Garden* styl'd his evil Genius.

Also generated here was a particularly persistent, damaging rumour which
claimed that Pope not only clung to the great dramatist to achieve his own
entrée to the great but also that he had gone so far as to compose a poem
praising his own *Pastorals* which he had later, audaciously, attributed to the
ingenuous Wycherley:

by this wise Proceeding [Pope] had the Benefit of the Encomium, and Mr. *W---*
had the Scandal of the Poetry; which it brought upon him to such a degree, that
'tis ten to one if ever he recovers the Reputation of a good Versifier.

But Pope's other early great friends were not quite so gullible, Dennis hinted,
and went on to claim that William Walsh had allowed Pope to accompany
him on occasion only as a sort of joke:

I remember a little young Gentleman, with all the Qualifications which we have
found to be in this Author, whom Mr. *Walsh* us'd sometimes to take into his
Company as a double Foil to his Person, and his Capacity.[1]

Time and malice honed these daggers hurled at Pope's reputation to a finer
cutting edge and added a few more charges to the list. By 1716 Dennis had
turned from crude taunting of Pope's physical defects to criticism on a
metaphysical plane; in that year he issued a *True Character of Pope* which
pronounced, with a solemn air of Biblical injunction, that

the Deformity of this Libeller, is Visible, Present, Lasting, Unalterable, and
Peculiar to Himself. 'Tis the mark of God and Nature upon him, to give us
warning that we should hold no Society with him, as a Creature not of our
Original, nor of our Species.[2]

By 1733 Lady Mary Wortley Montagu's sense of enmity was strong enough
for her to concur and, in verses addressed *To The Imitator Of The Second
Book Of Horace*, she advised Pope to follow the model of his Biblical ancestor:

And with the Emblem of thy crooked Mind,
Mark'd on thy Back, like *Cain*, by God's own Hand,
Wander, like him, accursed through the Land.

The most popular 'new' charge appearing in pamphlets after Dennis's *Reflections* was that Pope had become a rich man. Indeed, it has often been observed that what Pope's 'dunces' found really unforgiveable about him was his financial success and consequent literary independence of the professional writer's traditional bondage to patronage. Pope represented a literary landmark as the first English writer freed from the old necessity to flatter and to scheme and, although his motives may have been selfish ones, he revolutionised the position of the man of letters in society.

But despite his wealth and prestige, Pope was unable to ignore the pamphlet attacks. His original or, at least, avowed intention had been to maintain a stoical silence. In 1711 he remarked in a letter to his close friend John Caryll that he would not make the

> least reply to [Dennis], not only because you advise me, but because I've ever been of opinion that if a book can't answer for its self to the public, 'tis no sort of purpose for its author to do it.

Swift, too, advised Pope not to 'answer' his detractors, warning him that, like Virgil, he would only succeed in immortalising his enemies in his verse. But Pope's good intentions and his friends' counsel were overthrown by his naïve belief that his *Dunciad* might 'rid [him] of those insects'.

On one level the *Dunciad*, with its appendix of *A List of Books and Verses, in which our Author was Abused*—including thirty-four items derived from the pamphlet attacks—represents a fairly straightforward response to Pope's critics. What is not so obvious is that the letters Pope published in 1729, 1735, 1737 and 1741 equally represent a kind of rebuttal.

Pope had learned from Dennis, appropriately enough, that the publication of personal letters might be used in a course of attack and defence. In July 1729 Dennis published a letter Pope had sent him on 3 May 1721 in which Pope requested two sets of Dennis's *Original Letters* and thanked him for the 'Omissions you have been pleas'd to make in those Letters in my Favour'. Dennis included this letter in his *Reflections* on the *Dunciad* to make public what he construed as Pope's hypocrisy in, first, seeming to agree to a cessation of hostilities between them and, then, attacking the critic in that poem.

Pope quickly retaliated in kind. The second edition of the *Dunciad Variorum*, printed in November 1729, included Dennis's letter of 29 April 1721 to which his own had been a reply. In this letter Dennis admitted to removing from *Original Letters* the 'Footsteps' of their previous quarrels. The critic's integrity was thus indicted in the suggestion that, on his receiving Pope's subscription money, Dennis had removed from his publication all passages offensive to Pope.

Lewis Theobald, who had already provoked resentment by his scholarly disparagement of Pope's edition of Shakespeare, offered the poet another opportunity for vindication when he published his own letters. The occasion of their new quarrel was Theobald's publication of a volume of Wycherley's *Posthumous Works* in 1728 which included poetry Wycherley had once entrusted to Pope for revision and which, finally, Pope had advised him against publishing. Knowing that Wycherley had not intended these poems to be made public, that they could not enhance his old friend's reputation and, moreover, that some of the poems contained emendations or insertions supplied by Pope himself, he felt indignation at Theobald over and above the wounds inflicted to his vanity three years earlier by that critic's *Shakespeare Restored*.

In 1729 Pope issued—anonymously, of course—a second volume of Wycherley's *Posthumous Works*. He included twenty-six letters to and from Wycherley in this volume: eight written by himself and seventeen complete letters and two extracts from letters written by Wycherley. This selection from their correspondence fulfilled three functions. First, Pope's preface 'To the Reader' makes explicit his contempt, dismissing Theobald as one of the greedy adventurers who 'finger'd' Wycherley's inferior, unpublished work after his death 'without any Warrant but their own Arrogance, or motive but their own Lucre'. The accusation is repeated by Pope in his 1735 and 1737 editions in a footnote which deplores the fact that Wycherley's 'Papers . . . having the misfortune to fall into the hands of a Mercenary, were published in 1728'.

Second, Pope publicised the details of Wycherley's request that he 'improve' his poems. Eleven of the twenty-six letters published in 1729 discuss Wycherley's pleas for Pope's assistance, with their correspondence, then, serving as a chronicle of Pope's unsuccessful attempt to transform the mediocre verse, full of repetitions and clumsy phrasing, into passable writing.

Third, this publication of their correspondence illustrated Wycherley's admiration and affection for the young poet. Thirteen of his letters praised Pope, including four commending Pope's witty letters which 'at once pleas'd and instructed', another lauding Pope's 'vigorous Mind', and the two extracts and four other letters extolling Pope's *Pastorals*.

The connection between these Wycherley letters and pamphlet attacks upon himself was drawn by Pope in a footnote to a letter from Wycherley dated 13 May 1728 in which the dramatist told Pope he intended to commemorate his approval of the *Pastorals* by composing a poem in praise of them:

> This, and the following Extract, are a full Confutation of the lying Spirit of *John Dennis* and others, who impudently asserted that Mr. *Pope* wrote these Verses on himself.

The 'Extract' the footnote refers to consists of fragments of Wycherley's letters of 18 May and 28 July 1708 which Pope printed together and which opens with Wycherley's declaration that 'I Have made a damn'd Compliment in Verse, upon the printing your Pastorals'. This footnote also appears in the 1735 and 1737 editions.

To ensure a seemingly disinterested publication of these letters to and from Wycherley, Pope had first deposited their correspondence in Lord Oxford's famous Harleian Library. This tactic enabled him, in the preface to his second volume of Wycherley's *Posthumous Works*, to imply that his friend had been solely responsible for their publication; as he explained in a letter to Oxford of October 1729: 'I have made the Publishers say, that Your *Lordship permitted them a Copy* of some of the papers from the Library, where the Originals remain as Testimonies of the Truth.'

In the event, for reasons unknown, the second volume of Wycherley's 'remains' was suppressed. But the failure of this project did not prevent Pope from grasping the wider implications of what he might accomplish by publishing his own letters. Since 1726, when Curll had obtained his letters to Henry Cromwell from his former mistress and published them without permission, Pope had adopted the habit of recalling his own letters, making copies of those he sent, and preserving those which had been sent to him. By September 1729 he was ready to ask Oxford for his consent to deposit not only Wycherley's but also other friends' letters in his library, a request Pope said he had 'had at heart, for half a year & more'. In this letter to Oxford Pope described his hope that the correspondence he deposited in the Harleian Library might represent a true history of himself and his friends:

> As the rest of the Work I told you of, (that of Collecting the papers & Letters of many other Correspondents) advances now to some bulk; I think more & more of it; as finding what a number of Facts they will settle the truth of, both relating to History, & Criticisme, & part of private Life & Character of the eminent men of my time.

The chronology of events supports a strong link between the pamphlet attacks and Pope's first publication of his general correspondence in 1735. The appearance of the *Dunciad* in 1728 and the *Epistle to Burlington* in 1732 contributed to bring the ephemera warfare relating to Pope to a climax in 1733, which Guerinot describes as a 'year which produced more pamphlets for or against Pope than any other'. It was also in 1733 that Pope, having amassed a large number of letters, initiated his scheme to manoeuvre Curll into publishing them. In that year Pope responded by letter to Curll's advertisement for information for a life of the poet in the anonymous guise of 'P.T.', who offered Curll a 'large Collection of [Pope's] *Letters*, from the former Part of his Days to the Year 1727'.

Pope never admitted responsibility for the 1735 edition of *Letters of Mr. Pope and Several Eminent Persons*, delivered already-printed to Curll and which served as the basis of his *Mr. Pope's Literary Correspondence*, but he did acknowledge the 1737 edition which, as the first volume of the *Works in Prose*, was thus presented as the 'genuine, authorised' edition of his correspondence. As Pope's equal involvement in preparing both these editions for the press was conclusively established by Dilke's discovery of the Caryll transcripts in 1864, it is not surprising that the editions are similar. Both editions also bear distinct signs of their relation to the pamphlet attacks.

Both editions begin with a selection of Pope's correspondence with Wycherley. In 1735 Pope added two letters from himself to Wycherley to the eight he had printed in 1729. The first 'new' letter, dated 26 December 1704, opens the section and appears to serve as a formal introduction to Wycherley, identifying him as a friend of Pope's mentor, Dryden, and placing him within the circle of Pope's early friends, Congreve and Trumbull. The second 'new' letter, dated 23 June 1705, echoes one of Pope's favourite complaints: that his friends were too indulgent to him and that they lavished praise on his poetry rather than the criticism it deserved.

Pope somewhat distorted the picture of his epistolary relationship with Wycherley in the 1737 edition by neglecting to show how very two-sided and self-conscious a literary game they played in their early correspondence, heavily indebted as it was to the 'precious' style of letter writing inherited from Balzac and Voiture. This edition substantially reduced Wycherley's contribution, printing only five of his letters, while it includes nine by Pope. Six of Pope's letters object to Wycherley's compliments: a reproof deserved in their correspondence as printed here by Pope, for the letters from Wycherley that he included convey primarily the impression that the dramatist greatly admired the young poet. Too, while Wycherley's letters thank Pope for his friendship and assistance, they do not reply in kind with witty complaints of the flattery contained in Pope's actual letters to him. These distortions are partly attributable to Pope's vanity, but it is also instructive to place them in the context of the many pamphlets which had depicted Pope as a conniving flatterer who had attached himself to the unsuspecting Wycherley.[3]

The selections of his correspondence with William Walsh that Pope printed in 1735 and 1737 equally served to rehabilitate the public image of Pope's relationship with a famous friend. Pamphleteers had, in general, loyally followed the example set by Dennis in his *Remarks* in portraying Walsh's patronage of Pope as a refined form of entertainment or, as Charles Gildon described it in his *Memoirs* of Wycherley, a 'Man of Wit may find an agreeable Diversion in the Company of a pretending Fool sometimes, provided that the Interviews are short and seldome'. The letters Pope printed tell a very different story.

He included six Walsh letters in his 1735 edition and five in the 1737 edition. They serve a variety of functions. If Pope was proud of his friendship with Wycherley, who was widely considered one of his age's greatest writers, he was equally glad of a chance to advertise his intimacy with the eminent critic. Lest his readers failed to grasp Walsh's importance, a footnote in both editions described him as 'Author of several beautiful pieces in Prose and Verse, and in the Opinion of Mr. *Dryden* . . . the Best Critic of our Nation in his time'.

The letters Pope printed reveal that Pope was respected by Walsh as an astute expert on literary matters, with the two friends conversing on terms of equality on such topics as the proper definition of pastoral and pastoral comedy. They show, too, that Pope was not only loved by Walsh as a friend and admired as a critic but that his poetical precocity had early been recognised by him. In the first letter of the Walsh correspondence in the 1735 edition—a letter dropped in 1737—Walsh recommended the sixteen-year-old poet's pastorals to Wycherley in terms of a gratifying comparison: '*Virgil* had written nothing so good at his Age.'

Thus, if we allow that Pope selected for inclusion in his editions those letters to and from Wycherley which might vindicate both his own and the dramatist's reputation (although he cast aspersions on Wycherley's poetical ability in doing so), his selection of Walsh letters for publication followed a similar guideline: they redeemed Walsh from the charge of malice and Pope from that of fawning servility.

The Walsh letters, too, served another purpose. A major topic of this section of correspondence is the sensitive issue of literary 'borrowing'. The charge of plagiarism had dogged Pope for many years; here he could air Walsh's belief that Pope only followed literary tradition in drawing from classical precedent or, as Walsh observed in a letter Pope printed in both editions:

> in all the common Subjects of Poetry, the Thoughts are so obvious (at least if they are natural) that whoever writes last, must write things like what have been said before . . . it being evident in all such Cases, that whoever live first, must first find them out.

Pope also carefully selected and edited letters for publication in 1735 and 1737 which might explain his troubled relationship with a third famous friend—Addison. From 1714 until Pope's death a favourite accusation levelled at him by the pamphlets was that he had viciously turned against his erstwhile patron, the great Addison, who 'rais'd from Dust th'ungrateful Miscreant's Head'. Addison was generally depicted as one of Pope's earliest supporters and, in such pamphlets as *Pope Alexander's Supremacy*, as one of the most active of Pope's friends in procuring subscriptions for the projected *Iliad* translation. This pamphlet, issued in 1729 by Dennis and Duckett, claimed that the fickle Pope, seeing which way the winds of favour blew, had betrayed his old Whig friends and

> listed openly in the *Tory* Service, and every Week publish'd scandalous Invectives on those very *Whigs*, who had been his amplest Subscribers.[4]

But, while Pope always maintained that Addison had been the first to encourage him to undertake the translation, Addison apparently did not bother to solicit a single subscriber. He also sponsored and possibly collaborated on Tickell's rival translation and encouraged his circle at Button's coffee house in their manoeuvres to obstruct Pope's success.

It is simplest to consider the Addison letters as printed by Pope in the 1737 edition, where he allotted them a separate section. This section consists of five letters from Pope to Addison, two from Addison to Pope, one from

Charles Jervas to Pope and his reply, one to Lord Halifax, four to an unidentified 'Honourable', and one to the 'Hon. James Craggs'. Taken as a whole, these letters present a picture of the rise, growth and betrayal of Pope's affection for Addison. As most of the letters purportedly sent to Addison were demonstrably fabricated from letters Pope originally sent Caryll, it is most profitable to regard them in the light of a 'story' and to decipher Pope's message in its presentation.

Pope's early letters to Addison are full of expressions of eager admiration, with the 1737 section opening with a letter from him which exclaims: 'I Am more joy'd at your return than I should be at that of the Sun.' This is partly, of course, the cant of the Augustan letter-writer's *politesse* exaggerated to the point of humour, but one senses Pope was sincere in his early enthusiasm and respect for Addison. Always a fierce partisan where his friends were concerned, it was this esteem for Addison which prompted Pope's hilarious satire on Dennis, the *Narrative of Dr. Robert Norris*, which is the subject of this first letter and which a footnote in the 1735 and 1737 editions describes as 'occasion'd by *Dennis*'s Remarks upon *Cato*'. In the event, Addison was dismayed by Pope's defence of his play and, through Steele, he expressed his disapproval of the pamphlet to its publisher, Lintot. Lintot passed the letter on to Dennis, who printed it in 1729. This unfortunate tale of their early friendship, with Pope's affection rebuffed by Addison, presaged the course of their relationship as chronicled in Pope's editions of their letters.

In the second letter in the 1737 edition, a suspected fabrication, Addison voiced his support for Pope's project: 'I question not but your Translation will enrich our Tongue and do Honour to our Country.' In the context in which Pope prints this letter it represents, as Sherburn has observed (1956), a 'clear indictment of Addison's sincerity'.

The quarrel with Addison presented by Pope in his editions concerns, however, not only the contested *Iliad* translation but also the sensitive issue of party loyalty. Pope's friendship with Swift and Bolingbroke offended Addison's Whig sympathies, who advised Pope in one of his letters to avoid political faction and not to 'content your self with one half of the Nation for your Admirers, when you might command them all'.

In his letters to Addison as well as in the general correspondence he published in 1735 and 1737 Pope portrayed himself as a disinterested spectator of the contemporary political scene who detested the narrowness and animosity bred by the spirit of party so prominent in the eighteenth century. In one of the letters to Addison Pope drew a parallel between the intolerance and irrationality of party loyalty and the bigotry and dogma of religious fanaticism. Pope could not renounce Catholicism, fearing the pain his apostasy would cause his devout mother, but while religious faith or, at least, the appearance of it, was required, he refused also to adopt any exclusive political allegiances. As he observed in this letter: 'I confess I scorn narrow souls of all parties, and if I renounce my reason in religious matters, I'll hardly do it in any other.' Another letter to Addison concludes: 'I am ambitious of nothing but the good opinion of good men, on both sides.'

The remaining letters in the 1737 edition's section of Addison letters concern, directly or indirectly, Pope's quarrel with him. In his letter of 20 August 1714 to Pope, for example, Jervas recounted his efforts to reconcile the two friends, relating Addison's confession to him that he believed Swift had carried Pope 'too far among the enemy during the heat of the animosity'. Pope's letters to the unidentified 'Hon.' refer more obliquely to Addison in their descriptions of Ambrose Philips' partisan activities; Pope claimed that Philips was not only spreading malicious gossip about his suspected alliance with the Tories but that he also refused to relay to Pope subscription money for the *Iliad* which had been temporarily entrusted to him. The final letter of the section, to Craggs, includes a prose sketch of Addison as an envious 'great Turk in poetry, who can never bear a brother on the throne' which anticipates the 'Atticus' portrait in the *Epistle to Dr. Arbuthnot*.

The 'Atticus' portrait represents another instance of Pope's remarkable facility for learning from his enemies. Just as he learned from Dennis that the publication of a personal letter might serve to answer an attack on him, so he apparently abstracted this famous analogy of the envious Turk from Addison himself. Addison's review of the *Essay on Criticism* in a *Spectator* paper had described a phenomenon he suggested his readers might apply to Pope: 'In our own Country a Man seldom sets up for a Poet, without attacking the Reputation of all his Brothers in the Art.' Addison then proceeded to quote Sir John Denham's verse: 'Nor needs thy juster Title the foul Guilt/Of Eastern Kings, who to secure their Reign/Must have their Brothers, Sons, and Kindred Slain.'

In the opportunity for redress offered by a publication of their letters, Pope was anxious to counter not only the charge that he had been ungrateful to Addison but also that he had libelled him posthumously in this portrait, which was first printed in December 1722 in *St. James's Journal*—three years after Addison's death. The 1728 pamphlet *Characters of the Times*, included in the second of Pope's four volumes of attacks, echoed many others in its avowal that its denunciation of Pope was inspired by a need to

> expose the abominable Ingratitude of the Wretch who has dar'd to Insult [Addison] after his Death in a low and stupid Satyr, to insult the Man, to whom he intirely owes his undeserv'd Success, and to whose too great good Nature, he had been so infinitely oblig'd.

Pope acquitted himself of this second charge by adding to the 1737 edition a selection of his correspondence with Francis Atterbury. A letter of 26 February 1722 had contained the request that Pope send him a 'compleat copy of those verses on Mr. Addison', with Atterbury adding that the delineation of the satirical portrait was obviously where Pope's "real strength" lay and suggesting that Pope 'not suffer that talent to lye unemploy'd'. Pope appended a footnote to this letter which absolved him of responsibility for the first publication of the 'Atticus' portrait: 'An imperfect Copy was got out, very much to the Author's surprize, who never would give any.'

Publication of the Atterbury letters afforded another chance to redress the popular pamphlet claim that Pope was a 'rank Papist' and, hence, a treasonable subject plotting the return of the Stuarts to the throne. Atterbury's incarceration in the Tower in 1722, his subsequent conviction of Jacobite treason and exile to France, coupled with the suspicious circumstance of Pope's religion and his close friendship with the former Bishop of Rochester meant, as Pope was fully aware, that these letters would prove of special interest to his contemporaries.

Although Atterbury's guilt has since been conclusively established, Pope apparently never suspected him. As printed by Pope, their correspondence reveals that the two friends shared a fondness for literary criticism rather than for political conspiracy, and their publication thus gave Pope an opportunity to clear his own name and publicly to air his belief in Atterbury's innocence.

Pope's surreptitious publication of an edition of *Letters Between Dr. Swift, Mr. Pope, &c.* in 1741, which he reprinted in the second volume of his *Works in Prose*, represented yet another opportunity for him to vindicate his own reputation and that of some of his closest friends. The second volume of Pope's *Works in Prose* also included the *Memoirs of Martinus Scriblerus*, and the letters defended, appropriately enough, his relationship with former Scriblerians.

His association with the Scriblerus Club was a popular target of pamphlets attacking Pope. One of 1727 entitled *Gulliver Decypher'd*, for example, was devoted mainly to ironical 'proofs' that Gay, Pope and Arbuthnot had 'maliciously Father'd' *Gulliver's Travels* on Swift, but it deviated from this task to offer caricatures of each of them and to satirise their friendship. Gay's dependency on the patronage of the Duchess of Queensberry was mocked, while the three friends jointly were reviled for combining, in such works as *Three Hours After Marriage*, to form an 'Alliance offensive and defensive between each other'. This pamphlet, included in the second of Pope's four volumes, obviously attracted his attention. His copy is marked by X's and a number of underscorings; Pope also added an explanatory footnote and supplied names of individuals identified only by their initials.

A pamphlet of 1728, *The Twickenham Hotch-Potch*, similarly denigrated Arbuthnot, Swift, Gay and Pope by characterising them, respectively, as an 'impertinent *Scotch*-Quack, a Profligate *Irish*-Dean, the Lacquey of a Superanuated Dutchess, and a little virulent Papist'. *The Metamorphosis*, also published in 1728, narrowed its attack to Swift and Pope, likening them to dogs, a 'Spaniel P – – p – e; a *Mastiff Sw – – t*', that indiscriminately 'teize and bite what'er came next 'em,/But of pure Spite, tho' nothing vext 'em'. Pope's and Swift's literary collaborations were accordingly described as inhuman, malicious ravings: 'To bark, to insult, to run stark wild,/And foam at Woman, Man and Child;/To *foul* and *dirt* each Place they came in,/And play some Pranks, unfit for naming.'

Swift is represented by forty-two letters in *Letters Between Dr. Swift, Mr. Pope, &c.*, Pope by thirty, Bolingbroke by seven, and Gay by three. This collection is augmented by seven 'new' letters in the second volume of Pope's *Works in Prose*, including six additional letters written by Swift and a letter from Lord Orrery which deflects from Pope the responsibility for the first publication of his correspondence with Swift. Orrery claimed that Swift had delivered a number of letters to an unidentified individual who might be considering their publication.

Although Bolingbroke had not belonged to the Scriblerus Club, Pope's inclusion of his letters in this volume is partly attributable to the fact that he occasionally collaborated with him on letters to Swift. Too, in Swift's absence, Pope had come to rely increasingly on Bolingbroke's support and advice and, in a letter to Swift of 1732, written jointly with Bolingbroke, he suggested that the three friends might form a literary alliance reminiscent of the Scriblerus Club:

> I know nothing that moves strongly but Satire, and those who are asham'd of nothing else, are so of being ridiculous. I fancy if we three were together but for three years, some good might be done even upon this Age; or at least some punishment made effectual, toward the Example of posterity, between History, Philosophy, and Poetry.

That his friendship with Bolingbroke had frequently been condemned in the pamphlets undoubtedly represented one of the reasons Pope included these letters in the 1741 edition. Bolingbroke was usually charged with an attitude of insolence toward his contemporaries, with questionable morals verging on atheism and with treasonable conduct. In the 1735 *Epistle to Alexander Pope*, for example, Bolingbroke was characterised as Pope's evil genius who unscrupulously misled his friend into supporting his campaign against Walpole's government. Similarly, a 1739 pamphlet entitled *Characters: An Epistle to Alexander Pope Esq*, written by a 'Walpole hack' to discredit Pope's anti-government satires, accused Bolingbroke of treason and complained that Pope was unduly influenced by him.[5]

The letters Pope published 'answer' these attacks on the Scriblerians in a number of ways. He deleted, for example, references to Gay's dependence on the Duchess of Queensberry's patronage, thus perhaps directly responding to such pamphlets as *Gulliver Decypher'd* and *The Twickenham Hotch-Potch*. Also, he excised from the 1741 edition Swift's criticisms of such mutual friends as Mrs Howard and the Earl of Burlington, presenting his circle of intimates to the public eye as a united front. There is no talk of politics let alone of treason in this edition but, rather, it is full of the friends' reflections on their aversion to faction, political or religious, and their philosophic indifference to any ambition other than to devote themselves to writing works intended to reform their own and to enlighten future ages. Letter 48 of the second volume of *Works in Prose*, for example, is described in the table of contents as

> From [Bolingbroke]. Of his studies, particularly a Metaphysical work. Of Retirement and Exercise—Postscript by Mr. *P*. His wish that their studies were united in some work useful to Manners, and his distance of all Party-writings.

Pope's presentation of these letters deliberately enhanced the impression that the correspondence constituted the 'story' of a close-knit coterie characterized by its distrust of 'Party-spirit' and by its preoccupation with how one may lead a 'good life'.[6] The pamphlet image of a weak, indolent Gay, a Machiavellian Bolingbroke, and a Swift and Pope who are misanthropic dabblers in dirt and scandal is, thus, carefully undermined by these letters, whose theme might be described as a celebration of friendship and virtue.

The 1741 edition also 'answered' the pamphlets by commemorating the Scriblerus Club and by reaffirming its values; it demonstrated that humanist principles as well as practical reasons underlay their collaborations. The link between the Club and this edition is made explicit by Pope's decision to print the letters and the *Memoirs* together in the second volume of his *Works in Prose*. It is made implicitly by the style and content of the letters Pope included, in which Bolingbroke, Swift and Pope and, occasionally, Gay, join in good-natured mockery of abuses of taste and learning. The rationale behind these letters—and behind Pope's decision to print them—might be traced to Erasmus's letter which prefaces *The Praise of Folly* and dedicates that work to Thomas More: 'How unjust it is to allow every other walk of life its relaxations but none at all to learning, especially when trifling may lead to something more serious!' In publishing their letters, Pope both affirmed and demonstrated the Scriblerian belief in the utility of learned wit.

As for the insidious, because irrational, insinuations throughout the pamphlets which hint that Pope's physical defects were but the visible manifestations of a crippled mind, the letters Pope published in 1729, 1735, 1737 and 1741 represent an answer even to the belief that *mens curva in corpore curvo*. In a letter he sent Caryll shortly after Curll's unauthorised 1726 publication of his letters to Henry Cromwell, Pope accompanied his request that Caryll return his letters with the observation that he believed that his correspondence with 'good men' might vindicate his own character. Cicero's belief that 'friendship cannot exist except among good men' represented a humanist maxim which Pope self-consciously echoes here; as his correspondence

> serve[s] to bear testimony of my own love for good men, or theirs for me, I would not but keep [it] on all accounts, and shall think this very article more to my reputation than all my works put together.

The traditional view of Pope's editorship of his own letters holds that his main purpose was to pander to his own ego and that this is confirmed by the fact that Pope readdressed letters originally sent to Caryll to more famous individuals such as Addison and Steele, thereby advertising his intimacy with the great figures of his age. But while there is certainly justice in this conjecture, it does not explain the fact that Pope also readdressed some of the Caryll letters to such comparatively obscure friends as Hugh Bethel, Edward Blount and Robert Digby, nor does it account for the fact that he featured his relationship with these three men so prominently in the 1735 and 1737 editions, which include sections devoted to each of them.

Roscoe, in his 1824 edition of Pope's *Works*, offers the most plausible explanation in his observation that 'notwithstanding the acknowledged anxiety of Pope for the establishment of his literary fame', the importance he accorded his friendship with Bethel, Blount and Digby in the *Letters* 'may perhaps incline us to give credit to the asseveration he so frequently makes, that he was still more desirous of being esteemed a good man, than a great poet'.

Of course, one might also see Pope's featuring his intimacy with 'good men' as self-serving. We may return here to Tillotson's point: Pope's reputation after the *Dunciad* was at its shabbiest. Pope's awareness of this is reflected in his collection of pamphlet attacks, which includes a clipping from the *Daily Journal* of 11 May 1728, marked by Pope with lines and X's, which observed:

> this little turbulent Creature has endeavoured to decry and calumniate every Author who has excelled him, and shone in a superior Region to him, moved partly by his natural Envy and Malice, (the Deformity of *Mind* answering to that of his *Body*) and partly by that Ignorance and Stupidity which make a Dog howl at the Moon.

Pope also possessed a copy of Giles Jacob's *The Mirrour* which opened with a letter from Jacob to Dennis in which he observed that, although he had once been content to applaud Pope as a 'rising Genius', the publication of the *Dunciad*, with its 'most shameless and unprecedented Abuse of all his Contemporaries, without making any Distinction between Foe and Friend', had provoked Jacob to 'retract [his] good Opinion, and to draw [his] Pen against such an Adversary, and convince him of his great Error, Folly and Madness'.[7]

The letters Pope published serve as a mirror image of that poem. For those who condemned the author of the *Dunciad* as a vitriolic satirist, the letters show Pope in his other capacity: the public poet who denounces vice is revealed in his correspondence as the private individual who loves virtue. While the *Dunciad* dramatically evoked a world of bad writers and faithless friends trembling on the brink of cultural and moral collapse, the 1735, 1737 and 1741 editions of the letters vividly depict a private sphere in which humanist values are restated in contemporary terms. They portray a circle of loving friends dedicated to upholding the banner of civilisation bequeathed them by the classical writers. Just as the *Dunciad* had employed Pope's philosophy of the efficacy of a satire based on the example of actual individuals, these three editions operated on the same principle by presenting individuals worthy of imitation.

Pope may have felt that there was a certain ironic justice in 'answering' his detractors with letters in view of the fact that the majority of the pamphlets directed against him and his friends had themselves assumed the form of personal letters. But we must ultimately locate Pope's editorship of his own letters in the philosophy of satire which he explained in a letter to Arbuthnot included in the 1737 edition: 'General propositions are obscure, misty, and uncertain, compar'd with plain, full and home examples.'

The Augustans often ranked biography above history for its value as didactic literature. In his remarks on Plutarch which preface an edition of the *Lives* Dryden commended his work in these terms; it sets 'before us what we ought to shun, or to pursue, by the examples of the most famous men'. In the letters Pope published he not only substantiated his satiric ethos of the good man and the good poet, but he also commemorated his friends by presenting an epistolary tale which taught, by example, what Emrys Jones (1968) has identified as the 'great Augustan theme' and a 'lasting pre-occupation of humanism': 'the use of knowlege: how to make knowledge live by making it useful to the real business of learning'.

NOTES

1   In Pope's copy of this pamphlet, included in the first of the four volumes (preserved in the British Library, pressmark C.116.b.1–4), he inked in Wycherley's name in Dennis's claim that the poem praising the *Pastorals* had misleadingly been 'publish'd in Mr. W.– – –'s Name'. He also underlined 'ancient Wit' and identified him as Wycherley in the margin.

2   In Pope's copy of this pamphlet, included in the first volume, he marked these comments with a line down the margin and with two X's.

3   For this type of accusation see, for example, *Characters of the Times* (*London*: 1728) which describes Pope as a 'little Flatterer of, and Hanger upon the late Mr. *Wicherley*'. This pamphlet is included in the second of Pope's four volumes.

4   See *Mr. P[O]PE's Picture in Miniature* (London: 1743). *Characters of the Times* similarly had asserted that 'When [Pope] first set up for an Author, his Works lay for some Years in the Refuse and Rubbish of the Booksellers Stalls, and had continued in the same Obscurity until this Day, had not Mr. *Addison*, out of his uncommon Generosity taken Notice of him . . . No sooner had our great *Addison* given him a Figure in the Eye of Mankind, but he set himself to abuse and ridicule him, and all his Acquaintance.'

5   In *Characters* (London: 1739) Pope was advised: 'Now drop with *St. John* to the deepest Hell,/And unto Traitors there your Poems sell:/There let your Hawkers cry 'em on a String,/And spread Sedition to dethrone your King./Yet blot out all Encomiums ere you vend,/With which you dawb and flatter ev'ry Friend;/Or you'll be scourged severely for a Fool,/And double damn'd for an *Apostate*'s Tool.'

6   For an exhaustive catalogue of Pope's revisions of the letters for publication, see Vinton Dearing's unpublished PhD (Harvard: 1949) on 'A History of the Publication of Alexander Pope's Letters During his Lifetime' and Archibald C Elias's unpublished PhD (Yale: 1973) on 'Jonathan Swift and Letter Writing'.

7   See the third of Pope's four volumes. *The Mirrour* consisted of twenty letters followed by an 'Addenda' chronicling the 'legal *Tryal* and Conviction of Mr.

Alexander Pope of Dulness and *Scandal*'. Pope was found 'guilty' in his 'nonsensical and filthy *Dunciad*'; his sentence: 'The said *Alexander* was the same Day cast down from the high Mount of *Parnassus*, no longer to be rank'd among the Poets of Fame.'

References

Guerinot, J V *Pamphlet Attacks on Alexander Pope, 1711–1744* (London: Methuen, 1969)

Jones, E *Pope and Dulness* (London: Oxford University Press, 1968)

Sherburn, G *The Correspondence of Alexander Pope* (Oxford: Clarendon Press, 1956)

Tillotson, G *Pope and Human Nature* (Oxford: Clarendon Press, 1958).

Index